A WILDERNESS CALLED HOME

Dispatches from the Wild Heart of Canada

CHARLES WILKINS

PENGUIN

VIKING

VIKING

Published by the Penguin Group

Penguin Books Canada Ltd, 10 Alcorn Avenue, Toronto, Ontario, Canada M4V 3B2

Penguin Books Ltd, 80 Strand, London WC2R ORL, England

Penguin Putnam Inc., 375 Hudson Street, New York, New York 10014, U.S.A.

Penguin Books Australia Ltd, Ringwood, Victoria, Australia

Penguin Books (NZ) Ltd, cnr Rosedale and Airborne Roads, Albany, Auckland 1310, New Zealand

Penguin Books Ltd, Registered Offices: Harmondsworth, Middlesex, England

First published 2001

1 3 5 7 9 10 8 6 4 2

Author representation: Westwood Creative Artists
94 Harbord Street
Toronto, Ontario M5S 1G6

Printed and bound in Canada on acid free paper ∞

NATIONAL LIBRARY OF CANADA CATALOGUING IN PUBLICATION DATA

Wilkins, Charles

A wilderness called home : dispatches from the wild heart of Canada

ISBN 0-670-89416-8

1. Wilkins, Charles—Journeys—Canada. 2. Canada—Description and travel. I. Title.

FC75.W56 2001   917.104'648   C2001-901740-5   F1017.W54 2001

Visit Penguin Canada's website at **www.penguin.ca**

*In memory of my father, Hume Wilkins,
and for my sisters, Ann and Susan,
with gratitude and love.*

ACKNOWLEDGEMENTS

Many people made valued contributions to the creation of this book. For their help and support in any number of ways, I want to thank Kevin Parkinson, Pat and Vic Carpick, Rosalind Maki, Dorothy and Peter Colby, Peter Crooks, Jim Foulds, Doug Allen, Rob Lannon, Claude Liman, Mary Frost, Gerry Waldron, Elinor Barr, Ted and Erika Burton, Gary Genosko, Susan Carpick, George Morrissette, Jake MacDonald, Larry Krotz, Dan Diamond, Dr. Phillippe Mallhot and Gary Woodbeck.

I am also grateful to Larry Hebert of Thunder Bay Hydro for his generous provision of office space when I needed it, and to the Thunder Bay Arts and Heritage program for timely financial support.

Thanks are due especially to Don Paterson and N. M. Paterson and Sons for their unqualified hospitality and good will in allowing me to travel on the *M. V. Paterson*—and, of course, to the crew and officers of the *Paterson*.

ACKNOWLEDGEMENTS

This book might not exist at all had it not been for early inspiration from my former agent, Jennifer Barclay, and from my current agent, Jackie Kaiser, who has been a steady source of motivation and reassurance. My profound thanks to both of them.

And to my editor at Penguin Canada, Diane Turbide, who, throughout, has shown notable patience and perspective, and has provided both moral support and editorial wisdom. Many thanks, too, to my copy editor, Sharon Kirsch, who brought numerous valued improvements to the manuscript, and to Sandra Tooze for her exacting work in production.

Lastly, I want to acknowledge my family—first, my dad, Hume Wilkins, who, even when he was very sick during the spring of 2001, gave his attention to parts of the manuscript and encouraged my progress, as he always did. I regret deeply that he did not live to see the book in print. Many thanks to my sister, Ann, for her unflagging support during my father's illness.

And to my children, Matt, Georgia and Eden, whose love and inspiration are constant and indispensable. And to Betty Carpick, who has for years provided me with not just her editorial acumen, but the freedom to stay at my writing. For this book and the others, my debt to her is greater than I can put into words.

PART ONE

Chapter One

lacked the fat gold earring that, by the ancient code of the seafarer, would have paid for my burial in a foreign port should I have needed the service. And my tattoos, though many and detailed—and for the most part, self-inflicted—were entirely of the psychological variety. But on that bright morning of April 6, 2000, I did have a thousand dollars cash in my pocket, a sailor's collateral against the visions in my skull, and I was wearing new navy-blue suede shoes as I lugged my earthly necessities up the gangway of the freighter *M. V. Paterson* in my home port of Thunder Bay, on the north shore of Lake Superior. Eighteen days hence, in hallucinatory heat and a mood of gypsy abandonment, I would fling my alternative shoes, a pair of ripening Nike cross-trainers, into the molten recesses of a scrap converter at the Acme steel mill on the Calumet River in one of the grittier precincts of Chicago's South Side. But before their fiery transcendence, the shoes would feel the water of all five Great Lakes, and of the St. Lawrence River, and would take on a ghosting of the salt of the Atlantic Ocean. What's more, they would accumulate a lichenous-looking overlay of wheat dust and iron ore powder from my clandestine trudgings on deck in the pre-dawn hours.

But all of that was the furthest thing from my mind as I stepped across the bulwarks and was greeted by the ship's Australian-born third mate, Terry Holt. Terry is a one-time accountant who years ago renounced the modest stimulations of arithmetic, not to mention those of marriage, for a life at sea. The freedoms of that life have imparted to him an ambiguous liquid gaze and, as I would eventually learn, an almost pathological fear of having ever to return to a career on land.

Terry escorted me to the aft house, a structure about the size of a seven-storey apartment block, and led me up the interior stairs to Owner's Cabin #1 on the upper promenade deck. This lavish salon, my bivouac for the next three weeks, was perhaps twice as large and twice as well furnished as any bedroom or office I have ever rented or owned. But what pleased me more than its hard-wood cabinetry and wingback chairs was a pair of forward-facing windows that looked out along the full length of the ship to the bow and beyond. These enabled me to see the stars at night and whatever scape of water and land, or often just water, that we happened to be sailing into during a given hour of daylight. When I wasn't up in the wheelhouse or on deck, I would stand at those windows, sometimes for half an hour, gazing out at nothing more than, say, the spray that, in heavy weather, would soar up over the forecastle—or at a lone heron, the B-52 of the bird world, winging across Lake Erie or Ontario on its way to base camp on some distant island or shore.

I joked to Terry that the set-up would have to do, and, after he had quizzed me briefly on my life as a pen-pusher, he told me in his Aussie-inflected English that when his own book got written, it would be called *Horses, Swords, Violence, and Perverted Sex,* because, as Hemingway had mandated, "a writer should write about what he knows." Beneath the jokey depravity of his self-image, Terry was, in fact, something of a teddy bear and an egghead, well read and benign, albeit with a radical imagination and a teacherly passion for military history and for the writings of Lewis Carroll, whom he loved to quote ("We don't call those mountains where I come from, we call those valleys," etc.). But he contented himself now in telling me that a gale was being forecast for Lake Huron, on which we'd be sailing the following day, and that if, as projected, the waves hit five or six metres, life for anybody on board would assume the character of a slapstick ballet danced among quick-shifting props that might include anything from books to breakfast to television sets to airborne La-Z-Boy loungers. "You don't get seasick, do you?" he smiled.

"No," I predicted.

"Check this out," he said, and he crossed the broadloom to a double-doored closet that contained a neatly rolled Bayley Survival Suit, a kind of stiff rubber bunting bag, safety orange in colour and weighing seven or eight kilograms. A sheet of instructions explained that in an emergency, the suit, *if worn properly*, would keep a person alive for up to twenty-four hours in frigid water.

A few nights later, after a lengthy discussion of storms, wrecks and the plight of sailors lost at sea—a discussion that included an opinionated debate over the merits of the Bayley suit—I said good night to the wheelsman and second mate, went to my cabin and, as an exercise in curiosity, removed the suit from its bag and hauled it into the middle of the room. It was cut to fit a hippopotamus but, even so, I spent ten minutes struggling to get it on, its hood fastened, its zippers and Velcro closed. Having done this, I lurched out in front of the dresser mirror—a preposterous orange Teletubby, laughably impressed by my transformation. The problem was that in spite of the suit's "one size fits all" label, it was too short for me and so stiff, so inflexible, that it compressed my neck and spine to such a degree that I'd have been lucky to survive an hour in it in the comfort of my cabin, not to mention twenty-four hours amidst ice pans and five-metre waves, in the drink, in the dark, in a snowstorm. As I went to take it off, however, I realized that with my hands in the paddle-sized mittens that formed the ends of the sleeves—mittens that, like the suit, were made of stiff quarter-inch rubber—I was unable to grasp either the thick Velcroed flap at the throat, a most industrial appurtenance, or the cord on the all-important front zipper, which had somehow gotten lodged inside the suit.

I couldn't get it off—and at this point had not reasoned that it was the suit's *job* to stay on, at least until you were eased out of it by the blessed soul who, at two in the morning under a halogen spotlight, pulled you from Lake Superior into the safety of the rescue helicopter.

For five minutes or more, I writhed, pawed and sweated, pausing every few seconds to ponder my Houdini impersonation, then continuing to wriggle.

Half exhausted and temporarily resigned, I eventually went over and lay on the bed on my back and closed my eyes, drenched now within the airtight rubber, feeling dreamy and adrift, although unquestionably beached and safe, and as yet unwilling to seek help beyond the suffocating intimacy of my predicament. At a point, I looked down my front and realized that by raising my head, I had created a slight upward bowing in the throat section of the suit. I buried my chin in it and bit at the Velcro neck fastener, tugging at it like a teething puppy until I had worked it open. Then I went at the zipper cord until I had freed it to where I could grab it with my mitts and jerk it downwards a millimetre or so at a time.

On that first afternoon aboard, however, I simply closed the closet on the suit and, in Terry's company, went down to the galley for a lunch that contained more calories than I would have consumed in a day of feasting: clam chowder, coleslaw, pan-fried cod, green beans, beets, boiled potatoes, a side dish of Chinese pork, chocolate squares, cherry pie, and ice cream. The head cook, a savvy old Barbadian named Sam Newton (who, in the words of one of the ship's officers, had been aboard "since Solomon was a cowgirl"), reiterated Terry's storm warning and advised me that the anticipated heaving of the boat was a blessing, not a liability, because motion kept "the food going down" and that without it the meals would "all pack up in the middle."

As I bent to this initial packing, the second cook and lone female crew member, Marion Dorota, came into the captain's dining room, where I sat by myself, and welcomed me to the ship. Having travelled half the planet on water during more than twenty years, Marion knows well the privations and freedoms of life at sea and, perhaps more than others among the twenty-two-member crew, has evolved a poetic, even mystic, nexus with the deep, although she is entirely unaffected about it. When we had chatted for a few minutes, she told me self-consciously that she had visited a tarot-card reader during freeze-up. "It took this woman about three seconds to see that I spend a lot of time around water, and that I'm very deeply influenced by it," she said. "I told her I worked on a ship, and she said, 'Of course you do, dear,' and that if I wanted to maximize my inner strength and growth, I should go out on deck two or three times a day, right at the rail in the middle of the vessel where the only sound is the waves, and hold my arms wide, and sweep the spirit of the water into my lungs and heart."

"Do you do that?" I asked.

"In my way," she smiled. "If I did it her way, the guys on the bridge would have a helicopter out here within twenty minutes to take me for psychiatric assessment."

During my weeks on board, I would have almost daily conversations with Marion, chats that invariably circled back to her extraordinary intimacy, as well as her occasional breaches and battles, with the lakes and sea. "Sometimes when the water's rough, I just want to *scream* at it," she told me one windy afternoon as we stood on the second-level catwalk powering north up the middle of Lake Michigan somewhere west of Petosky. "I just want to tell it to stop harassing me, stop beating up on me. That's how it feels. Oh, a ship can get small in rough weather." From where we stood, we could see across a vast plain of white caps to the distant sand cliffs of the lake's east shore—the so-called Gold Coast of the tourist brochures. "The good thing"—Marion brightened—"is that because you can't go anywhere, you're thrown back on your own resources, your own capabilities to survive and to heal. Eventually the wind drops, and you go out on deck and stare at the water, and it restores you."

On another day, she described how during a "particular bout of melancholy" more than a year ago, she had gone on deck as the *Paterson* passed the mouth of the Saguenay River on the lower St. Lawrence, and how at that moment an enormous grey whale had come alongside the boat within metres of where she stood. "When his head was so close I could have jumped onto it, he did a sort of log roll and brought that one big eye out of the water and just looked right at me. I said, 'Oh yes, thank you, God.' I mean the reminders don't always come that directly that things'll be okay. Sometimes you have to dig for them. But there was no mistaking that one. At that moment, I just felt so powerful and blessed to be connected to the water and to that big, intelligent animal."

Compared with her existence as a sailor, Marion said she found city life "noisy and short," and told me she didn't sleep well in the absence of "the swelling and swaying." When her father died during the late eighties, she stayed home with her mother for a while, and figured she should probably stay longer. "Then one day, reality hit me. I told my mother, 'I've gotta go, Mom,' and a few days later I was back on the water."

In addition to making desserts and acting as an occasional confidante to those on board, Marion was responsible for stocking the refrigerator in the passenger lounge down the hallway from my cabin. On that first run of the season, I was the only passenger on board. Nonetheless, she fulfilled her responsibility with a daily smorg that would have sated the most decadent of Romans during the last days of the Empire: fresh fruit, exotic juices, homemade pies, five-layer tortes, crabmeat sandwiches—all in addition to the three-a-day belly-packers I was eating in the galley. The first of my lounge snacks appeared late that first afternoon, accompanied by a handwritten note that included a surprise quotation from John F. Kennedy: " 'All of us have the same percentage of salt in our blood, in our sweat and in our tears. We are tied to the oceans, and when we go back to the sea, whether it is to sail or to watch, we are going back whence we came.' . . . p.s. We are headed for salt water.'"

At dinner, I told Marion about a quixotic Canadian mathematician who'd recently been gunned down on diplomatic service in Yemen or Kuwait (I couldn't think of his name). The story was that he'd come into northwestern Ontario bush country during the year or so before he died, to try to get a feel for what he called "this land of ancient rocks." He had stayed several weeks and had returned raving to friends that in the wonders of the Precambrian world, in the mosses and lichens and ravens, he had discovered a new truth, and believed now that the primeval forest and billion-year-old granite, as much as the sea, represented the beginnings of life on the planet.

Marion countered with a story that we had both heard concerning a marine scientist who, using seismic recording equipment somewhere off the coast of South America, had detected in the ocean floor traces of a massive heartbeat. The readings had been gathered over several years and across several thousand square kilometres of the Pacific. Suddenly Marion was laughing. "I could have told them about it without any equipment at all!" she announced. A minute later, as she stood to resume her duties in the galley, she said softly, "I dunno about these guys with their scanners and sonar—we're supposed to be impressed at what they figure out. As far as I'm concerned, it's the guy who *can't* find a beat somewhere out there on the bottom that we should be watching. It's that guy we've gotta worry about."

———

Just before eight that evening, our holds brimming with 25,000 tonnes of Number One Durham Red Wheat—enough, I was told, to make a hundred million loaves of bread, give or take a crabmeat sandwich—we cast off lines and, with a vast boiling of silt from beneath the stern rail, dieselled out of Thunder Bay Harbour.

My itinerary during the next twelve weeks would total some twelve thousand kilometres—the eastern half of the continent on water, the western half on land. It would touch Great Lakes and great rivers, as well as prairie and forests and five ranges of mountains; would take in whales and seals on two coasts, ospreys on the Seaway, eagles in the mountains, and would come to count among the most intense and memorable travels of my life.

When at the end of April the *M. V. Paterson* arrived back in Thunder Bay, I packed my aging green van, a vehicle as ripe in its way as the corporate clodhoppers I had incinerated in Illinois, and took off in the opposite direction across the dense boreal bushlands of northwestern Ontario. It is easily overlooked that the distance westward from Lake Superior—the fabled "inland sea"—to Canada's next oceanic expanse is less than a day's travel by car. The evidence of that ocean is obscured by twelve thousand years of drainage, erosion and revegetation, but by the time the westward traveller reaches Prawda and East Braintree, on the edge of the Manitoba gumbo lands, he or she is in fact voyaging across silted deposits laid down by the largest body of fresh water in history, Lake Agassiz.

At another remove downwards, in central Manitoba, are the remains of the ancient Ordovician Sea that covered the area 300 million years ago, leaving a bed of intricately fossilled limestone, which, quarried and slabbed, dresses more public buildings in Canada, including the interior of the House of Parliament, than any stone from anywhere. The bluish-grey version of the stone is as sombre as a tomb, while the amber version is said to radiate the sunlight it absorbed in its formative years—in the way that, perhaps, light from Andromeda might brighten the astronomer's telescope after millions of years in no man's land. But in reality, worms, not sunlight, are the founders of the feast, in that their embedded castings make the Kandinsky-like squiggles that are the stone's unique appeal to the eye.

I lived long enough in Winnipeg to know that the lush beaches and tropical temperatures of 300 million years ago are a decidedly moot point to anyone standing at Portage and Main when the wind out of the north has dropped the temperature in his pant leg to −40°C. But on that day, on the fringe of the prairie, I could not have been more aware of the benevolent seabed beneath me. My attention was particularly keen at a point near St. Anne, Manitoba, where, on an intuition, I touched the brake pedal and felt it drop to the floor, producing no effect whatsoever on the forward motion of the car. The happy coincidence of having my brakes fail on the world's widest stretch of dead-flat sea floor—as opposed to, say, in the Rocky Mountains, where it would have been a more emphatic inconvenience—did not escape me. If anything, it renewed my lifelong meditation on the link between destiny and geography (if someone was attempting to murder me, they were clearly now dealing with a higher power), and of course enabled me to inch along at ten or twelve kilometres an hour into Winnipeg, where I got the van's broken rear brake line repaired.

My westward roll would cross grasslands, gas lands and highlands, and would hit its western terminus two weeks later at the extreme edge of the continent, on a spit of boulders pointed more or less directly at Japan. It would continue on to Port Alberni and Comox and the seventeenth floor of the Young Women's Christian Association in Vancouver. There, my twelve-year-old son Matt and I spent a stewardly night, exchanging hallway glances with women in velour dressing gowns, rapping gently on the door of the floor's coed toilet, or trilling discreetly from inside when the knocks came—"Just a minute!"

In the meantime I was a sailor, and when Terry Holt's first-day warnings of a gale on Lake Huron came to nothing, I was (despite a wheelhouse reproof that I should never wish for a storm at sea) silently disappointed. In the end, Lake Huron did not let me down. On the way back west, as we came up the Detroit River out of Lake Erie, the sky darkened to a point where its colour rivalled the glassy black cladding on the now-visible Renaissance

Center in downtown Detroit. A coil of lightning buzzed the Ambassador Bridge as we were about to pass beneath it, and by the time we'd emerged from the St. Clair River into Lake Huron "a black-assed gale," as one of the ship's engineers called it, was bearing down on us out of the northeast, across a fetch of water some four hundred kilometres in length. The ship rolled heavily as we steered into open water, and, that night, I made the mistake of leaving one of my windows open. When I wakened just after dawn, an intense sleet was being driven three or four metres into my cabin. My books and papers were strewn across the floor, some of them soaked beyond reclamation, and two of the room's four chairs had been dumped onto their backs.

The challenge of my first few minutes out of bed was simply to stay upright. Even a manoeuvre as straightforward as crossing the floor to shut the window recalled lurching through the funhouse on a Paddy Conklin midway. A form letter from the captain, explaining aspects of protocol aboard, had somehow been plastered to the ceiling, where it remained until a day or so later, when it fluttered down dry. I bumped my forehead on the mirror and my tailbone on the shower stall while brushing my teeth, and then stumbled down to the poop deck for breakfast. Marion and Sam were working in wide, oblique stances, and the eggs, when they hit the grill, shot ten centimetres to port and then ten centimetres back to starboard before they had stiffened enough to stay put.

The captain, Ken Strong, chose this particular morning to tell me about the sinking of the *Carl C. Bradley*, a bulk carrier that he had toured as a young sailor and that had gone down in a storm on Lake Michigan during the late 1950s, taking all but three members of its crew of twenty-nine to the bottom. Sailors disagree as to whether ships built earlier in the century of thicker, more brittle steel than what is used in contemporary vessels were better able to withstand the pounding of the storms, or whether their brittleness made them more likely to split and break up, as the *Edmund Fitzgerald* did in 1975. The *Bradley*'s hull plates were not welded like those of newer vessels but were joined with hundreds of thousands of heavy steel rivets. The ship's trio of harrowed survivors reported that, before the boat broke in two, they and the rest of the crew could hear the hull rivets snapping, dozens at a time, like gunshots going off, audible right up into the wheelhouse, and that in those last despairing hours, they pretty much knew what the fate of the vessel would be.

Our own vessel, by comparison, was built of lighter, more flexible steel—"high tensile" steel—and was intended to bend and flow with the waves, rather than simply deflect them. It was constructed in 1985 in the shipyards in Collingwood, Ontario, and to this day is the newest and last of the Canadian lake freighters. Because of the vessel's tendency to flex and twist with the waves—its "whippiness"—a former officer on the ship is said to have nicknamed it "the noodle." I had seen it working to a degree on the Gulf of St. Lawrence, but to see it in heavier weather, flexing anywhere up to half a metre off its axis, was impressive, if not entirely reassuring. Under certain pressures from below or from the port or starboard, a vast and visible "ripple" would come undulating back through the hull and holds and deck.

"They tell us it's safe," the captain told me, "and you've gotta have confidence. On the other hand, you've got to know that any vessel is vulnerable."

The wildness of life at sea—the "outlandishness," as the early etymologists had it—is understandably impressive to a species whose stability on dry land has been honed by a million years of ongoing mutation and selection. It is both seductive and unsettling and, like all forms of the unknowable in nature, induces an ever-shifting warp in one's perspective on the planet and on oneself. Ken Strong's father was shipwrecked three times on the lakes. The last time was at Isle Royale, off Thunder Bay, where in an autumn storm he was left clinging to the wreckage after a forced grounding sent hundred-tonne boulders through the decks and hatch covers of the vessel on which he was an officer. "At the beginning of the next season," Ken told me, "he walked up to the ship he was supposed to work on, and he stopped at the foot of the gangway and realized he couldn't do it, that his life on water was over."

Even at its simplest, the sailor's life rolls a measure of prison hard time into a lyric saga of, among other things, long views, non-stop motion and a thousand variations of ongoing seascape and light. During my weeks on board, I saw sunsets so fiery and vivid that long after they had peaked and faded, I was left standing at the window or rail with an irreducible red knot in my residual view.

On one of the few mornings I was up at dawn, the sunrise made an apocalyptic flare of the hotels and skyscrapers of Quebec City. The light over lakes Erie and Ontario was soft, Floridian, while that above Superior was as hard and glaring as the ice cap. Bridges invariably drew me out on deck: the elegant longbow of the Pont Laviolette at Trois-Rivières; the collapsible-looking bat wing that is the Ivy Lea at Gananoque; Detroit's gritty old Ambassador; and the "holy" Mackinac, the longest suspension bridge on earth, which links lower Michigan with the state's Upper Peninsula. The Big Mack is so massive and spans so much water that, passing beneath it, you get a sense not so much of any human plan or activity as of the spectacles of Genesis and of Creation (the spidery suspension lines you saw from ten kilometres away turn out to be five-thousand-tonne steel trunks, the imponderables of whose place-ment are on a scale with those of Stonehenge, or the pyramids, or Easter Island).

The cities too brought me onto the bridge or decks—Detroit, Chicago, Montreal—as did the lonely little towns of the lower St. Lawrence, with their silver spires and brooding, ambivalent histo-ries. These tiny ancient ports are rooted in the fields and rock cliffs—and in the repressive traditions of the seigneury and parish—but they are juiced by the sea.

On the morning of April 22, I had the first mate, Dan Mac-Donald, who was on early morning watch, wake me twenty min-utes before dawn. I wanted to be up and alert as we passed Cornwall, Ontario, where I had lived for seven years as a boy and still have close friends. I stood shivering on deck in a low-level fog as we slipped past this old bilingual city. But from the perspective of the water, I could get no sense of intimacy or even attachment from its remote smokestacks and church spires, or from its bleak international bridge, on which a couple of teenage acquaintances had died in drunken car crashes during the 1960s. The scenery, though, was as rich as ever: the pastoral islands, like something out of a Gainsborough painting; the accelerated eddying of the current where the channel narrows by Cornwall Island; the Adirondack Mountains in the distance to the south.

My one significant lift on this stretch of my home water came at Hamilton Island, just east of the city, where I got a nostalgic look at the home of one of my all-time best teachers, Emily MacInnes, who is now nearly a hundred years old and who taught me high school Latin with such passion and intelligence that, even today, I can recite tracts of *The Aeneid* and take a better than passing shot at the meaning of obscure Latin-based words. It was, in fact, from the lawn of Emily's home, on a foggy morning in August 1959, that, as a child, I saw Queen Elizabeth sail past on the royal yacht, on her way downriver, having just opened the St. Lawrence Seaway.

From the window of my cabin, one afternoon, I saw a dead man fished swollen and moss-coloured out of the antique miracle that is the Welland Canal. On another day, through binoculars on the bridge, I viewed the skeletal remains of an ancient and unsettling steel wreck protruding from the surface of Lake Michigan. And on dozens of occasions, I caught glimpses of animals whose populations and communities are as intricate and ancient as our own, but are of course a good deal more innocent and vulnerable in their pact with the planet: moose, deer, coyotes, foxes, seals.

One night as I stood by the rail, at a time when no large bird should rightly have been abroad, a shadowy winged creature—a heron? an owl? a raven?—brushed by me at close range and was gone into the darkness. On another night, in the Gulf of St. Lawrence, under a near-full moon, a grey whale as big as an eighteen-wheeler breached within twenty metres of the starboard rail where I was standing. It surged up and forward in a protracted arc, shedding water in all directions, as shiny as rubber in the moonlight.

As much as anything, I loved going up into the wheelhouse in the middle of the night, when the only interior light was the dim glow of the radar or computer screen, or the flickering red digits of the depth gauge and compass readouts. Sometimes the darkness was so profound I'd have to pause at the top of the entry stairs for as much as ten or fifteen seconds before groping my way past the dim silhouettes of the gyrocompasses and chart table to a rickety swivel stool where I'd sit swigging coffee and swapping stories with the second mate, Serge Masse, and his (aptly named) wheels-man, Don Wheeler. We'd talk till 3 A.M.—about storms and shipwrecks and navigation; the Arctic and the South Seas; politics and the environment; foreign ports and, sometimes, foreign women.

Serge, the son of a Montreal judge, is a man of extensive inner range who can comment with equal trenchancy on Quebec separatism, continental cuisine, poetic nuance and the price of escorts—"international nurses," as he calls them—in any number of the world's great seaports. He is placid and heavy-set with Mediterranean blue eyes and a hedgehog haircut—and is, among other things, an unabashed lady's man and gambler. In a tavern in Port Cartier, where we offloaded wheat, I saw him blithely dump two thousand dollars' worth of twenty-dollar bills into a video lottery terminal, and leave with well over a thousand dollars in net winnings. But he is no less a man of the planet, having farmed for ten years, first near Mirabel, Quebec, where he kept cattle, and then on a commune on the red-clay coast of the Gaspé. "It was like a poem," he told me one night, "the fields, the soil, the river, the animals. I used to look around and wonder if my neighbours saw the same poem I saw."

Serge's reinvention as a sailor began in 1983 with the purchase of a small fishing boat in which he once rowed sixty kilometres round trip across the lower St. Lawrence. He said, "One day it hit me that, even though I loved the soil, it was never going to support me properly and that, in the long run, I'd be happiest on water, where I could make a decent living and always be going somewhere."

He applied for entry to the coast guard but was refused—"which was good," he says now, "because I wouldn't have been happy in the little smurf uniform without much to do." Instead he went to marine college in Rimouski, on the south shore of the Gulf of St. Lawrence. Today, he shares a home there with his eighteen-year-old son, who is afflicted with Down's syndrome and with whom Serge spends an hour or so a day conversing via cellphone. As planned, Serge's graduation as a navigator and ship handler became his ticket to five continents, seven seas and, of course, now to the Seaway and to the wheelhouse of the *Paterson*, where he described himself as being "perpetually drunk" on the pleasures of the water and of the job.

Don Wheeler came more directly both to shipping and to drunkenness. He is an impassioned middle-aged Newfoundlander, a redhead, who, in his salad days, on seagoing vessels, thought nothing of guzzling as many as twenty-four bottles of beer a day, plus what he calls "a forty-pounder of hard stuff." These days he's on the wagon, having replaced alcohol with fifteen or twenty cups of coffee a day and an endless succession of cigarettes. When he is not on board he lives on Newfoundland's wild east coast, at Summerford, in a house surrounded on three sides by the sea. The place was once owned by his grandfather, a boat builder, who bequeathed to Don not only his tools and design models but also a yearning for the water which, by the time Don was twelve, had him working on a packet freighter up and down the coast of Newfoundland.

Don told me one night that, as a young deckhand in the Arctic, he had fallen overboard into the perishing waters of the Beaufort Sea, and that it had taken eight months of heating pads, warm baths and whisky to get the savage aching chill out of his bones. On another occasion he was left clinging to a ring bolt on deck, flat out, as a fifteen-metre wave submerged him for thirty seconds or more, causing him to wonder if he'd ever "breathe daylight" again.

"I thank the guy upstairs that I'm still out here working," he told me at about 2 A.M. on a night in mid-April as we cruised down Lake Ontario. "Some guys may be doing this for the money, but I have to do it! It's my life. And I'll tell ya, there's been times when I've been out on the open sea in storms that I was damn sure were gonna take it all away from me. But they didn't, because it wasn't my turn. And I only hope I'll still be out here when it is my turn, because I love the water, and I'd rather end up at the bottom of it than in some bone park somewhere."

On another night, when I had quizzed Don and Serge for perhaps fifteen minutes, Don fixed me with a squint and said, "How about you answering some questions for us now—like, what are you doing out here?" And I explained to him, among other things, that I was writing a book about Canadians and the planet—about the way so many people had lost touch with it and, more importantly, about people who'd kept some meaningful connection.

"Like who?" he said skeptically.

"Like you," I said.

"You mean with the water and so on."

"Yeah," I said, and I told him that a few months earlier, when I'd mentioned the book to Don Paterson, the vice-president of N. M. Paterson and Sons, he had suggested immediately that I take a trip on the lakes and the St. Lawrence on the company flagship. "So, here I am!" I said, adding that I had been going to travel the country anyway, and figured I couldn't do better than to see the eastern half of it by ship.

After a longish silence, Don said in a conspiratorial hush, "Do you write about sex?"

Serge, who had been eavesdropping from the other side of the wheelhouse, piped up, "If you do, you're in the wrong place! Hasn't sex been outlawed in Newfoundland?" he said to Don. "Aren't there enough of you guys already?"

"It's about the only thing that hasn't been outlawed!" Don shot back. "Seal hunting's gone. Cod fishing's gone. We got sex and scenery! . . . And the black market!" After a silence, he said out of the darkness, "You can buy anything you want in Newfoundland."

"Like what?" I said.

"Lobster. Wild game. A quarter of moose costs fifty bucks. Ya say to the guy, 'How much have you got?' He says, 'How much do you need?'"

———

When the talk ran out, as it tended to do in the wee hours, I'd often just sit there, staring out at the constellations and moon, the lights of passing ships, the distant glow of the cities and towns. There is an almost tranquilizing dreaminess to the wheelhouse at such times; but there is a ghostliness, too, and if I sat up there long enough, I'd sooner or later find myself thinking about the darkness below, the second darkness, with its thousand-year secrets, the ghosts of old ships and drowned seamen, and of the gales and cataclysms that had put them where they were.

The shipping routes on the Great Lakes tend to be relatively narrow, so that sailors are constantly passing directly over the spectres and wreckage of the past. There is no equivalent on land— except to imagine, say, a freeway, such as the one in the movie *Road Warriors*, that could simply swallow wrecked cars and buses, as well as the fractured bodies of the dead, eliminating the evidence and allowing traffic to flow heedlessly and immediately overtop. Ships are down there by the hundreds. And the connection to them is anything but remote. I have been told that toward the west end of Lake Superior there is a wreck that sits on end in some two hundred metres of water, so that its prow or stern rises to within a few metres of the surface. When I heard this, I could not help considering what it might be like to cruise over it unawares in, say, a smallish sailboat, on a summer day, and suddenly see its monstrous deathly presence beneath the waves.

Except for a trough along the south shore of Lake Superior, where the water is nearly four hundred metres deep, there is no place on the Great Lakes where the distance between a boat on the surface and the ghost hulks on the bottom is greater than the length

———

of the 230-metre *Paterson*. Lake Superior is so clear that at, say, Gargantua Harbour, on a remote section of the north shore, you can see the wreck of a century-old steamer in thirty metres of water. If the St. Lawrence River were that clear, you'd see, among other vessels, the wreck of the *Roy Jodrey* in the American Narrows at Brockville barely twenty-five metres beneath the keels of passing ships; and the *Heathcliffe Hall*, which went down in the early 1960s when a drunken helmsman hit Chrysler Shoal near Morrisburg, drowning several sailors and a couple of members of the chief engineer's family. It is said that when the *Jodrey* slid to the bottom on a summer night in 1966, its lights went out when the engine room flooded but were dramatically rekindled when an emergency generator kicked in, with the result that the boat could be seen receding into the depths like a doomed but well-lit Atlantis.

Lake Superior is the eeriest of the lakes, inasmuch as the remains of those who drown in it are generally never found. The reason for this is that the gases created when a drowned body begins to decompose—gases that eventually bring the body to the surface—do not form in Superior. The water is simply too cold to support the necessary bacteria. Michigan novelist Jim Harrison, who lives at Marquette on Superior's south shore, has speculated fictionally on the possibility that Aboriginals who drowned in the lake centuries ago may still be down there, in effect cryogenically preserved. Divers who explored the wreck of the *Edmund Fitzgerald* during the mid-nineties are said to have reported discreetly that those on board looked much as they must have on the night they went down.

On some parts of the Seaway, particularly between lakes, and on stretches of the St. Lawrence River, the water is barely deeper than the eight-metre draft of the vessels. The Great Lakes water has been so low in recent years that, as we left the Soo on our downstream trip, there was doubt about whether we'd get into Lake Huron through the West Neebish Channel, an underwater rock cut several kilometres long. While the captains of other vessels deliberated, our own gave the go-ahead and, with a gunslinger's eye on the clearance readout—eight inches, eleven inches, thirteen inches—guided his monstrous payload over the treacherously shallow rock.

On the way up the Calumet River in South Chicago—a river so profoundly contaminated that no dredging is allowed for fear of stirring deadly combinations of toxins off the bottom—I could hear the hull of the *Paterson* scraping what I was told were old cars and machinery on the riverbed. A watchman at the Acme steel mill, where we offloaded the iron ore we had hauled from Pointe Noire, Quebec, explained to me that the earliest of these cars dated to the Capone era and, in some cases, "still held the stiffs" that had been in them when they were pushed off the piers during Prohibition. When I questioned whether the chemicals wouldn't have dissolved the cars' inhabitants, or at least unstiffened them— or perhaps dissolved the cars themselves—he said with no apparent irony, "What chemicals?"

At some point nearly every night, I'd leave the wheelhouse and go down onto the spar deck and outside into the blackness, and stand alone at the rail, or walk up to the bow, where on windy nights the swells would throw spray right over the bulwarks on the forecastle. Or I'd stand between the hatch covers listening to the groaning and creaking of the hull.

One night in a strong east wind and significant roll on the Gulf of St. Lawrence—at a point where the Gulf is perhaps seventy kilometres wide—I shuffled forward along the deck (where I had been more or less advised not to go on such a night), holding tight to whatever I could grab to steady myself. I fumbled up the steel steps that led onto the forecastle deck, and shoe-skated past the huge anchor windlass, past the shadow of the hawse pipe, and latched onto the bow rail with all the strength of both hands. With the forecastle heaving three or four metres at a plunge, the ship rolled into a trough, angling my sight line so that, whereas a second ago my ambient element had been air, it was suddenly water, a black wall of it, surging up and toward me. The boat rose again and fell, and, in an instant, a blinding briny spray exploded up around me, into my nose and eyes and ears, up my pant legs and sleeves, tearing at my hands on the rail for seconds on end, before it dropped as abruptly as it had risen, leaving a tidal runoff streaming past my ankles. I considered backing off, but at first wasn't sure of my timing between waves, and before I could move got ripped again. Then again. But each time I was better prepared, had my feet wider spread, my chin better tucked, although it was impossible not to take the spray in the face and still cling hard to the rail.

It is no particular credit to me that I was dumb enough to be out there where and when if I'd gone overboard (as sailors without lifelines occasionally do in rough weather), no one would have missed me until noon the next day. But to stand up there in the blackness, on my own, with whatever risk might have been involved, and to feel my nerve and adrenaline cranked to the limit by the wildness of the water, was an exhilaration that I was reluctant to exchange immediately for a warm bunk. There were times on deck at night when, driven by urges that I cannot explain, I felt a temptation just to go with it all, to fold everything into the big foreboding comforter, and to plunge, as I had sometimes felt tempted to do when I lived by the Niagara Escarpment and would find myself walking within centimetres of the unprotected gorge at Tews Falls. On this night, however, I wanted nothing more than to hang on tight as I plotted my safe retreat.

I had been latched to the bow rail for perhaps ten minutes when Serge, who was at the helm, switched on one of the gazillion-watt searchlights atop the aft house, not for my benefit apparently, or as any sort of signal to me (as far as I knew, he was unaware I was out there), but to get a fix on whatever it was he wanted to see off the starboard bow. Then it was gone, and the blackness was deeper than ever. However, something about the light's platinum tunnel boring deep into the water had spooked me, and within seconds I was hustling back along the catwalk, up to my cabin for dry clothes, and then further up still into the warmth and camaraderie of the wheelhouse.

There were days on board when I must have asked five hundred questions. How thick was the hull? Was there a sextant on board? What was the purpose of the black ball on the mast stays? The "bulbous bow"? Which of the lakes was trickiest in a storm? Could anyone still navigate by the stars? Where did the *Roy Jodrey* go down? The *Edmund Fitzgerald*? *The Heathcliffe Hall*? What about "Dirty" Gertie, the one-time Lake Erie pirate—where did he operate? What was a "water hole"? A nautical mile? A "shot" of chain? When did the bow thruster come into play? What were those hundreds of tiny black crosses on the chart of Lake Erie (as it turned out, they were not wrecks, as I had suspected, but oil wells, unseen and unacknowledged on the lake bed)? I asked about tonnage and towns, current and horsepower and ship construction; about depths and drafts, sea lingo and foreign vessels; the cost of our endeavour and the frequency of seal sightings. And, of course, about the lives of those on board.

Questions are a prelude to discovery and, in that sense, are as much a part of a writer's capital as are his childhood and travels and imagination. The problem is that answering them can wear people down. One evening when I had asked perhaps fifty of them during a couple of hours on the bridge, I noticed a distinct lull in the general communication. It wasn't until the captain had gone to bed that I asked Terry Holt, who was at the helm, if anybody had said anything about my near-constant badgering. He reflected for a moment, and in his tangential way ("We don't call those mountains around here . . .") quoted what I believe was a Chinese proverb. "To ask a question can mean a moment of shame," he submitted with literary poise. "Not to ask can mean a lifetime of shame."

It was good enough for me, and I kept on asking.

And they kept on answering.

Chapter Two

hen I got back to Thunder Bay, I carried the same
tolerance for momentary shame into my westward
push overland. The sailors had told me it took them
a week or more to regain their shore legs when
they got off the boat at the end of the season. In rare moments
well out onto the prairie I found myself in an unnecessarily wide
stance, or leaning into a phantom roll, or seeming to float momentarily as I lay down, the inner ear still compensating, perhaps even
longing for its too-brief sojourn in the source.

If the prairie seas of the past provide a reminder of the water
they were, it is less in their flatness than in the wind that tears
across them, as relentless as the Trades but, unlike sea wind, as
gritty as 50-grade sandpaper. There is an urgency to it that, during
a dozen years away from Manitoba, I had forgotten existed in the
extremes of flatland weather. Even in the van, with the windows
up, the wind whistled in around the weather stripping and through
the vents into my sinuses and skull. I stopped for gasoline at a

truckstop near Brandon, and walked out behind to examine a tee-tering shed of century-old farm implements. The wind was so severe that I wrenched open the door and stepped inside, emerg-ing a minute later sneezing from the dust but in possession of a greasy, deteriorated book entitled *The Prairie Farmer*, written by Albert J. Heintz and published in 1904. "Greetings, countrymen," its introduction began. "You are farming on the spoils of what, eons ago, was a mineral-rich body of water."

I have never used maps on the prairie, perhaps because even from the height of a car seat you can see pretty much to the edge of the earth—or think you can. The same grain elevator will appear just off your port fender sometimes for ten or twelve min-utes. The old joke is that if you miss the sunset in Winnipeg, you can go up to the second floor and watch it in Regina (above the corn). You can see weather developing a hundred kilometres away, and as I crossed into Saskatchewan, a low-pressure front—for me, a migraine in the making—was coming out of the west under a fast-flowing avalanche of clouds.

By the time I reached Grenfell, the sky was the colour of mica and was as busy as a clothes drier. An almost occult light had turned the new willow and poplar leaves an intense yellowy green. When the lightning came, it was as if an artillery cannon had been mounted directly on the roof of the van, and the rain fell so hard it was quickly a couple of centimetres deep on the highway. Accord-ing to CBC Radio, a half metre of snow was forecast for Canmore and Banff, and fire storms were devouring the brushlands around Los Alamos, New Mexico.

I took a motel room in Swift Current, and wakened to find twenty centimetres of snow on the lilacs. The Trans-Canada hardly seemed to exist beneath the tires, and on the humpy rangelands of eastern Alberta a hard north wind pushed the van around as if an unpredictable quarter horse had been yoked to the fender.

At a highway doughnut shop in Medicine Hat, I spoke to a pie-eyed trucker who had come through the mountains with a load of raspberries from Abbotsford, British Columbia, and who acknowledged having risked his life in the cause of getting them to market before they went bad. He said that on half a dozen occasions through the night he had sensed a perceptible slide of the trailer toward the edge of a precipice as he came around a bend. "Wasn't long ago," he said, "when you didn't *have* fresh raspberries in Toronto at this time of year. And they still wouldn't if dimwits like me didn't risk our lives getting them there." He sipped at his coffee and, with no particular malice, said, "If I had the balls, I'd roll a load of them off the mountainside for the hell of it. But I'd probably end up going with them."

———————

I had flown over the Canadian Rockies perhaps a dozen times in recent years, but had not driven into them for more than two decades, and as I ascended into the easternmost passes late on the evening of May 11, I was struck by an almost crushing sense of their power, not to mention their silence and (in a land-borne echo of the moodiness of Lake Superior) their indifference to my dwarfish concerns and mortality.

At noon the next day, I sat on the deck of the Drake Hotel in downtown Canmore, Alberta, with Caroline Marion and Doug Leonard, looking up and around at the mile-high stronghold of peaks that have surrounded the area for perhaps a hundred million years and will, according to the geologists, eventually weather to the point where they are low-lying grassy plains. In the meantime, they are axe heads and cleavers and saw teeth, weird misshapen tetrahedrons, like dream figments, not so much "timeless," as the travel literature would have us believe, as dense with time and foreboding. "Climbers talk about 'conquering' mountains," said Doug at one point with a sardonic smile. "But nobody ever conquers them—people test their wits and determination against them for a day or two and then retreat."

Doug is the director of the Whyte Museum of the Rockies, in Banff, and, at the time of our visit, Caroline was the acting superintendent of three national parks: Yoho, Kootenay and Lake

Louise. In much the way that, say, Marion Dorota and Don Wheeler might define themselves by their affinity for water, Caroline and Doug are intrinsically creatures of the mountains, whose destinies seem somehow to have been forged on a vertical rather than a horizontal plane.

Caroline discovered mountains as a teenage skier in the Laurentians near her home in Ottawa. In her mid-twenties, disoriented by what she calls "a series of pathetic relationships," and desperate for self-affirmation, she took up rock climbing. She progressed quickly from follower to leader and, on training expeditions to the Adirondacks in Upstate New York, was soon confidently out front, urging muscular young men to keep up, take a few deep breaths and hang in there. "I'd never done anything that made me feel so totally confident and alive," she said, "and so scared at the same time."

When she travelled to Canmore for her first course in high-altitude mountaineering, in 1988, Caroline met Doug, who was visiting from Winnipeg. "By this time," she said, "climbing was my lifeline, my meaning; it was who I was." It is something of an irony that the first six years of the pair's marriage were spent in a version of altitude denial, in Winnipeg, climbing mostly on faults in the Precambrian Shield, near Minaki, Ontario.

Doug, a flatlander since childhood, describes his initial trip to the Rockies with a pair of buddies during the late 1970s, as "the Three Stooges come to Lake Louise." The trio had no proper footwear, no weather protection and one short length of rope. "I had an old pack from Army Surplus," Doug said. "I was wearing street pants! Corduroys!"

But they were determined to climb Mount Victoria, near Lake Louise. Having completed the most manageable part of the ascent, they made camp the first night in a hut at Abbot's Pass, with a group of experienced mountaineers. "When we got up in the morning," Doug said, "surprise! All these real climbers had gone back down. We couldn't figure out why—I mean, it was such a beautiful sunny day!" What the prairie Stooges could hardly have known was that the combination of warm sun and a recent snow-fall would, within hours, begin to send deadly acreages of surface snow sloughing off the mountain. By the time the trio had climbed a hundred metres or so (and had in fact wandered off Victoria onto a precarious tongue of ice called the Death Trap), they were on footing that Doug, the leader, likens to "a pile of dinner plates"—extremely unstable. A providential midday rain forced them back to Abbot's Pass before they could get into more trouble. "In fact," Doug said, "our big accomplishment was just getting off the mountain alive."

Since their marriage, Doug and Caroline have climbed in Italy, in France, in various parts of the United States, and all over the Rockies: on Athabasca, on Andromeda, on Mount Edith Cavell. They had climbed two mountains within sight of the table where we sat: Little Sister and Chinaman's Peak (recently renamed Hai Ling Peak for reasons of political correctness).

As we ate, Caroline looked at the latter and scowled. "Doug used to talk me into these climbs that I had no business being on. He'd be, like, 'C'mon, Honey, you don't need a rope.' On the China-man, I was almost in tears. It was all loose rock! Finally, he put a rope on me, and a minute later, I stepped on a boulder the size of a car and sent it wailing down the mountain. I could easily have gone with it."

Whereas Doug is small-boned and patrician, Caroline is robust and jocular, with boy-cut brown hair and a strapping laugh. In their climbing, at least, they are a kind of high-voltage yin-yang, whose lives as mountaineers have wedded the intricacies of staying alive on high-altitude cliff faces with the precarious mechanics of marriage. Both of them are as bright and energetic as sunlight. But where she is cautious, he is a daredevil, apparently without fear, who has several times been on climbs where his life hung not so much in the balance as over the edge of the balance.

Caroline described a time in the Joshua Tree area of California when Doug completed the upper part of a highly dangerous climb without a rope or any other protection for his life. Another time, on Mount Andromeda, with one of the most experienced guides in the Rockies, he was forced, first, to save the guide's life, seriously risking his own, when the latter fell through a snow cornice and was left dangling—and, later, to rappel down a line affixed to nothing more than a bollard of ice that the pair had carved out of the hardpack on the peak's upper slope.

"When I met him he was a lunatic," Caroline told me quietly after Doug had left the table to greet friends. "He'd say to me when we were up on a mountain, 'Honey, look what I just did!' and it would be some horrific life-risking manoeuvre. I'd say, 'Well, that's *great*, Doug!' When I'm up there, I'm paralyzed with fear the whole time. In the back of my head there's always this little voice reminding me that the next step could be my last. Don't get me wrong—I love the mountains. I feel whole up here. I feel more myself than I do anywhere on earth."

Caroline felt sufficiently herself as we spoke to reveal an almost confessional array of attitudes toward the peaks she has climbed or attempted to climb—or has refused to climb. As their names arose in connection with one point of discussion or another, she responded by turns cynically, hatefully, romantically, at times almost erotically. She "just *loves*" the Red Rocks in southern Nevada, for example—the heat, the colours, the light, the dreaminess of the setting, the sweat-drenched exhaustion that accompanies a day's climb.

Mention Mount Everest, however, and both she and Doug make it clear they have little patience for bravura, or what they call "prestige," climbing. "If you love climbing, you're happy just to be out there," Doug said. "You don't need the badge of having climbed Everest. And that's what it is, a badge. I mean, if the weather's good and there's lots of time, a good guide can get a relatively novice climber up Everest. At the same time, there are climbs here in the Rockies that only a very adept climber could manage—climbs that, technically, are more difficult than Everest."

I asked them to name one, and they said simultaneously, "Mount Alberta," and exchanged what appeared to be a meaningful glance.

After a silence, Caroline said, "It's so dangerous, I've forbidden Doug to do it. Sorry, Honey," she said, turning to him.

Doug said, "To get to the summit, you have to climb through a yellow rock band, really rotten rock; it's very deathly, very spooky. The north face is the ideal route up because it retains its ice into the summer, but it's extremely steep."

"Ice can crack and fall off," Caroline said solemnly, adding something to the effect that Mount Alberta was another Rocky Mountain obituary just waiting to get written.

Doug explained that the climb would require four days: one to walk to the base of the mountain, another to make the ascent, another to descend and a fourth to walk out. He added quite cheerfully that he would probably attempt it this summer.

In the ensuing silence, I stared off at Hai Ling Peak and chewed twenty times on a single bite of my dinner—after which Caroline put her arm around Doug and said with almost telepathic tenderness, "I'll stay at base camp and cook."

The pair recently built a home in the coniferous wilds at the foot of Mount Lady Macdonald—"Lady Mac," as they call it. "Part of the beauty of being out here," Caroline said, "is that you never know what you're going to see when you step out your back door—an elk? a mountain lion? a grizzly?" A while back while Caroline and a friend were walking their dogs, they came directly into the path of a cougar. "We called the dogs, turned around and walked briskly toward home," she said. "It was only later that I had time to think about what it might feel like to have that big mouth full of teeth hit full force at the base of the skull."

Doug is fifty this year—a radically youthful fifty, but nonetheless an age at which many climbers have either quit the big climbs or have pared back considerably in their ambitions. Caroline is forty. "I don't climb as much as I used to," she said late that afternoon. "I enjoy hiking more now—just getting out there. And yet my connection to the mountains is probably stronger than ever—it's just more internalized. There's an old Native saying that the mountains will bring peace to the people. And they've certainly done that for me."

"When you start out," Doug said, "climbing is this huge spiritual quest that becomes a sort of analog for everything about life: the difficulties, the achievements, the getting to the top, the understanding of self. Your connection to the rocks and mountains is totally obsessive—there's hardly a minute when you're not thinking about it. Then gradually over the years, you begin to appreciate the mountains more clearly for what they are—see them for their own huge spirit and presence—and not just for what they are in relation to you."

———

That night, at Golden, British Columbia, I lay with the drapes of my motel room as wide as they would go, looking out at the hemlocks and peaks, thinking not just about mountains but about the method and meaning of what I was up to. I felt buzzed by the altitude and couldn't sleep, so at about 2 A.M., hoping a dose of fresh air would help, I left the room and walked up a narrow gravel road behind the motel. Eventually, I reached a meadow, perhaps half a kilometre above the lights of town. I sat on a boulder under a comet-clear sky in the moonlight and, for perhaps half an hour, luxuriated in the silence, the smell of fir trees and grasses, and the long open view across the valley to the snowy peaks maybe ten kilometres away.

Several years earlier, and a thousand kilometres to the south, in Vail, Colorado, I had visited the former NHL hockey player Eric Nesterenko. He is now nearly seventy and is a ski guide and mountaineer, a man of profound curiosity, who for a month or so every year hikes, sometimes alone, into the formidable mountains of the Wind River country of Wyoming.

"I really believe human beings need a lot of silence," he told me as we strolled though Vail Village one night in an early December snowfall. "We spend half our lives surrounded by electronic distractions and entertainments," by which he meant television and computers and recorded music and the like. Eric sensed that these create "a reality but a very superficial one" which demands little or

———

no effort, so that people end up getting lost in it, drifting, without a sense of time or focus.

"In the backcountry," he said, "way out there by yourself, you have to create your own reality, in a sense create yourself, deal with who and what you are. And as you do this, you shake off all this dehumanizing passiveness and conformity—life becomes childlike again; it becomes magical."

If I was even remotely disconcerted in the Alpine clearing above Golden, it was partly because of Caroline's story about the cougar, and partly because the motel clerk had told me a cougar had been seen near town the previous week, although he thought "some fascist" had shot it.

"Do they actually shoot them?" I had asked.

"Oh, yeah, they plug 'em."

"Who's 'they'?"

"I guess the police or the game warden would do it if it was right in town here. Out on the back roads, lotsa jerks'd put a shell through a cougar's head if they thought they could get away with it, or if they thought it was gonna eat their dog or something."

This was several months before the well-publicized killing of a woman by a cougar at Banff. So, when I asked if anybody had ever been attacked by a cougar, he said, "Not that I've heard about— 'course there aren't many of them around here." Nevertheless, I kept to my boulder, away from the cedars and firs, where I would at least not be pounced on from above.

Back at the motel, I curled into my blankets, and in a lyric dream stood with my twelve-year-old son, Matt, at the top of a glacier, the two of us grinning like chimps. Matt had his snow-board and, because I know nothing about the sport, urged me to join him on it for the long run into the valley. We swooped down effortlessly, carving across the face of the mountain, taking leaps into fresh powder, and finally going over a cliff from which we sailed into free flight, laughing and kibitzing as we zipped across the treetops to the wonderment of those on the slope. It was only as we descended that I realized the forest was full of cougars, hundreds of them, roiling like sharks in a tank. At a point, Matt turned to me and was not Matt at all but a bearded teenager who said in Matt's voice, "Don't be afraid, old man. Just try to learn."

Forty-eight hours later, I met Matt at the airport in Vancouver. He had flown from Thunder Bay to travel with me for a couple of weeks, and by noon the next day, at his instigation, we were walking across a ten-metre-deep snowpack, in our T-shirts, well above the treeline on Whistler Mountain, where a high-level snowboard competition was taking place. On the way up in the gondola, we had watched eagles and ravens and jays, and had seen a bear amble across the mountain, sniffing the newly exposed meadow for bits of fresh browse or an aperitif of spring grubs.

The next day, we caught the ferry to Nanaimo and crossed Vancouver Island to Long Beach, where for an hour or more we strolled around in a receptive stupor, watching the waves break in mile-long rolls across the shallows. For those of us from the middle of the continent, the West Coast, with its blossoms and rain forest and tidal zones, is the equivalent of a hot, sweet bath after the parching cold of winter in the interior. Everything about it seems swollen: the air and smells, the soil and vegetation. Even the light seems somehow thicker and denser than back home, so that almost from the minute you get there, you experience a corresponding swelling of the psyche and senses.

My friend, Maija Sarkka, a Finnish reflexologist in Thunder Bay, told me recently that we receive the earth's energy most directly and naturally through the soles of our feet, and that we commit a cardinal act of separation from the planet when we put on shoes. Babies and tribesmen know better—as do those who go barefoot in the dew to absorb the earliest and subtlest of what the planet has to give.

At the water's edge, Matt and I took off our shoes and waded in, at first cat-like because of the temperature of the water, but gradually warming (or cooling) to it. We walked a kilometre or so up the beach, taking care to dodge the sea urchins in the tidal pools. I am sensitive about them, because once, in Nassau, where

I lived for a year during my mid-twenties, I stepped on one that put half a dozen spines into my heel. The doctor who treated me got me to stand and turn my back to him, then himself turned so that we were standing back-to-back. In the way a blacksmith would take a horse's hoof, he bent my leg at the knee, took my foot between his lower thighs and gave me a sharp rap on the heel with an inch-thick board that he kept for that purpose. When I had finished hollering, he said, "That'll pulverize them; your body'll dissolve the calcium—or else it won't, and you'll carry a bit of sea life with you forever."

———

During the late afternoon, Matt and I drove to the docks in nearby Tofino, where we were met by Steve Lawson, his wife, Suzanne Hare, and their nine-year-old son, Oren. The notion is hypothetical in the extreme, but if ever you were forced to survive in the wilds and you could take along one person as a warranty on your well-being, you could do no better than to seek out Steve Lawson, one of the toughest, gentlest, most knowledgeable wilderness men anywhere.

The Lawsons ferried us immediately up Clayoquot Sound to the wilds of Wickininnish Island, the continent's westernmost breakwater. There the family lives in a ramified home of heavy timbers and hand-milled lumber, without power or phone lines, plumbing or motorized vehicles—or schools (all of the Lawsons' four children have been home-taught on a curriculum rich in the lessons of the rain forest and sea). Their existence on the island is, as Steve puts it, an "exercise in faith," attuned to tides and whales and wolves, and to the Pacific crashing up under their deck, and foot-thick mosses and thousand-year-old cedars and firs at their back door.

Steve was born during the late 1940s on the Sioux Narrows Indian Reserve on Lake of the Woods in northwestern Ontario. When he was four, his mother, who had been raising him, died, and within months his father and stepmother had abandoned him in Victoria. He spent much of the next nine years in a succession of foster homes in that city (and eventually agreed to adoption on the condition that he keep his own name).

"I hated school," he told me. "I couldn't see why I should spend six hours a day cooped up in a room, when there was so much life out there waiting to be discovered."

During summers and vacations, Steve was turned loose with other foster children, under light supervision, and lived, as he puts it, "like a little animal" in the B.C. coastal mountains and, later, on the shore of the Pacific at Long Beach. Centuries from civilization, the resourceful irregulars embraced a clockless existence that took all the old assumptions about wasted time or energy—or aimlessness or troublemaking—and recycled them into a passionately applied education and into the gruelling satisfactions of self-reliance. "They never gave us enough food," Steve said, "so we learned how to catch fish, pick berries, find edible plants—anything to stay fed."

As he honed his instincts both for physical and for psychological survival, Steve also learned how to make crude shelters and watercraft, and learned the character of fauna and flora. Today, he navigates the sea with the same knowledge and confidence that he takes to the forest. He is at ease among bears, whales and timber wolves, and can build a house from scratch, including making his own lumber and shingles.

About halfway between the Lawsons' house on the open Pacific and their beachfront moorage on the lee side of the island is a large skylit shed, rough in construction and virtually covered with moss and evergreen needles. Inside, bathed in the remote greenish light of the rain forest, is a fifty-one-foot wooden boat made of red and yellow cedar, yew and fir. Steve hand-cut and shaped every plank of it—not from a pre-set design, but from his profoundly artful intuitions about the age-old allegiance between wood and water. "I just drew the shape of the hull on the floor, full scale," he told me. "Then I figured each piece out from there." He has worked twenty years on the boat, has built its hull and decks and superstructure and, at the time of our visit, had just finished caulking its planks with a kind of cotton oakum. Thirty years ago, he built an even bigger wooden boat, in a tenth the time. But with the new one, homesteading and family have intervened.

What's more, for most of two decades, Suzanne and Steve have poured thousands of hours a year—as well as notable passion and intelligence—into altering attitudes toward the rain forest and the ocean and animals. In 1984, during the early days of the movement to preserve West Coast forests, when the oldest of their four children, Mat, was just seven, and the youngest, Misty, was a baby, the family waited alone in a cabin on the back side of Meares Island, off Tofino, to meet boatloads of loggers who were due to arrive the next morning with chainsaws and skidders to begin clear-cutting fir trees and hemlocks, some of them three metres across. The trees were by no means earmarked as prime lumber, as might have been assumed of such Promethean specimens, but were as likely as not to have become pulpwood for the Yellow Pages and tabloids of Los Angeles and San Diego, as even the biggest trees often did.

"It was a very stressful time for us," Steve told me. "We were under threat of jail sentences. The authorities had told us that if we continued to defy the law, we'd not only be thrown in jail, we'd be found delinquent as parents, and that our children would be seized by the social services." But the Lawsons felt deeply that what the loggers were going to do was wrong, and they were determined to prevent them from destroying what Steve calls "the magnificence of these billion-year-old islands." The protest was complicated by the fact that the protesters had to address not just the logging companies, but also a provincial government that sanctioned the companies and benefited immensely from their endeavours—indeed, encouraged them to log.

"They have the courts, the police, all the firepower—they can put the cuffs on you and throw you in the dungeon," Steve said. "One of our main fears, of course, was that they'd take away the kids. Suzanne would probably have preferred to vacate at that point and take the kids to safety. But I was staying for sure, and then Mat, our seven-year-old, said, 'Mom, we can't go. If we go now they'll cut down the trees.' So, Sue and the kids stayed. We had a radio phone up there and people were calling up from town—they were afraid for us, because we were right in the middle of the logging plan. We knew we had a lot of moral support; what we didn't know was whether anybody else would show up. I don't think they knew themselves. So it was a long day. Then just before dark, the first of their boats started arriving, and by morning we had more than a hundred people on the island."

The loggers arrived as scheduled. "They had their timber licences and their court orders to clear us out, and their chainsaws ready to go," said Steve. "And we stood at the edge of the woods, and blocked their passage with our bodies. And we told them how it was: 'You're not going to do this.' "

In the end, not a chainsaw was started or a tree cut. "It was a great happening, a very important step for us," Steve said. "For one thing it was the first time that Natives and non-Natives in this area had worked co-operatively toward a goal. But the most important thing was it introduced hope into the overall picture. As far as anybody knew, it was also the first time that a small group of people, whose only weapons were their beliefs and their ties to the planet, had stood up to this sort of power and turned it back."

Four years later, during the winter of 1988, Suzanne and Steve and the family took a tent, some blankets, and the power of their convictions and, with "a few other people," as Steve put it, installed themselves in Strathcona Park, the oldest park in British Columbia, in the middle of Vancouver Island—this time to resist what they and many others considered an unwarranted mining initiative. "I love that park and those mountains; it was one of the places where I spent my summers as a kid," Steve said, "so it was very personal for me. The place had been protected since 1911, and now a mining company had negotiated rights to go in and start tearing it up."

For weeks, the family camped in the mountains—in rain, in snow, sometimes short of food. Steve said, "There were days when it got pretty miserable. After a while your bedding and clothes are just damp right through. Then I got arrested and jailed, which was stressful for everybody. The good thing was that by the time I got arrested, the protest had developed into a big blockade, lots of support. And eventually we proved our point and the government backed down."

Suzanne said, "I think the outcome of these early standoffs helped people recognize a very old truth: that there's power among people who are connected to the land. But it's only there for them if they know it and can locate it and are prepared to use it."

A logging initiative at Sulphur Pass on Clayoquot Sound in May of that same year triggered a significant decision among a growing contingent of those who opposed such endeavours. "These confrontations take a tremendous toll on everybody," Steve said. "And at this point we agreed that, if we were going in again, if we were going to endure the stress, we were going to make it count not just for an individual island or tract of forest but for the whole of Clayoquot Sound, more than a thousand square kilometres of ocean and islands and animal populations."

And so, during the summer of 1988, the movement to preserve Clayoquot Sound—which would quickly gain international notoriety—was forged.

————

Today, because of twenty years of hard work by Suzanne, Steve and many others, Clayoquot Sound is recognized as a United Nations Biosphere Reserve. However, the designation has by no means brought peace of mind or a sense of victory to those closest to the battleground. Steve believes that by bringing the United Nations label to Clayoquot Sound, the authorities have, in a broad sense, *facilitated* logging and development—particularly in the vast tracts of sensitive forest that remain undesignated.

"Those of us who dare to speak up are contained now," he says.

————

"We're cut off by the fancy name, as if it didn't matter what happened on equally vulnerable sounds to the north or south. Really, it hasn't yet been decided what's going to happen even *within* the designated area. Logging plans for Clayoquot Sound are being made right now, and unfortunately, when the battle comes again, the debate won't be whether it's right or wrong to destroy these grand old forests and islands, but only whether it's right or wrong to do it in one relatively tiny area."

Steve is half Ojibwa and half Irish (some might say 90 percent Ojibwa and half Irish). His face is broad and unlined, and he is missing a front tooth, which gives him a rakish look. But his eyes suggest the patience of generations, and he can bring to an issue almost any mixture of old-world Irish fluency and even older-world mysticism. Needless to say, he can also bring a fierce practicality when it is called for.

"Our biggest problem all along," he told me at one point during our first long conversation, "was that every time we made some progress, won a battle, made a bit of difference, I'd see in retrospect that the people who opposed us had been shrewd enough and powerful enough to be able to do damage control, limit us by making small concessions, so that a larger change of attitude or consciousness couldn't take place. At a certain point I was so frustrated by this I decided that, if it became necessary, I was ready to lay down my life for this cause—in fact, I felt maybe it was *only* from that level of commitment that others would find the courage and strength to go on and to get the job done."

———

Given their commitment, it is hardly surprising that the Lawsons have chosen to live as lightly as possible on the earth. They build and heat with driftwood and deadfall, consume no hydro power or natural gas, and cook and bathe in collected rain water. They recycle to a degree that is perhaps best exemplified by a living-room furnace meticulously crafted from an old navigation buoy—or by their forays onto neighbouring islands to gather seashells, which they sell to the tourists in Tofino. Their "facili-ties" consist of a hand-carved wooden bathtub in the living room—a kind of stubby dugout canoe made of rich, reddish cedar and varnished to a showroom gleam—and, in a less-travelled part of the house, a composting toilet whose chief components are a light plastic seat, a twenty-litre plastic pail, and a bucket of cedar sawdust swept from the floor of the shed where Steve is building his boat.

The Lawsons pick berries and mushrooms and wild herbs, and Suzanne keeps a garden of herbs and vegetables. She and Steve put up dozens of Mason jars of salmon as the family either catches them or are given them by friends. Steve is happy enough to fish, but does so with reverence. "When I catch a fish," he says, "I always stop and thank it for giving up its life to feed my family. I get some funny looks from people who go fishing with me. But I don't make any explanations. They understand. Now, even the most redneck guys around here, friends of mine who fish, do the same thing."

Before I knew any of this, I had asked Steve if he was a vegetar-ian. "Yes, I am," he had said—and then, echoing Gandhi's famous response to the same question, "except when I eat meat." He and the family will eat a roast of venison or a roadkill deer when it is given to them, but do not hunt. "I once killed a deer," Steve told me, "and once was enough." When the Lawsons receive a carcass, they respectfully employ every part of it, so that nothing goes to waste. For example, Suzanne uses the hides—along with wood, metal, feathers and the like—in the mixed-media wall sculptures that she creates either by commission or private impulse.

In Steve's younger days, his senses were so finely attuned to the nuances of his surroundings, he could smell fish beneath the ocean at forty kilometres an hour in a motorboat. "I could differentiate between herring, anchovies, coho, anything. I'd just stop the boat, throw out a lure and we'd catch the species I'd smelled. Commer-cial fishermen used to look at me as if I were a madman, or just a liar. Then years later, a couple of them came up to me and said,

'You know what you used to tell us about smelling the fish—well, you're right. It's the fishes' essential oil floating to the surface. The more agitated they are in their feeding, the more of it rises, and the better you can detect them.' "

Steve reflected for a moment and said, "One of our problems is we've stopped trusting our senses—we don't believe what they have to tell us until we see it corroborated in print, or on television. The senses are like muscles, in that you either use them or lose them. And once they're lost, so much else is lost, too, in the way we know and understand the world."

That evening for dinner, Suzanne served a savoury vegetarian stew made in part from the vegetables and herbs that come from her garden preseasoned by the salt mist off the ocean. She also served bread made in the immense wood-burning range that is at the centre of the family's kitchen and dining area. Suzanne is an intense, artistic woman, a mystic like Steve, protective of the land and of the animals, and with an exacting sense of right and wrong, between whose poles there does not always appear to be much middle ground. She is intuitive and motherly, and is stylish in an artfully earthy sort of way. She has no Aboriginal blood, but, by a curious inversion of genetics—indeed, a kind of fated compliance with her life's path—looks more Native than Steve, with her black eyes, high cheekbones and fine-edged nose and chin. She grew up on the prairies, in Winnipeg, but has had vivid intimations of past lives as an ancient inhabitant of the land and seashore on which the Lawsons live. Steve says, "I could live other places, as long as I'm on the coast. But for Sue it goes deeper, she's more attached to this particular piece of the planet."

Were it not for Sue, in fact, "this particular piece of the planet" would, today, quite likely, be either a gentrified tourist resort or a wasteland stripped of its trees and devoid of its animal and bird populations—or both. During the early 1970s, Suzanne and her first husband lived on the 250-hectare island with the permission of the Seattle doctor who owned it and kept a cabin there. One summer afternoon, a seaplane landed off the island's east shore and disgorged a group of Americans, who proceeded to enjoy a champagne picnic on the beach and to discuss openly their intention to buy Wickininnish and make a grand hotel of it, complete with breakwater, docks and tennis courts. All of this, Suzanne learned from them, was to be paid for by logging the place.

"What often happens on the coast," Steve said. "is that people put a down payment on a piece of land, log the bejesus out of it and then walk away from the payments, so that it reverts to the original owner minus the trees. But in this case, the doctor who owned it stipulated that it was not to be logged until it was fully paid for. So there was a snag."

Inspired to act, Suzanne quickly masterminded her own purchase plan, and with a dozen or so friends and family members, had, within days, arranged to buy the island out from under the champagne-swilling chatterboxes. It is both an artful and a delicious irony that Suzanne's group's fiscal validity at the bank was based largely on the value of the island's timber rights. Today there are fourteen common shareholders at Wickininnish, many of whom own cabins on the island, although Steve and Suzanne and the family (Steve and Suzanne came together during the mid-seventies) remain the island's only year-round residents.

———

As we ate, a raccoon that lives just off the back corner of the house stole tentatively onto the deck and watched us through the screen door at the far end of the living room. Wild-eyed gulls and ravens with heads the size of tomahawks perched sporadically on the deck rail, looking in the window. It was low tide, and after dinner I walked out onto the rocks in front of the house to watch the sunset. Perhaps twenty-five metres from the edge of the forest, I turned to get some perspective on the land and the dwelling, only to realize that the latter, with its unobtrusive architecture and unfinished wood surfaces, was entirely camouflaged by its surroundings. From a few metres further out I could see into the cove just to the south of the house, where a pair of adult deer had come down out of the forest and were stepping gingerly among the sea-weed piles and driftwood.

Later, as Steve and I walked across the island to the sheltered beach where several family boats are moored, he told me that of all the fauna the Lawsons have befriended and known on Wickininnish and on surrounding islands—a bestiary that includes wolves, whales, sea lions, eagles, foxes, bears, sea otters, owls, even an occasional cougar—his "best friends" are the deer.

"They've taught me a lot," he said, citing in particular three deer that were brought to the island for the family and have been raised and protected by them. "One of the females just loved playing with the kids," Steve said. "But her favourite thing of all was to come and take us for a walk through the forest. Literally. She'd come up to the house when Suzanne and I were outdoors, and she'd indicate to us with her face and ears that she wanted us to go with her, and we'd follow her off through the forest. When she wanted to show us something, she'd look back at us and direct our attention to, say, a flower, or a squirrel's burrow, or maybe some little beetle crossing through the moss. And when we'd seen it she'd tiptoe on ahead."

Steve and Suzanne are convinced—through intuition and through their understanding of the old Native teachings—that one of the reasons the human race is in such difficult throes is because we have abused our connections with the animals. It was not the first time I had been exposed to the notion. A Native elder of the Little Pic River Band on the north shore of Lake Superior—a knowledgeable old woodsman and trailblazer named Proddy Goodchild—told me several years ago when I visited him at Pukaskwa National Park that a culture that had lost its respect for its animal populations had little hope of respecting itself or respecting other cultures or individual human beings.

I asked Steve if he thought the disconnection with animals had been a *cause* of other difficulties, or was more a *result*, among others, of a variety of planetary breakdowns. He thought for a moment and said, "Both." Then he said, "Native cultures themselves have drifted away from their connection with the spirit energy of animals. Traditionally, the animals were our spirit helpers, you might say a kind of focusing link into the realm of the spirit. But they were also teachers more directly, through their economies and self-sufficiency, and so on."

Steve acknowledged that this was likely to "sound very strange" to those not accustomed to Native mysticism—or to the ancient Tibetan teachings to which he also adheres. "What brings the disconnection into focus for some people," he said, "is realizing, for example, that even our Ministry of Natural Resources, a representative of our government, our highest earthly power, is in the business not of caring for but of killing, say, bears or wolves if they happen to get in the way of human activity. We wipe out the salmon; we wipe out the cod. The government helps start a salmon farm up the sound in a fenced enclosure, and essentially sanctions the killing of any animal that might see a feed of fish in it. They dump antibiotics into the water that destroy all sorts of other sea life for miles around."

Steve reported with undiminished cynicism how some thirty years ago he had heard a B.C. Fisheries officer brag about having shot an eagle. "I said to him, 'Why on earth would you do that?' As it happens the eagle is my particular spirit helper. And he said, 'Eagles eat fish, don't they?'. . . Well? I had to admit that they did. And that bears and wolves and human beings did, too. And so did other fish. But this guy was a Fisheries officer, and in some confused way, I guess he just figured he was fulfilling his duty."

In Steve's view, the lapse in our connection with the animals extends to a myriad of nature's forces—to water, wind, fire, forests, everything right up to whole ecosystems. In keeping with Native tradition, he does not believe anything in nature operates entirely independently of anything else. Nor does he believe human consciousness is disconnected from even the most powerful forces in nature.

"But we act as if it were," he says, "often to a point where we seem to be doing nothing more than defending ourselves against nature. The truth is that we can work *with* nature's forces. We can love them and know them, and they can love and know us. Or we can work against them, and they can brush us off like bits of dust. I realize all this sounds highly impractical, but the possibility of a co-operative relationship with forces so powerful but also so graceful and compassionate is certainly much more than what I ever learned in school."

As the household came gradually to rest on that first night of our stay on Wickininnish, I went out on the deck and sat watching the stars, luxuriating in the musky fragrance that combines rain forest and tidal life and sea. Back inside, Matt and I blew out the candles that Suzanne had lit in our room and, with the roar of the Pacific in our ears, passed easily from one dream to another.

———

Four days later, in a bristling rain, Steve and Suzanne's oldest son, Mat—a coast guard sailor who moonlights as a driver and guide on whale-watching vessels—and their oldest daughter, Cosy, who also pilots whale watchers, taxied Matt and me back to the docks in Tofino. At the offices of competing tourist operators in town, the young Lawsons met their first whale watchers of the day, walked them amicably down to the water and tore off up the Sound with them in a pair of fourteen-seater Zodiacs.

Meanwhile, my own Matt and I took off across the island to Nanaimo, and then north up the Georgia Strait to Comox to visit our old friends Anne Gardner and Ted Holekamp who, incidentally, own a cabin on the lee side of Wickininnish Island, in the area where the Lawsons moor their boats.

That evening, Anne told me a story about the Lawson family's uncanny connection with the animals. "This happened on a terribly foul day in March a couple of years ago out at Wickininnish," she said. "The wind was gale-force. The rain was coming horizontally against the windows. It was icy. The waves were enormous. I remember how bad it was," she laughed, "because I had just decided that no matter how much rain gear and warmth I might be able to pack on I couldn't bring myself to go up the trail to the outhouse. Then, in that very instant, I caught sight of Mat Lawson running down the beach in his wetsuit to his boat. I said to Ted, 'Mat must be going surfing.' I mean, the thought was preposterous, but less preposterous than anything else he might be doing out there in this weather. Then Suzanne came running up the steps, drenched—could we look after Oren for a while? And she poured out this breathless story about how three grey whales had swum right up into their little cove, virtually under their deck. You've got to understand that, except for the odd instance in the past when they'd had, say, a single killer whale come in there, this sort of thing just didn't happen."

While the three whales churned and breached near shore, Steve spotted a fourth grey whale, offshore, entangled in ropes, apparently from a crab trap, and floundering on its side. "He could see that this fourth one was in real trouble," Anne said, "and realized that the three in the cove had obviously come signalling them for help."

Anne is an energetic, intensely focused woman—by profession a speech therapist—whose face is an almost constant study in low-key surprise. "What's uncanny," she said with redoubled intensity, "is not just that the whales would come to human beings for help but that they seemed to know *which* human beings to come to—as if they'd been watching and assessing, and knew where their connections were likely to be most useful to them. And of course they were bang on."

Within seconds, Steve, Mat and the Lawsons' two daughters, eighteen-year-old Cosy (who was pregnant with her own daughter, Laterra) and Misty, who was then fifteen, were girding to deal not just with rough seas but also with a distressed mammal that outweighed and outmuscled the lot of them by perhaps a factor of a hundred.

"As it happened, Mat's snorkelling gear was in Tofino," Anne said, "so he had to race all the way into town to get it."

While he did that, Steve and the rest—a group that now included

Anne's husband, Ted Holekamp, a Comox lawyer—went out around the island in Steve's twenty-foot utility boat, onto the open Pacific, which was by now a survival test in its own right, so that they could assess the situation and at least offer company to the whale.

Immediately on joining them—apparently without overture or consultation—Mat dove into the water, found the tightest rope and sawed through it with his diving knife. "Unfortunately, when the whale became aware of him," Anne said, "it instinctively threw him back, and wouldn't let him approach again. So all he could do was get back into the boat and wait for another opening."

Gradually the drama moved north up the coast, the whale propelling itself with its ineffectual lurching.

"It was a day," Anne told me in summary, "when no normal human being would even have been out there. Ted and Misty eventually had to be brought in because they were close to hypothermia. I guess it was Cosy who brought them in and then went back out with food and hot water bottles that Suzanne had prepared. The thing was that, through all of this, not one of them ever remotely considered leaving the whale on its own for even a minute. I'm sure they'd have stayed out there all night if they'd had to. I mean, a whale was in trouble, and Steve and his kids were determined not to let it die."

After six hours of watching and manoeuvring and waiting—under a continued assault from the elements—Mat's initial work bore fruit and the ropes that bound the whale began to fall away.

"Then suddenly they were off," Anne said. "And right away, the whale righted itself, regained its symmetry and swimming ability, and began moving around as if nothing had happened. So they were all jubilant. They'd saved its life. One of the most amazing things, however, was that, throughout these six hours, the three original whales, the signallers, had entirely disappeared. Obviously, they were communicating somehow. But it wasn't until the tangled whale was free that they reappeared within sight of the boats to acknowledge what had been done. And then all four of them were gone out to sea."

———

Whereas once Canadians went west for the riches and risks of the frontier, accepting whatever pain the process entailed, they now go to *soothe* pain, to shorten the winter and to live comfy with a view of the orchards. It is a westward migration that, thanks to pensioners and the retirement industry, has made the Comox area Canada's second-fastest growing municipality (after Kelowna). The municipality's planning code of late might well be described as: If it ain't developed, develop it. If the trees are standing, cut 'em down. If the green-thinkers are standing, cut them down, too. If they're already down, sit on them.

At the time of our visit to Comox, a land battle more compact but no less compelling than those across the island at Clayoquot Sound had off and on for nearly seven years consumed a sizeable helping of the town's political and media focus, not to mention its deeply conflicted ideological energy. It had engendered threats, lies, tears, bullying, lawsuits—and, very nearly, hand-to-hand combat.

On the morning after our arrival, Matt and I had an opportunity to inspect the battlefield, a densely forested four-hectare site called Macdonald Wood at the east end of town on Comox Bay. We were accompanied by Wayne and Diane Maxted (he a B.C. ferry captain, she a Comox librarian), who generously shared with us both the glories of the site—the deer, the eagles, the ancient Aboriginal encampments—and of the strategic, drag-'em-out war that, once won, had prevented the wood from being 'dozed and ditched, its life as an ancient repository of culture and nature buried beneath sewer pipes, parking lots and the consummate banalities of the "adult lifestyle" (which, almost by definition, seems more destructive and insensate than anything that might be imagined as a "children's" lifestyle).

Diane and Wayne, along with our friends Anne and Ted, and hundreds of other vigorously committed residents, had battled cronyism, cretinism, powermongering and stupidity, as well as

———

plenty of plain old greed. They had mortgaged their houses, begged relatives and friends for loans, cashed insurance policies, refinanced cars, and had finally purchased an old chip wagon from which they raised money at local events either by catering lunches or selling burritos and baking—all to save the last local piece of natural seashore and rain forest on Comox Bay.

None of it would have been necessary had the wood, a de facto park site in the community since before anybody could remember, not fallen into the hands of a gold-bedecked Vancouver developer, Ivan Noort, in 1993. To his credit, Mr. Noort agreed reluctantly to put off building nearly a hundred condos on the site while those who wanted to save it—by name, The Macdonald Wood Park Society—battled to raise the nearly $1.8 million that would be necessary to purchase it from him and turn it over to the town as a park.

"One thing that was really remarkable," said Diane, "was the way our public image changed over those first few months. At first we were praised in the local media as progressive community-minded citizens." However, as soon as the "progressive citizens" enlisted three branches of government—town, provincial and regional—to commit a half-million dollars each toward the creation of the park (the region eventually withdrew its support), the stakes changed. "Suddenly, we weren't pushovers for these developers any more. On the opinions page of the newspaper, and in the letters to the editor, we went from decent people with a will to save a valuable piece of land to some sort of scrubby, conspiratorial commies—greasy old hippies determined to betray the best interests of Comox for our own selfish purposes. Of course it was all about power. A lot of people in the town wanted to see those condominiums built—it was good for business. And they just happened to be people who more or less controlled the public press through advertising. If the local paper ran even a faintly positive story about us, the advertisers came down hard on them to get with the development program—this is what we call freedom of speech, democracy in action."

Several times, the movement to save Macdonald Wood was confronted by surprise cash-delivery deadlines, involving hundreds of
thousands of dollars, the message from the developer being pay up
or we'll start knocking down trees. Which on one occasion they
did, early on a December morning, bringing the faithful running,
some still in their nightgowns, to stand by the hemlocks and firs to
protect them from the chainsaws.

One of the battle's more operatic moments came during a
debate of the Regional District Council on whether or not to
make good its promise of half a million dollars toward the creation
of the park.

"Macdonald Wood isn't legally within the Regional District's
jurisdiction," said Anne Gardner. "It's in Comox proper, whereas
the Regional District is rural. So the council's support had been
contentious all along, and now the developers were threatening
the council members with lawsuits if they didn't back off and
mind their own business. Anyway, the antipark forces had done a
phone poll—some spuriously worded thing that showed that the
constituents of the Regional District didn't want the park. And
they were going to present this at the District Council meeting
where the issue of financial support was to be debated. Well, I got
word of it on a Friday night. The council meeting was Monday."

Anne is a long-time acquaintance of the famous national poll
conductor Angus Reid, and she immediately called him. "I said,
'Angus, I need a poll that shows what the people of this regional
district think about saving an important piece of old forest and
seashore here in town.'

"He said, 'I can do that.'

"I said, 'The bad news is I need it immediately—like in two
days.'

"He said, 'We'll get right on it then.'

" 'Oh,' I said, 'and I can't pay a cent for it.' "

As expected, the antipark group presented its poll at the meeting
Monday night. "There was kind of a big sigh of relief in the
council chamber," said Anne. "The fix was in, the poll showed the

constituents didn't want the park, and the council could now with-draw its support with dignity, blah, blah, blah—which by this time was what a majority of the council members wanted to do anyway to end all the controversy that had arisen. But at that point, I jumped up, yelling 'Wait a minute! I have an Angus Reid poll here that shows the people of the Regional District *want* the park!' Well, of course Angus Reid trumped this local poll, and the mayor jumps up and yells, 'That's good enough for us! The polls cancel. Our support is on!' Eventually, their support was voted down in a refer-endum, but for the time being we were flying high."

What was at stake in Macdonald Wood was not just a chunk of forest or tidal zone or beach, of course, but herons, pileated wood-peckers, deer, otter, raccoons, plus spectacular purple trilliums and a stream that in spring is crowded with cohos and steelheads that have been spawning in the fresh water for thousands of years.

What's more, about fifty metres back from the beach, there is an ancient Native midden, a soil ridge, built up over some 3500 years from the leavings and burials of the Aboriginal tribes who have lived along the bay.

"Can you imagine a developer just piling all that stuff into trucks—the trilliums, the spawning beds, the bones of the dead—and hauling it to the dump?" Anne said with a kind of dispos-sessed laugh.

"One thing I've often felt was important about all this," Wayne told me as we walked through a diffuse shower of sunlight that slanted through the greenery, "is that this piece of property was saved by women. There were a couple of guys on the board of directors, but basically it was women, many of them elderly. And what was bizarre about that was that, for months, these affluent pro-development people were basically beating up on a bunch of little old ladies. It absolutely outraged me to see how far some of them were willing to go to discredit these committed older women, many of whom were citizens of this community long before these developers got here. In fact, the developers said at one point, 'These women have no credibility because they're just living off the fruits of their dead husbands' labours. They don't know the value either of a dollar or of a piece of undeveloped land.'"

"In fact," said Diane, "they knew very well the value of a piece of undeveloped land, a last bit of the wilds in an otherwise over-developed community. And that's why, in the crunch, even though many of them had very little, they mortgaged their properties, gave what they had and, when more was needed, baked cookies to sell at our fundraisers."

One of the pivotal points of the protracted battle was the Macdonald Wood Park Society's loss of the aforementioned public referendum. "The night we lost we drove back to what everybody hoped would be a victory party, and some of us were in tears," said Diane. "And it was that night that we realized that the time had passed when we should be trying to explain ourselves and to find support among those whose views we didn't know. We just said, 'From now on we simply have to identify those who support us, who want this forest preserved, get our backs to the wall and carry on.' And that's what we did."

And in the end, that is what saved Macdonald Wood. That very night, Anne and Ted, Diane and Wayne, and an elderly librarian named Fran Johnson, who had, since the beginning, been the matriarchal spirit of the movement, made a commitment to remortgage their homes. Within a few days, a dozen more individuals or families did likewise. And in the weeks that followed, nearly two hundred families and local businesses agreed to pay twenty dollars a month each, until the mortgages were paid off.

It is a nice bit of synchronicity (unknown to me at the time) that, of the two funding foundations that supported Macdonald Wood—two of a hundred or more that were begged for help, and refused—one was the Paterson Foundation of Thunder Bay, whose chairman is my friend Don Paterson, and on whose ship, the *M. V. Paterson*, I sailed.

As Diane, Wayne, Matt and I walked out of the woods into the sea grass above the tide line along Comox Bay, Wayne said, "Everybody pays lip service to the fact that the public is supposed to be involved in land-use decisions. But everybody who has money and private property knows, in fact, that the last thing they want is to have the citizens involved in deciding what happens to valuable land in their own backyards. We were involved. This park was purchased by little people. The business community made us out to be treasonists, eco-terrorists, scumbags—parasites who couldn't afford to do anything without public funds. They said, 'If you want to save this land, write the cheque—c'mon, write it! Three-quarters of a million.' And we did."

———

Two nights later in Vancouver, Matt and I fulfilled a promise to ourselves to rollerblade around the sea wall in Stanley Park, a distance of nine or ten kilometres. As we sat on the curb on Alberni Street pulling on our skates in the presence of rose gardens and pastel hydrangeas, a luxuriantly coated skunk came strolling up the sidewalk toward the core of the city, imperturbably self-possessed while pedestrians (as in a parody of what anybody ought to do in the presence of a skunk) bounded several metres across the boulevard to get out of its way. On the outer tip of the park, under the Lion's Gate Bridge, we spotted a sea otter moving in syrupy loops down the Burrard Inlet, and taking an occasional torpedo lunge forward to make up distance against the incoming tide.

We ate in a Japanese restaurant on Robson Street and, unable to quit gorging on the city, walked till three in the morning. Sometime after midnight, on Denman Street, I smoked a smelly cigar and felt like Huck Finn's pappy, with my truant kid and our irredeemable affinity for the wee hours. Even amidst the garbage smells and car exhaust at the south end of Robson Street, the downtown air hints of dogwood and evergreen from neighbouring gardens and parks, and the smell of the sea comes faintly up from English Bay and from the Burrard Inlet.

Matt and I have travelled thousands of kilometres together, including several weeks with the Great Wallenda Circus in 1997 and, despite being temperamentally disposed to quarrelling, know pretty well one another's requirements and preferences. I enjoy night driving, particularly in moonlight, and as we cruised the sea coast, or climbed into the mountains, or sailed out onto the prairie, I would, as he slept in the seat beside me, speak softly to him about our good fortune at being out on the road with one another, about the way life passes so fleetingly and elusively or, in a drowsy presentiment of some future sag into nostalgia, how we would remember these times (although I entertained such thoughts less, I would say, out of certainty than out of a kind of winsome longing bewilderment that has dogged me for much of my adult life and tends to surface in times of solitude). Even the most resonant platitudes are unequal to the connection one feels in such circumstances, and at times I would simply reach over and hold Matt's smooth hand as we sought out yet another wayside motel or all-night café, where I could get a bump of caffeine as Matt poured himself groggily into his snowboarding or skateboarding magazines—or sometimes into intense conversations about why things were the way they were.

One night in the interior of British Columbia (as if, even in his innocence, he had seen as much as he needed to of life's tantalizing caprices), he said, "Isn't it strange how we're doing what we're doing and other people are doing what *they're* doing?" On another night, he wakened abruptly as I made the turn off the Trans-Canada into the village of Lake Louise, Alberta, and agreed to run in and check the cost of a room at one of the splashier local hotels. He came back with a figure that topped two hundred and fifty dollars, and I said, "Let's check that place over there—I saw some kids going in." And we drove through a little copse of firs, and across the main road through town, into the parking lot of a magnificent piney lodge, made mostly of foot-thick logs, obviously newly built, with stone pathways and splendid side buildings but with no identification that I could see. Matt came back giddy to report that it would be twenty-six bucks for me, thirteen for him, and that they had one booking left. "Well, get in there and get it," I enthused, not realizing until I reached the desk that we had come into the magisterial local version, the Ritz model, of the contemporary International Youth Hostel.

The place had a baronial library and archive, a forty-table restaurant for granola gourmands, cathedral windows and ceilings, and a great, hand-hewn lounge with a medieval hearth. We forked over cash for a "dorm" accommodation that we were told we would be sharing with four others. I had not slept in a youth hostel in perhaps twenty-five years, and remembered them as joyless fart-ridden barracks, sometimes crumbling estates, where men and women were separated by thick walls and by the dour watch of security matrons who delighted in their officiousness and doled out breakfast so that no one got an extra lump of powdered milk or dribble of semolina (the hated "white porridge" of my childhood, preferred only to the satanic "yellow porridge").

We unlocked the door to our room and stepped inside. If at that moment my surprise had been an animal, it would have been something big and fuzzy and would have been up on its back legs on the grey carpet in the middle of the room. Within an instant, four black-haired heads rose simultaneously from four bunk beds, showing at first surprise and then wide oriental (unmistakably female) smiles. Our roommates for the night were four fetching, university-aged women from mainland China, only one of whom spoke any English. That one, wearing royal blue Umbro shorts and a blue cotton sports bra of some sort, was immediately on her feet, seemingly as surprised as I was.

"I guess maybe we've got the wrong room," I said.

"Hrong Hroom?" she said with a tilt of her head.

"*Not our room*," I said emphatically, my heel still propped against the open door.

"Yes, yes," she said as she advanced on us, then "No, no, no," as I turned to go back into the hall. "Hwun bed, hwun bed," and she beckoned us in, pointing up behind us to a loft above the door, where there was still space for two for the night.

As we brought in our bags, one of the young women went into fits of giggles underneath her blankets. By the time she emerged, she seemed merely curious, and in retrospect, I view the night as a gratifying exercise in community, in that Matt and I and these decidedly foreign women so easily transcended what might have been gender or language or cultural barriers—or even privacy or domestic concerns—and simply lived together, however briefly, as peacable citizens of the planet.

Just after dawn, I looked over the rail and found all four of them up and packing. Three of them were fully dressed, while the fourth stood unselfconsciously in the middle of the floor in thick-ish wool underwear that I will not attempt to describe, except to say that Victoria's lacy secret is well-kept from at least one Chinese university student. A few minutes later, when they were about to leave, the one who spoke English glanced up to where I was now sitting in the loft, and said with stentorian aplomb, "Canada many hundred more beautiful than *many* beautiful lily!" She pointed out the window at a dense stand of fir, and at the sunlit snow peaks behind, and said (in more or less these words), "Canada many more beautiful with many more long trees on a mountain!" The others chimed in not with words but with nodding and confirmation of posture.

Momentarily disarmed by her poetics, I had gone into a mental stall, and was merely gazing at the four of them, when it occurred to me that some response, some closure, was in order. "Yes!" I blurted. "Thank you!" And with a cheery string of goodbyes, they were gone out the door.

————

The following day, on the Saskatchewan prairie, we bucked north-east winds so savage that, every time a semi passed on the two-lane Trans-Canada, trapping us momentarily in its blast, the combined forces of truck and wind knocked us half a metre toward the ditch. What made things worse was that the primary hood latch on the van had broken in Medicine Hat, meaning that every new wallop of air threatened literally to peel back the hood. But at midnight, just east of the Manitoba border, the wind dropped almost to nothing, and I realized at a point that the northern lights were raging above us, having somehow picked up the work of the wind.

We pulled off near Virden for a better look, and stepped across the spring-matted grass of the road allowance and out into the freshly ploughed furrows beyond. The sky was a bowl of bristling green gases, and for ten minutes or more we watched the show, until quite suddenly it tailed off. However, as we were about to return to the vehicle, we noticed an immense oval of light the colour of molten steel behind the trees on the southeast horizon. It was partially covered by cloud wisps that divided it into a head shape and abdomen, and was so unlike anything either of us had seen, we simply stared at it, transfixed by its colour and intensity, and by our own inability to make sense of it. I know the story of the man who mistook his wife for a fedora hat, and his reflection for himself—and a minute later felt humbled having to admit to Matt that our bright alien light, our message from Garcia, had risen perceptibly in the sky and was obviously the moon (which, of course, we did not normally see as low and bright and huge as it can be seen above a prairie horizon).

But the truth seemed no less subtle for the letdown. We are haunted by the ghosts of our phylogeny—the cats, the hunters, the lunar idolaters—and we had been mesmerized briefly into seeing something more than we would otherwise have read into the night sky. My dad described to me years ago how my mother, a lifelong Christian, had, in a moment of private crisis, asked him how much of the Bible he thought was metaphor and how much should be taken literally. "I thought about it," he said, "and realized the only answer I was comfortable with was that we had to see it as a mixture, undivided, the poetic and the literal as one." Likewise, the moon that night was a union of its own transfiguring glitter—at first unrecognizable—and the glitter of perhaps the best-travelled metaphor in history.

PART TWO

Chapter Three

I would have taken these travels for their own sake, because I love the Canadian landscape, and I love being on the road—whether it is a literal ribbon of pavement, or a trail through the mountains or forest, or a wide flow of water beneath a ship or sailboat or canoe. What's more, during the early months of the year 2000, my personal life was somewhat tattered, and as a tonic for emotional distraction I have never known anything that is at once more soothing and stimulating than time on the road.

But I had another reason, too, a more Euclidean reason. It is obvious to anyone with an eye for the evidence that, as a culture, we have drifted decidedly from our detailed and long-standing links with the earth—from our one-time empathy with its processes and powers and messages. My purpose in going was not so much to collect proof of this disengagement but, rather—accepting my complicity in it—to regain a sense of personal acquaintance with the land and water, and also with the proportions of the country from one coast to the other. What's more, I wanted to explore the countless connections that remain—and to meet people who embody those connections, through some spirited affinity for the wilds and wildlife around them.

It hardly needs saying that an immense range of such affinities exists, a range accentuated in Canada both by the vastness of the country and by our extremes of terrain and climate. Even within our borders, the landscape and climate constitute thousands, if not millions, of overlapping determinants of history, the economy, industry, transportation, cuisine, recreation, shelter, clothing, art, language, literature, politics and communication.

A recent television commercial for Molson's Canadian beer parodies our stock identity as Canadians—true-hearted backcountry trailblazers. But whether in practice or at heart (and among a host of more global characteristics), we are indeed rail-riders, summer worshippers, cottagers, berry pickers, toque-heads, nature photographers, curlers, ice-skaters, sleigh riders, snowboarders, bird feeders, parka and Sorel wearers, lumbermen, trappers, hunters, foresters, miners and mining investors; people of the highway and the long journey, accustomed to light deprivation, to the politics of vastness, regionality, consensus, uncertainty, social compromise (and sometimes parochialism) . . . fur garments, long underwear, large farms, good water (with recent notable exceptions), cheap bread and lumber, maple syrup, open spaces, buffalo-wool sweaters, down comforters and sleeping bags, Hudson's Bay blankets, triple-pane windows, R20 insulation, ice-rutted streets, salt-eroded cars, McIntosh apples, autumn colours, wood-frame houses, wood-burning stoves, cedar-strip canoes, maple and pine furniture, snow-burdened winters, real Christmas trees, white Christmases, wool mittens, frozen cheeks, winter depression, northern ice roads, Arctic char, Canada geese, smoked lake trout, tourtière, moose tongue, cod tongues, network radio (born of territorial spread).

Even the most common and banal of our household knick-knacks and crafts—*especially* the most common and banal—are larded with likenesses of loons, moose, rainbow trout, great grey owls, polar bears, Canada geese. Toronto Mayor Mel Lastman's idea of gussying up his city for the tourists last summer was to place big cartoon moose sculptures, most of them intricately painted, in hundreds of locations across the city. Not surprisingly, the endeavour showed less instinct for the animals, or even interest in them, than a third-rate cartoonist might show for the subtleties of human nature. It was kitsch gone wild(s)—minus the wilds, where, in reality, you are less likely to see a sculptured moose than to see one standing eerily in the twilight on the highway shoulder, or dead in the ditch with its legs up, or ripped up by wolves, or surrounded by pecking ravens. The food chain is relentless and so efficient here in northwestern Ontario, where nature is still allowed to go to work, that when a collared moose died recently in Pukaskwa National Park on Lake Superior, by the time park officials got to its location, via the radio collar attached to its neck, there was nothing left but a few bits of hair and the radio itself, without even the leather collar. The lot of it had been chewed up by a cast of predators that might have included anything from wolves, lynx, bears, foxes, marten, weasels and skunks, through to ravens, jays, mice, shrews and maggots.

Our currency and coinage have, for decades, carried more or less the same images as our kitsch crafts, and our flag bears a likeness of the leaf of the sugar maple. Our iconic paintings, whatever one might think of them, are, predominantly, of evergreens, granite and lake water, and the homes of half the affluent families in the country display an item or two of Native or Inuit art.

Despite urbanization, we are a culture familiar with rock cuts, roadkill and rifle kill, and, even when we are not familiar, are inclined, it has occurred to me, to take a more than passing interest in the Gothic rawness of the carnage of the highways and hunt. And, of course, in fishing, which comes up routinely in our movies, our literature, our visual art and our newspapers. The sports sections of even those newspapers sworn to such bloated enterprises such as the NHL, NFL, and major league baseball continue to carry weekly columns on how best to catch a speckled trout or pickerel—and on birdwatching and bird-feeding. Not long ago in *The Globe and Mail*, I saw a story on dirty dealings and trash talk among three-hundred-pound NFL linemen, and beside it a column on how to attract red-eyed vireos to your woodlot feeder (not with dirty dealings and trash talk). During a recent forty-eight-hour stretch, the central Canadian media lavished more attention on a moose that had been stranded on the ice of Lake Superior (and died of trauma after being rescued) than they did in total on the Middle East peace talks, the collapse of the NASDAQ and the Bush-Gore election farce.

In Deep River, Ontario, the Atomic Energy of Canada town where I lived as a boy—and that is, pound for pound, the most educated community in Canada—dozens of sophisticated scientists dropped everything at a point each year in autumn and hit the woods. They appeared a few days later, like sixteenth-century musketeers, with slaughtered deer and moose roped to the fenders of their latter-day steeds. I have writer friends who, while steeped in artistic nuance, are obsessed with hunting and fishing to a point where, when they meet, their talk of these supplants any talk of books or ideas or cultural abstraction. As a boy in Muskoka, I watched the wife of one of Canada's most successful developers spend hours on end, all summer, standing on her dock on Clear Lake, casting in futility for smallmouth bass. And I remember my stepgrandmother Wilkins, a staid and corseted paragon of Germanic Ontario values, whooping ecstatically from the rear seat of the rowboat as she pulled in a twelve-inch bass in front of the family cabin.

In the autumn, here in the north, I am likely to see any number of pickup trucks on the road, or even in town, ferrying formidable fresh-killed moose from the forest to the garage floor, where the carcasses get butchered into roasts the colour of Welch's Grape Juice. Even in Toronto, as a teenager, I saw occasional dead deer tied to the fenders of cars, and during the early seventies a girl-friend and I saw a slain moose in a truck on an East York back street in late November. I remember it particularly because of our curiosity and how, as we sidled over to it, we were startled to see its big black tongue lolling out into a pool of thickened blood.

My friend Dan Diamond's father owned a cold storage facility in Winnipeg during the 1960s, and in autumn would occasionally store a fresh-killed deer or moose for a hunter who had not yet had a chance to butcher his kill. To this day, Dan, a Toronto publisher, swears that when he went to view a moose shot by the famous Winnipeg Blue Bombers football coach Bud Grant, this particular creature possessed the X-shaped eyes of the Bullwinkle cartoon—as well as a tongue that Dan described as "hanging out like a scarf."

At Thanksgiving 1999, as I drove with my family through the northwestern Ontario town of Ignace, we spotted a gutted moose suspended by its back legs from a steel arch at a hunting lodge by the Trans-Canada Highway. What caught our attention was not so much its being there—it was one of perhaps five thousand such carcasses on display somewhere across Canada that day—as its *tremendous size* (and, for me, at least, a sense, however false, of the disproportionate ecological responsibility that would seem to go with killing such a beast). Stretched out, it was well over four metres long, had a chest a metre deep and a body cavity as big as a clothes closet (my daughter, Eden, then four, referred to it later, distastefully, as "that horse with no stomach"). I have a photograph of my Grandfather Scholey, as a young man, with his Toronto hunting club—eight of them—standing in the woods beside eight newly killed white-tailed deer. And I have seen Muskoka photos from perhaps the 1920s in which as few as two or three fishermen display horizontal strings bearing as many as three hundred pickerel or trout.

Last spring in Banff—where it is easier these days to buy a twenty-thousand-dollar fur coat, or two-thousand-dollar après-ski duds, than to track down a loaf of bread—Matt and I asked directions to the skateboard park and were told to go "straight out Wolf Street, take a right on Squirrel, and a left on Muskrat." Practically every town in Canada has a Maple Street, a Pine Street and a

Spruce Street—an avenue des Pins, or rue d'Érable. Our apartment blocks and retirement homes are named Oak Manor, Maple Ridge and Larchwood Lodge. Sometimes such names are an all-but-savage irony. The ostentatious housing development and golf course developed recently by friends of the Ontario premier, Mike Harris, on the shores of Lake Nipissing—a development that was pushed heedlessly ahead as the Harris government's own environmentalists warned that it would ruin irreplaceable pickerel spawning beds and disrupt the $94-million annual sport fishing industry—bears the poetic dub Osprey Links (citing a bird that may well be wiped out in the area by the development).

The landscape is honoured even in the breach these days by the view that "serious" culture in contemporary Canada owes little or nothing to the realities that inspired A. Y. Jackson and Emily Carr and E. J. Pratt—not to mention, say, the now-devalued Cornelius Krieghoff, or Jean de Brébeuf, who risked papal censure by rewriting the Christmas story in the images and landscape of the Huron Indians.

During the nineteenth century, eastern and central Canadians lived from (pine) cradle to (pine) coffin on the beneficence of the great white pine forests of the Maritimes, Quebec and Ontario. Pine was housing, barns, churches, bridges, boats, wagons, rail cars, rail ties, mine timbers, sidewalks, furnishings. For thousands of farmers, it was little more than an obstacle to be cleared and burned. But for tens of thousands, it was jobs—in the sawmills and finishing factories, and in the hundreds of boisterous logging camps, where lumberjacks worked from sunrise to sunset, generally in the company of draft horses, oxen, or, in one reported case, a team of domesticated moose.

The demographics of our "Frenchness" and "Englishness" were themselves determined in some part by the land and its life forms—notably, beaver pelts, and to a lesser degree, "mast" pine and available arable land. Likewise, we are, say, Finnish, because the boreal forests of northwestern Ontario (home, today, to the largest population of Finns outside Scandinavia) are indistinguishable from those around Helsinki. And Chinese, at least in part, because when navvies were needed to build the planet's longest and most complicated railway (a response to the land and its vastness, if ever there was one in this country), impoverished Chinese villagers and peasants were available and exploitable. While the sprawling Chinese populations of contemporary Vancouver and Toronto are largely a result of more recent immigration, there are still hundreds of Chinese families in towns across the country—in Grenfell, Saskatchewan, and Brooks, Alberta, and Sutton, Ontario—who can trace their roots in Canada to the construction of the railway, and to the CPR's grandiloquent offer to transport the single young men who laid the rail to any place the railway made a stop.

Urban cynics might benefit from a reminder that even the character of our cities is largely a response to land forms and water—and, increasingly, to extremes of climate. Winnipeg, Saskatoon and Edmonton, for example (and to a lesser degree, Toronto and Hamilton), have all been reconfigured and excavated in recent decades, so that people can get around without going outdoors during the cold months. Not surprisingly, Canadians constructed the world's first indoor mall, Yorkdale, in Toronto, during the late 1950s. We build in the valley between mountains, or on the ridge by the salt marsh, or on the south side of the hill, with south-facing windows. Or on the water. There is hardly a town or city in Canada that is not on some significant eighteenth- or ninteenth-century water route—a river, or lake, or protected ocean harbour. Those that aren't grew up to service rail lines, highways, forestry, agriculture, mines—which are themselves responses to the earth.

And yet the notion persists among our cultural and economic realists that contemporary Canada has little to do with the raw planet or wilds, and that the image of Canadians as "hewers of wood and haulers of water" (as they invariably put it) is defunct. And, of course, they're right. We are certainly no longer hewers and haulers (the H&H have been reborn as cultural and economic realists). Nevertheless, the woods and waters that we hewed and hauled are still out there, big time, and are (the futurists tell us) getting bigger. As a measure of the role they play in the "real" lives of Canadians—not to mention the country's spirit and mythology—we need only remind ourselves that an estimated fifteen million Canadians vacate our cities at some point during the summer to spend time among the lakes and forests (joining five million who are already in a landscape that many city dwellers would consider "wild"). We might further remind ourselves that a vast chunk of the country's literal wealth is still in metals, minerals, wood products and farmland, as opposed to technological or financial expertise.

In an era when billions of dollars' worth of NASDAQ shares can be vapourized in seconds, we should perhaps be more grateful than we are for such hopelessly old-fashioned commodities as gold and nickel and palladium. And, of course, water—which we are reminded almost daily will be the "oil of the twenty-first century," or "blue gold," as some have called it. With per capita supplies of fresh water shrinking dramatically relative to exploding populations and industry—and in an era of globally threatening climatic changes—Canada is in an almost inconceivably privileged position. Of the world's total supply of water, just 2.6 percent is fresh. But more than half of that 2.6 percent is locked up in ice caps and icebergs, leaving just 1 percent of the world's water available for human use. Canada controls more than 20 percent of what's available, about a fifth of it within view of where I sit writing on the shores of Lake Superior. It is the sort of vastly inequitable distribution of wealth that, historically, has been known to trigger wars—and may yet threaten our sovereignty as the need for fresh water gets more desperate, particularly among the desperate rich of, say, Silicon Valley and Los Angeles and Arizona.

Jingo-talk aside, Canadians will have to be most judicious during the next few decades as we grow into our globally dominant position. Will we allow this greatest of natural resources to be "privatized" and gobbled up by the parched cities and corporations of the U.S. south (both NAFTA and the World Trade Organization advance the notion of water as a global commodity to be bought and sold subject to market forces)? Or will we resist the demands of affluent golf course and swimming pool owners, and use our influence democratically to help ensure that people everywhere have access to good water, and to ensure that ecosystems are not fatally weakened or destroyed in the rush to make wealth out of lakes Nipissing and Superior and Athabasca?

As a friend once pointed out, no matter how much distance we may believe we have put between ourselves and our wilds, the land does get a last honest lick, in that our tombstones are carved almost exclusively out of the granite of the Canadian Shield. At the same time, the land's licks are getting increasingly tiny and precious, and the perspective of the realists and cynics are increasingly hard to ignore. And here my argument languishes, inasmuch as, for many, our wilds have indeed become an irrelevancy, or at very least a pale and deodorized impression of themselves. It requires no great insight to see that much of what our grandparents and great-grandparents knew of the planet, their capability to "read" its messages and respond to them, has been lost or compromised to our hugely accelerated and depersonalized way of life. Instead of snow-shoeing or skiing through the forest, attuned to the subtleties of its sounds and sights—or sailing or canoeing, or riding in carriages or sleighs (the design of early cars approximated open or convertible horse carriages)—we blast across the landscape on snowmobiles, or in motorboats or air-tight vehicles. My ancestors, I am told, knew every pothole, ever piece of gravel—not to mention every clump of orange lilies or marsh marigolds—between their town and the next. What's more, they had an implicit awareness of the vastness and proportions of the planet. Jet travel has, for the most part, deprived us of that sense. Even driving does that. My five-year-old daughter, Eden, asked me recently why, when we drove someplace, it wasn't nearly as far as when we walked.

Distances that are, today, covered in two hours in the air were, at one time, covered during months on foot or in a canoe by the likes of the French fur trader Jean Baptiste Laguimodière, who during the winter of 1815, walked from what is now Manitoba to Montreal to deliver news to Lord Selkirk. Those in Montreal expressed dismay that he had walked the distance, but he is reputed to have answered, "Actually, I ran most of the way." By contrast, my Uncle Ralph Currie (whom I love well and in no way intend to demean) drives the weekly green bag of garbage from his cottage on Clear Lake in Muskoka thirty or forty metres up the lane to the main road, where the bag is picked up by the municipality. My neighbour drives to the corner convenience store, a distance barely greater than what he has to walk to get to his car behind the house. The literature of travel is revealing. Any piece of writing about a character in a jet is invariably about what goes on inside the fuselage. A story about a car traveller more often than not takes in the rivers and forests or cityscape beyond the car's windows. Stories about walkers, on the other hand, are almost exclusively about surroundings—smells, factories, rose gardens, riverbanks.

Last spring, on one of the final days of skiing in the Nor'Wester Mountains southwest of Thunder Bay, I drove out to Loch Lomond with my daughter Georgia to pick up my son, Matt, who had been snowboarding. We went early, and on a whim decided to walk up one of the runs, which was closed because much of the snow on it had melted. But we met skiers from other runs and, as we gained altitude, were asked with increasing incredulity how we'd gotten there—the upper part of the mountain was simply not a place anyone got to on foot. The ascent took us an hour, and the payoff as we climbed was a stream of subtle revelations about the way spring comes to the Nor'Westers: late-blooming pussy willows (higher altitude), tender red shoots poking from between the ice patches, drowsy squirrels, opportunistic ravens gliding low over the terrain, looking for a spring-intoxicated mouse or vole. At one point, we came across a garden of last year's puffballs, maybe a thousand of them, and stamped them into clouds of brown smoke.

Our reward at the top was, among other things, an exhausted and tantalizing hunger—for me, an almost dizzying hypoglycemia—that we satisfied at the bottom with a meal of coq au vin, fiddleheads and fresh strawberries (well, at least that's what the french fries tasted like in our state of craving). The richer reward was the satisfaction of having done it, *on foot*, combined with a heady mountaintop view of Lake Superior in the distance to the east, of an endless lowland of wilderness to the west, and the feel of the soft south wind coming in across the spruce tops, carrying the fragrance of newly bared soil and of the wakening forest.

The farmers of old watched the skies and barometer for coming weather, while sailors looked to the stars for navigation. Today, electric lights have, for the most part, robbed us of the opportunity even of *seeing* the night sky. Our capabilities to read the wind and humidity have been forfeited to computerized forecasts, our knowledge of food and its sources to shrink-wrapping and to the global economy. Whereas, once, a community's food came largely from farms, fields and orchards within miles of its borders, almost everything we eat these days comes tidy and taste-deficient from somewhere else. Peaches and pears arrive as hard as India rubber, tomatoes as pale as chicken parts. To this day, traditionalists from certain isolated valleys in the Italian Alps will eat no food from anywhere else, in that, by definition, it will have taken two days to reach them and must, therefore, either be stale or have been rendered inferior by the trip. Virtually every village in rural France or Italy has its own wines, cheeses, hams, curing methods, vegetables and fruits, the tastes of many of which are distinguished by the soil in which they grew. Why can't champagne be made from champagne grapes grown in other parts of the world? Because the true product comes from grapes grown in the Champagne soil, in the Champagne air, with the subtly imparted nuances of each. The Romans and Greeks are said to have had such educated palates that they could tell by taste which rivers, lakes or seas their fish had come from.

Unfortunately, profits and market ethics—or lack thereof—have replaced flavour as a determining ingredient in the production of many contemporary foods. I heard recently about an American cheese made from unpasteurized milk and cured among cut cedar boughs in open caves in rural Wisconsin, where the area's distinctive pollen, soil dust and humidity circulate around it, giving it its prized flavour and texture. Not surprisingly, the big corporate cheese manufacturers are petitioning the U.S. Food and Drug Administration to outlaw not only the Wisconsin cheese, but also others made from unpasteurized milk (as most European cheeses are). It would be nice to think that the burger flipper at McDonald's didn't hork onto the grill in a dissatisfied moment, but who knows, or really cares, in an era when food—not to mention those who prepare it, or the laboratories in which it is invented, or the depredations that are enacted on it—can be an all-but-impenetrable mystery? What's really in an Eskimo Pie? a Hot Rod? a Slurpee? The listed ingredients of even the humble English muffin read like a pharmacological catalogue.

Likewise our houses, once constructed of local rock and wood—oftentimes collected from within sight of the house itself—are today mysterious agglomerations of materials known perhaps by name but seldom by source or composition. Not long ago, I visited the site where a friend is building a lavish country home, and within minutes, had noted U.S. aluminum, Korean vinyl, Saskatchewan gyproc, Philippine light fixtures, and what appeared to be Quebec plywood. A box of Christmas lights by the front door had been made in China, undoubtedly by rural penny labourers, perhaps children, whose only notion of our age-old cultural and religious holiday was the coloured plastic that passed before them on the rickety assembly line.

When the Incas built the stone city of Machu Picchu in the Andes during the sixteenth century, they are said to have studied the surrounding mountains not for weeks or months, but for generations, as they waited for a vision—in essence, for a revelation from the land—as to what they should build and how they should go about it. It is not a gross exaggeration to suggest that today's builders have a vision Monday, get a building permit Tuesday, knock the trees over Wednesday and, by Christmas, have erected a building just like every other shoebox in the industrial park.

During the mid-1990s, Costco Stores, determined to establish themselves in northwestern Ontario, bought a wooded site on the Thunder Bay waterfront and, before they gained municipal clearance to put up their cracker box, bulldozed a couple of hectares of prime poplar and birch, part of a dwindling tract of second-growth forest that had for years supported a sizeable herd of deer. The problem was that, in the end, they weren't granted a building permit. So there the site sits, five years later, ditched, padlocked, of no use to animal- or humankind, sprouting a few spindly saplings, while a shrunken generation of deer ekes out a shrunken existence, perhaps with phylogenic memories of its one-time survival ground and Eden.

We can no longer even *name* plants that for centuries kept whole cultures alive on this continent. And it is a rare person these days who can identify half a dozen trees in the forest. My grandfather Scholey, a nineteenth-century lumberman, could identify twenty or more by smell alone. The Inuit, who for eight thousand years hunted whales and lived in igloos, now keep snow off the rooftop dish so as not to miss an instalment of *The Young and the Restless* or TV Action News from the Murder Capital of North America.

My great-great-grandfather George Allendorf—a custom weaver whose shuttle boards sat for years on the back of my father's desk—spent six days a week during the mid-1800s at a loom by the back window of the family home on Queen Street in Hespeler, Ontario, where he had enough light to work and could look out at the Speed River when his eyes needed a break. The mechanics of his work involved throwing the shuttles back and forth between hands, simultaneously, thousands of times a day. He did this with such skill for sixty years that, five generations later, I still hear it said proudly of him that, in all his years, he never put a shuttle through the window. He wove local linen and wool, as well as imported cotton, and sold the fabric for one York shilling—twelve and a half cents—a yard. As often as not, however, he got paid in chickens, beef, vegetables, dried peas or flour, all of which came from neighbouring farms and gardens. His customers knew the source of their suits and dresses—not just which loom but which sheep, or which fields of flax—and the Allendorfs knew where their vegetables and chickens came from. And it was the same place, because the soil that they knew by smell and sight nourished the vegetables, grain and grass, and the grain and grass nourished the chickens and cattle and sheep, and the sheep sprouted the wool, and the wool went from shearer to spinner to weaver to seamstress, all of them of the neighbourhood. And everything connected within the purview of the Allendorfs' world.

In those days in Hespeler, one of the great entertainments for the children—whose world was as much of the planet as was that of their parents—came on the day in spring when the farmers hauled their sheep out into the Speed River to wash their coats before shearing them. The townschildren would wait by the riverbanks, cheering and jeering, secretly hoping that a farmer might get thrown into the drink, as the animals balked and bleated over their treatment.

Which is not to idealize the era. George Allendorf's son, Baltzer, took a job in the local carriage works at sixteen, got his arm caught in the machinery and was killed. No compensation. He is buried in Hope Cemetery in Hespeler beside my grandmother, "Birdie" Brock Wilkins, who in 1912, at age twenty-four, died of an abdominal infection after giving birth to my father.

———————

I talked recently to school-aged kids in Toronto who have never skated on natural ice, or swum in anything but a chlorinated pool—and therefore know nothing of the ponds and rivers that, during my own childhood, were both a field for unstructured play and a primer on the mysteries of water and ice, and of everything else that existed around them in the way of wildlife, weather and sensory stimulation.

In 1998, my friend Jari Sarkka went north to teach at the Summer Beaver Reserve in far Northern Ontario. He returned with a beautiful story of how, in late November, to inaugurate both the hockey season and the winter, the entire able-bodied community enacted a historic local tradition by donning skates, grabbing hockey sticks and taking to the newly frozen lake for a mass game of shinny. For anywhere up to four or five hours, this free-flowing party, with as many as fifty players a side, moved up and down, back and forth, restricted only by distant shorelines. Each team's aim was simply to keep possession of the puck, while the other team tried to take it away. At times, Jari said, a single player would break free and skate a kilometre or more up the lake, swooping and teasing as the others followed in a scattered parade. In the old days, Jari was told, during the week or so of grace between freeze-up and the first heavy snowfall, the kids would play so heedlessly that, at sunset, they'd occasionally find themselves miles off at the north end of the lake, with only the lights of the community to guide them home.

Jari, who now coaches in the Thunder Bay minor hockey system, said to me one day, "If you could somehow bottle the spirit of the way they played the game at Summer Beaver, you could use it to cure almost anything that's wrong with contemporary organized hockey"—a game that, by common assessment, is psychologically oppressive, physically violent and too often lacking in anything recognizable as fun.

Eric Nesterenko told me that one of the happiest days of his career with the Chicago Blackhawks—a career spent in the service of what he called "nasty, greedy, vicious, self-serving people"— came on a day in January, during the late 1960s, when he was driving along Lake Michigan and spotted an expanse of natural ice stretching as far as he could see offshore.

"It was a clear, crisp afternoon," he said, "and dammit if I didn't pull over and put on my skates. I took off my camel-hair coat. I was just in a suit jacket. Nobody was there. The wind was blowing from the north, and with a good wind behind you you can wheel and dive and turn; you can lay yourself into impossible angles that you never could walking or running. You stretch yourself out at a forty-five-degree angle, your elbow practically touching the ice— it's as if gravity didn't exist. I have a feeling that to overcome gravity must be the innate desire of humanity. It's a feeling you never quite get in a uniform, or with a crowd or a coach to play for. I was a kid again—oh, I was happy. Just like on the outdoor rinks back in Flin Flon where I grew up."

Eric has lectured at the university level on the sociology of play and on the importance of a child's connection with the earth. One of his many thoughts on the subject is that we destroy our children's innate affinity for the planet not just with television and oppressive play structures, but also with overly ambitious attempts to teach them about the world. "We say look at this, do that, play here, analyze this, when all we really have to say is, 'There's the field, there's the forest, there's the snowbank—go ahead,' and let their native curiosity and creativity, and their sensuality, take care of the rest."

In November 1993, the Vancouver ecologist Andrea Schluter, an unwitting Nesterenko cohort, wrote in a personal essay in *The Globe and Mail*:

It is more important that a child care about and wish to know more about her environment than to be initiated into all the heavy particulars of, for example, biology. . . . We gather most information about our world through our eyes, but we must learn to use our ears and noses, our senses of taste and touch. Rachel Carson said that "impressions of the senses are the fertile soil in which facts and wisdom can grow." Teaching the science of a pond ecosystem has its merits, but if you really want to understand the life of a pond, jump in!

———————

When I jumped into my travels, it was, as I have noted, with the intention of looking afresh at the land and of visiting a range of men and women who, against the flow, have maintained some impassioned tie with their natural surroundings.

Or, for argument, no tie.

It may be presumptuous to say so (certainly, it invokes all the risks incumbent on those who live in glass houses), but it surprised me at times during my travels how otherwise knowledgeable people—people who, in some cases, prided themselves on being accredited citizens of the Information Age—knew so little about even the most basic geography of their part of the planet. On several occasions, when I told people about travelling by ship from Thunder Bay to the Gulf of St. Lawrence, and docking in Chicago en route, they asked unselfconsciously how I went about doing that—"via the Mississippi?" someone asked.

"I didn't even know Chicago was *on* the Seaway!" one said to me. "I thought it was on Lake Michigan."

A respected magazine editor in Toronto asked how much of the trip I had to do overland.

"None," I said. "I was on the Seaway."

"But I mean to get from one lake to another," she said. "Aren't there a lot of rapids, that sort of thing?"

I was confronted just as often by my own unflattering ignorance—though was hardly surprised by it, having dined and slept with it for the best part of half a century. I could fill a chapter with examples of same. But at this point, I will limit myself to reporting that one night in the wheelhouse of the *M. V. Paterson*, during a discussion of the comparative significance of the Great Lakes to Canada and to the United States, it was brought to my attention that while the lakes border on just one province, Ontario (I knew this), they touch eight U.S. states.

"*Eight!*" I blurted, aware even as the word left my mouth that one should never question a sailor's knowledge of geography, inasmuch as the bits and bytes of his programming are compass points, time zones, distances, place names, borders and jurisdictions. And yet I was certain I had either heard wrong or the number had been overstated.

"Minnesota, Wisconsin, Michigan, Illinois, Indiana, Ohio, Pennsylvania and New York," piped Terry Holt. "Most people forget Indiana and Pennsylvania."

Others I met impressed me by the (sometimes unexpected) thoroughness and intricacy of their knowledge. Some of the deckhands on the *Paterson*, for example, were founts of knowledge about the sea and sea towns and coastal lore. The captain of the *Paterson*, Ken Strong, was an intriguing resource, in that he seemed to retain aspects of what he knew not so much by use of the typical storehouse of memory, the cerebellum, but in a more primitive reserve of muscle and nerve tissue, where the knowledge was available intuitively if not always factually. He is, by anybody's assessment, one of the world's finest helmsmen, but he seemed to puzzle at times over having to put his knowledge and skills into words. "Oh, geez," he said one day, when I asked him about the length of a nautical mile, "I'm afraid you've got me on that one. I know when I've sailed one!" When I asked about the location of the ship's depth-sensing devices, he said, "I'm afraid you've got me on that one."

I took notes anyway, determined that the fuel for the book would come not from facts or science, at least not in any direct sense, but from *people*, from their stories and lives, the exotica of their work and interactions—and, in the broadest sense, from their twentieth- and twenty-first-century survival mechanisms. It would come, too, of course, from my own journey, connections and projections. I was determined, for one thing, to give good play to my time on water, both east and west, and to the people who know it best. Given the enormous role water plays, and has played, in the lives of Canadians, it seems somewhat underexplored as a part of our experience.

"Water is the greatest of all forces affecting life on earth," Steve Lawson told me one day.

"We have all this water," said a sailor on the *Paterson*, "and hardly anybody has a clue what goes on out here."

In my most hopeful moments, I imagined that, if all went according to plan, the resulting piece of work might project some paradigm of sorts through which readers could themselves connect with the planet, rediscover its messages and therapies.

"Sounds like some sort of New Age how-to," said my long-time friend Jake MacDonald, much of whose own good writing is about as far from New Age how-to as one can get in the absence of rods, guns and hip waders.

I said, "It's going to be a 'story' book—about sea captains and stargazers and trappers . . . and nudists."

"Nudists?" He perked up.

"They're in there," I told him.

I was determined to write with one eye on the future, in that the next century is going to heighten dramatically the importance not just of our water, but also of our forests, our Arctic, our soil and air, as well as those seldom-consulted coefficients of survival, our intelligence and imagination. Environmental futurists tell us that, in decades to come, Canada's great forests must be viewed not as a grand pulpwood and lumber resource, to be divvied up among voracious corporate claimants, but as a vital universal entitlement, a sustainer of water, air, and species differentiation—and education and natural history.

When I mentioned this to my friend Greg Adams one day, he looked at me rather sadly and said, "Too bad nobody listens to what the environmentalists tell us." I told him that a group of European futurologists had predicted that the north, including Canada's, would one day support cities of a million people.

"The day there's a million people up here," he said, "is the day I move out."

"You'll have already moved," I told him. "They're talking about the twenty-second century."

Chapter Four

att and I had barely arrived home in Thunder Bay, in June, when I began a new round of visits and travels—these ones more compact than the long trips east and west. During the third week in June, for example, I rendezvoused with Susan Burkos, a middle-aged truck-driving acquaintance, at a service centre at Grand Marais, Minnesota. She is an ordained Episcopalian priest, and was one of the first women to do full-time long-haul driving back in the 1970s. She works in Levi's jeans, Red Wing hiking boots and little hoop earrings.

"I'm not sure whether it's a gender thing," she told me over a cup of coffee, "but I'm different from most drivers in that I don't judge a route by mileage or truck stops or traffic patterns, any of that stuff, but by how many real good highs I'm going to get off the landscape. You know—big views, mountains, coastal cliffs, that sort of thing." She described a place on the I-75, heading south into Florida, "where you come over a rise, and there in front of you is this endless expanse of deep rolling green, about a hundred square miles of orange groves. It always just blows me away." And another place in the Saint John River Valley, near Fredericton, where she has experienced a similar deciduous kick.

Susan has seen the sun come out after snowstorms in Wisconsin and Minnesota, and "do things to the landscape" that made her question whether she was dreaming. She said, "One time in fall, I was coming down through Vermont from Montreal with a reefer full of bacon, or something. I came around a mountain outside Burlington, and the trees in the valley were just one huge orange-red flame. It was like being on drugs, except I wasn't—I don't need them. There just happened to be a rest stop and a lookout a mile down the road, and I stopped my truck, shut it off, and got up on the hood and just sat there with my back against the windshield. I guess I got into some sort of trance, because when I went to get down ten minutes later, I looked at my watch and realized an hour and a half had passed."

On another occasion, somewhere in rural Indiana, she saw what she called "this weird green glow above the highway" in the distance ahead. "It was the middle of the night," she said, "and at first I thought I was hallucinating. Then suddenly I was in the middle of a massive swarm of fireflies, billions of them—it was like driving through stars, mile after mile." Susan said she often stopped in a forest, or on a mountainside, or in the desert, on a Sunday morning, to watch what she called "the play of light" as the sun came up. "And then, because I'm a priest, I get out my little communion kit and serve myself the sacraments—serve other truckers, too, if they're around and want them." She told me that just seeing the land unfold day after day was a kind of sacramental thing and was in some ways as much a part of her awareness of the spirit as anything else she did. When we had talked for an hour, she said that if there was one thing she'd like to do, it would be to haul over the ice roads in northern Canada—"kind of extreme trucking," she smiled. "A friend of mine's done it—it'd sure be a test of a person's faith."

On another day in June, I sat with Freda MacDonald, one of Canada's most respected and knowledgeable Native elders, in a birchbark wigwam she had helped build in the Indian Encampment outside Old Fort William, on the Kaministiquia River a few kilometres southwest of Thunder Bay. At one point she told me that, in the 1930s, when she was a child, her mother would occasionally get a craving that could be satisfied only by the meat of a rather unlikely mammal. "She'd say, 'I feel like eating porcupine,' " Freda laughed. "And my brothers and I would run off and find one and knock it out of its tree. But when we killed it I always felt sorry that it had to die, and I'd pet the poor thing. But we never wasted even a bit of it. We'd use the quills and hair in our crafts, and when we'd eaten, we'd put the bones into the fire as an offering of thanks to the Creator."

During Freda's years of employment at the fort, which ended with her retirement during the mid-1990s, I several times heard her refer to the Indian Encampment as her "office." The place is a decidedly low-tech business address, where, apart from the human voice, the most sophisticated means of communication is a collection of deerskin drums that, when beaten, can be heard up and down the river for four or five kilometres. The office is air-conditioned by river breezes, and the only warmth in winter comes from the poplar fires that burn in the cooking shelter, or occasionally in the winter wigwam.

Beyond the spiritual leadership Freda provides in the Aboriginal community, she is a kind of one-woman heritage institution who can tan a moosehide, build a wigwam, make a rabbit robe, or craft a birchbark pot so sound that it can be used to boil water. "Many people don't believe you can boil water in bark," she said to me during my visit, "but I've known the technique since I saw my great-grandmother do it back at Fort Alexander, in Manitoba, when I was little." The trick, she explained, is to fold and fasten the birchbark so that it doesn't leak. "Then you suspend the container over smouldering coals so that it isn't in contact with open flame. If your coals are hot enough, and you have enough patience, eventually your water will boil." The scientific explanation of the phenomenon is that water cools the birchbark by drawing heat from it. The water will boil at 100°C while the birchbark, like paper, will not ignite unless it reaches a temperature of more than 200°C.

As we sat in the wigwam that afternoon, smoke from a poplar fire rose through the centre hole of the dwelling, and spruce boughs covered the floor to a depth of eight or ten centimetres. Freda explained that the spruce boughs are not just insulation from the ground and a comfortable mattress, but a natural deodorizer for the wigwam and a repellent for snakes, frogs and "other creepy crawlers" that might try to come inside. Poplar, she pointed out, is the preferred interior fuel because it burns cooler than birch or ash, produces minimal smoke and, unlike resinous woods such as pine or spruce, does not throw sparks that might ignite the highly flammable surroundings.

Freda is slightly built, and her cap of greying hair crosses her forehead in fine, even bangs. Her smile radiates from every part of her face. Like her ancestors, she is devoted to tobacco—in the form of du Maurier cigarettes, which she consumes at a longshoreman's pace. She incinerated several of them as we chatted that day in the wigwam, an emphatic No Smoking zone from which she peeked regularly to see if any visitors were coming. "The last thing they want in here is an old Indian with a du Maurier hanging out of her mouth," she laughed.

With her profound knowledge of the old ways, Freda can look at an artifact from another era and, judging by the natural materials used, make a telling assessment of the environment in which the tribe that produced it lived. What's more, she can tell *how* the tribe lived, the level of sophistication of its tools, skills and work habits. "If you know what you're looking for and use your imagination, you can get a sense of the whole relationship between the craftsperson and his or her world."

In keeping with the Ojibwa notion that all aspects of a culture are interrelated, Freda sees craft-making not just as manual or historical but spiritual—"a centring and healing thing." And Freda as much as anyone knows the importance of healing. At the age of five, she and her sister were taken from their reserve home and thrust into a residential school where, for ten years, they were deprived of their language, their community and, except during summers, their family. "It was heartbreaking," she said, speaking so solemnly and quietly as she told me the story that, at times, her voice left no decipherable impression on my tape recorder. What she said, however, was so vivid that I will not soon forget her account, say, of the sisters playing secretly with a doll their father had made for them, knowing that if the nuns discovered their play, they would be punished and the doll confiscated, as it eventually was.

Freda's cultural disinheritance was sealed in 1948 with her marriage and subsequent expulsion from the reserve (she still has the loathsome document in which she was "deemed not to be an Indian"). Still teenagers, she and her husband began a peripatetic existence that, twenty-nine years later, would bring them and their seven children to Thunder Bay, where treatment was available for a disabled son.

Shortly after arriving, Freda learned that the recently reconstructed Old Fort William was seeking seamstresses for its costuming department. "I went out to the fort to apply," she said, "but when I told them my background, they were more interested in employing me in the Indian Encampment. In those days the camp was just a single wigwam in a clearing, hardly developed at all. But I took one look at it and knew this was where I wanted to work. It was as if, after all those years in exile, I'd come home. A few days later," she laughed, "I started work as an Indian."

Freda brought with her to the fort a dimly recalled knowledge of traditional crafts that she had acquired as a child through her mother, grandmother and great-grandmother. More important, she brought a willingness to learn. Over the years, by reading and studying artifacts—and by experimenting with different types of crafts—she taught herself what she knows today. "I immersed myself in the work and began gradually to reconnect with myself and my culture. It was like coming full circle to my childhood and starting from the place where I got lost."

For years, during the Wednesday-night craft classes she has conducted in her home, Freda has imparted the same sense of focus and reconnection that she herself derived from her studies and handiwork. "Natives and non-Natives alike are hungry for this sort of renewal," she says. "Both cultures have lost their connection with the Spirit. They're caught up in greed and excess. They don't share. They don't do things for themselves any more. My people were stopped from doing for themselves. They became totally dependent. My generation was the first to receive family allowance, social assistance. Before that we were independent."

On an optimistic note, Freda observes that the old ways, the self-reliance and spiritual awareness, "seem to be coming back. Things are slowly getting straightened out."

One of the last things Freda told me that afternoon was that, during her years at the fort, visitors often came to the Encampment with expectations of what she called "a Hollywood-type" Indian. "They'd whoop and laugh and make jokes. And sometimes I'd go up to them and say, 'Are you here to learn or to make fun of people?' That always stopped them short, and I'd say, 'Let me tell you about my culture.'"

And she would.

"And I still do," she smiled. "I tell anybody who wants to listen—any time I get the chance."

————

On yet another day, in mid-September, I met with five of the members of the Traditional Finnish Sauna Society, a group of essentially nudist women who meet periodically, as one of them described it, to "sit in the sauna, meditate, bathe, talk, laugh, free the senses and imagination." I had heard about the group from an acquaintance who belongs, and had asked at the time if it might be possible to talk to one or two of them in the context of the book I was writing. She told me later that she had mentioned it to some of the others, and that the idea had (except for the pun) been rebuffed.

A few days later, however, I got a phone call from another of the women in the group—a woman I did not know, but who informed me that a few of them had decided to talk to me, and that I could come with them to a fall get-together at a lakeside property west of Thunder Bay. The group had maintained pretty much total anonymity throughout the sixteen years of its existence. So the stipulation was that we'd do our interview first names only and that, if I used the material in the book, I'd protect their identities, as well as the specifics of where we met. "We're not ashamed," she said. "Far from it. It's just that it's a small city, and people's imaginations get working. Besides," she said, "some of our people don't want this to happen."

I agreed and, on the day of the get-together, drove fifty kilometres out of the city to a small lake north of the Trans-Canada, on which there were just three or four cabins that I could see, and, beside one of them, a large cedar-log sauna. There was a woodpile between the cabin and the sauna, and as the women arrived, I picked up an axe and, wanting to make a favourable impression, went to work splitting kindling and piling it by the sauna door. Like all saunas before they are lit, this one was clammy and uninspired. But in the presence of fire, it came alive with the fragrance of woodsmoke and cedar.

The women were articulate and self-confident and treated me with easygoing affability. They ranged in age from mid-thirties to perhaps fifty. It is typical of Finns (which three of them were) to go naked in the sauna, but perhaps for my benefit, or for their own, they did not remove all of their personal effects. Two left their earrings on, another a small beaded anklet she had made, and another a pair of blue-framed glasses. The last wore a barrette and a rubber Timex watch.

One of the women, Sharon, who was perhaps in her mid-forties and who described herself as "something of an ecofeminist," said she came to the sauna with the women "to corroborate," to build both self- and mutual esteem. She looked at me with heavy-eyed forbearance and said, "Women communicate differently from men—not just with one another but with the planet." The gist of what she told me next was that women would certainly not have "messed up the earth in the way men have" if they'd had more say in its destiny. I said I thought the view was oversimplified, and asked if women in positions of power in, say, the mining or logging industry—the Peggy Whites of the world—were really any more nurturing toward the earth than were men. She trumped me with the thought that even women can and do abdicate what she called "the feminine earth spirit." Moreover, she explained, because the spirit exists in all of us in varying proportions, "men can embody and nurture it in proportions that even women, at times, do not. This is just first-year women's studies stuff," she said, "really just basic psychology."

During an hour or so when the sauna was at its hottest, the women took turns "schmising" one another, which is to say beating one another's backs with clumps of leafed birch branches somehow preserved from the summer. The women being schmised would stand, leaning forward, hands on the sauna's mid-level bench, while their partners in the exercise rained down a flogging. The sound was a succession of satisfying *thwaps* that seemed to combine physical stimulation with some sort of ritual cleansing or penance. The woman in the beaded anklet sighed as the schmise lit up her back, bringing it to more or less the colour of Barbie-doll packaging and leaving occasional birch leaves clinging to her wet skin. "It's very freeing," she said, and about two minutes later, left the sauna, walked onto the dock and dived into the September-cold lake. Another of the women told me that to smell the birch sap and cedar and the spruce smoke, and to see the sunlight slanting in on the forest, and to hear the fire—to be taking it all in through every cleansed pore—was as close as she ever felt to the earth. "When you get this close to yourself in a sensory way," she said, "it does more than expel the toxins. It relaxes you internally—frees the heart, opens a communion. There's an old Finnish saying that the sauna cleanses you from the inside out."

A quiet, pretty, grey-haired woman, whose overheated face was draining rivulets of sweat, added that cultures have understood the link between "heat and soul" since the Romans met in their steam baths, or Native tribes first gathered in their sweat lodges to awaken and celebrate the spirit. She was silent for several seconds, then told us about the day several years ago when, during a solo sauna at her family's camp on Lake Superior, she had, out of some inner compulsion, stayed in longer and at a hotter temperature than she was accustomed to. "I just kept throwing water on the stones," she said, and she explained how at a certain point she had begun "to feel very drifty, very free of time. I don't think I ever really lost the sense that I was physically there in the sauna, I wasn't dreaming. It was just that a different part of my awareness, way down in the subconscious, began to open and to offer me these images."

The marrow of the experience was that she had seen herself as a child, walking in the forest in winter, in a landscape that she took to be the northern forests of Finland, where her father and mother had grown up. "It was very dark," she said, "but even being a little girl out there on my own, for some reason I wasn't the least bit frightened. I saw a building ahead of me, a house that seemed familiar to me, and I went up to it and let myself in the back door. When I got inside, there was my father at the kitchen table, just sitting there. He was a young man. No one else was around, and yet we couldn't talk, because when I went to open my mouth, it was as if I was reminded that I didn't speak his language—nothing would come out. Then he stood up, and I noticed there was a little spot of what seemed to be blood on the table. I followed him into another room, but I lost track of him, and when I went back into the kitchen the blood was gone, and I seemed to be in a house we'd lived in when I was a child here in Canada."

The woman said that she and her father had not been close at the time, but that the next time she'd spoken to him, she'd asked about his life back in Finland—specifically about the house in which he'd grown up—discovering that it was "exactly" like the one she had envisioned. What's more, she'd inquired whether or not he had ever suffered depression.

"It just seemed there was some subliminal connection here that had impressed itself on me. And he told me that, yes, in the past, he'd often gotten very discouraged with himself. Then I just came right out and said it. I said, 'Dad, have you ever been so depressed you've considered suicide?' And he said, 'Why are you asking?' And I told him I'd had this strange reverie, and that somehow this was the question that had arisen out of it. And suddenly, he just opened right up to me—he said that when he was a young guy, before he came to Canada, he'd been so despondent about his life—about his failures and so on—that he *had* given serious thought to suicide. It was powerful for me, seeing this vulnerability in him. We hugged one another; I started crying. He did, too, which is really rare for most Finnish men. I came out of it with a whole new sense of who he is—and, really, who I am, too, because I've started to see some of my own impulses in his."

The woman told me later that, in the months since the "shake-down," as she called it, she and her dad had been "a hundred times closer," and she knew in her heart that the connection had been forged out of some mutual attachment to the earth. "I really do believe," she said, "that some of our deepest connections as human beings are preserved right in the physical world if we can find a way to get to them." The Finns, she told me, had at one time been more mystic than they are now (a notion I had heard expressed by the Lakehead poet Elizabeth Kouhi). "You see it far more in the women than in the men. And that's where the sauna comes in. For all of us. It's as if the closer we are to the earth through the senses, the more enlightened we tend to be about one another."

Chapter Five

One day shortly after my sauna visit, when I had begun writing all this down, it struck me that I had spent much of the past few months living the dreams and stories of others, experiencing the forests and waters and mountains more or less on their terms. As a consequence, I was gripped by a notion that I should go into the wilderness alone—not so much as a survival or proving exercise, in that I really had nothing to prove, but as a means of rediscovering on my own the life forms and lessons of the earth, as well as any capability I might have for interpreting and dealing with them.

And that is what I did. One Thursday afternoon in late September, when the bugs were gone from the forest, and the highways were empty of tourists, I decamped Thunder Bay and headed east on the Trans-Canada for one of the wildest stretches of Lake Superior's uninhabited north shore, in the Rhyolite Cove area east of Wawa. The sixteen-kilometre dirt trail in from the highway—a one-time wagon road that, at the beginning of the century, had led to a nearby fishing colony now seventy years extinct—has been improved off and on over the years. But lately it has been allowed to deteriorate into a menacing succession of washouts, potholes and half-extruded boulders. It winds and bumps over creeks and rock outcrops, through beaver swamps and, at one point, through what must be the largest stand of yellow birches on earth. The road is better suited these days to bears and lynx and wolves—all of which inhabit its precincts—than to motorized vehicles, and is best travelled (if at all) in daylight.

Unfortunately, by the time I got to it, at about 10 P.M., it was as dark and claustrophobic as a mine drift, and as I pitched and joggled over its ruts and grasses in the inky blackness—branches swatting at the windows and doors, the headlights forming an erratic tunnel ahead—I became preoccupied, even spooked, by the way the forest sealed itself constantly around and behind me. This worked itelf into a sense of impending misadventure: a washout too deep to navigate, a wigged-out driver coming the opposite way, a wendigo, any of which seemed possible in the blackness in my state of apprehension. I had been unable to shake the image of a dead wolf I had seen on the highway shoulder near Marathon—a sable-black monster, lying on the gravel with its eyes open, unmutilated except for a patch of shocking cherry-coloured flesh where a saddle of skin had been ripped off its back. At one point, a great grey owl swooped low across in front of the van, and at another, a half-dozen swallows swept up out of the underbrush and flew away wildly ahead, twisting and looping in the beam of the headlights, staying just beyond me for three or four kilometres, until they disappeared suddenly into the canopy.

At the clearing where this oppressive tunnel ended within a hundred metres of the lake, I threw open the door and swung my legs out, hugely relieved to be free of what was by then an almost nighmarish confinement. Eventually, I switched off the headlights, then the engine, stood up, and took my first tentative steps away from the van. I was able to hear the wind in the trees and the waves crashing onto the beach, and if I looked straight up

I could differentiate between treetops and sky. But in any other direction I was blind. I knew, certainly, that, whatever else, I could not at that point begin hiking the seven or eight kilometres to where I wanted to pitch camp.

When I had sorted through my pack in the back seat, I took my sleeping bag and groundsheet and a little doll-carriage pillow that I had borrowed from my daughter and, having bundled up to the chin, shut the door to the van, with its last bit of light, and stumbled over a heaped ridge of boulders down onto the beach. Feeling infinitely inept and forlorn, but determined not to spend the first night of my venture in the relative hominess of the vehicle, I knelt in the sand halfway between the boulders and the water, spread my groundsheet and sleeping bag, and crawled in.

––––––––––

During the hours before I had left home, my son, Matt, said to me discreetly, "Dad, you don't have to do this." I told him I was doing it because I wanted to, although my assurance was far from perfect. I had asked my friend Ted Burton, a former bush pilot and district Crown attorney, if he thought such a trip was safe. He had said, "Sure it is, but not for you," and he had advised me that, if I persisted in such foolishness, I should take a handgun, just in case. My friend Jake MacDonald, an experienced woodsman and hunter, had advised me to watch out for bears, which would be fattening up on anything they could find at that point in the fall. He also tried to deter me by saying there would be more bears, and hungrier bears, than ever, because of the cancellation of the spring bear hunt in northern Ontario. However, my experience with bears had always been good—I had seen dozens of them in the wilds over the years—and I felt it would be ill-omened to go into the woods with even the faintest reservations about them. Ted described to me the odyssey of a young woman who had gone into the wilds of Northern Ontario to live during a recent winter, and had been driven out by wolves which, as their hunger deepened, had become increasingly aggressive around her cabin, finally waiting on the roof for her to emerge.

In the end, all of this only whetted my appetite for a spell amidst the perils and attractions of the wilderness. My friends Jari and Maija Sarkka applauded my plan, Maija telling me she didn't feel people stayed long *enough* when they went into the woods, because it took a while just to locate the friendship of what she called "the spirits." It was only gradually, she said, that a visitor to the wilds could realize that "more is out there than you'd imagined. You start in fear," she said, "and end up wanting to stay on, thanking the spirits for letting you be there."

In the days leading up to my sojourn, I had read with fascination about the four-day vision quests of young Ojibwa warriors, and of the traditional initiation of the Inuit hunter, wherein young men are sent out onto the ice or tundra alone to confront the great white bear. They go seeking visions, confronting fears, looking for irreducible parts of themselves, corroboration of their aliveness and spirit, in what the writer Barry Lopez calls "a harsh land, where life takes insight and patience and humour."

Certainly, I had no illusions about visions or quests. In coming to the wilds alone, I would have been quite happy to get an inkling of what it had been like merely to exist on these shores and in these forests before the arrival of my own white ancestors—or what it had been like for the newcomers themselves. Failing that, I would have been happy to discover what it is like to exist there now for eight or nine days. There was, of course, the ever-present option of civilization, of a road out, if things went badly—not to mention the advantage of nylon tenting, antibiotics and steel tools. I knew enough of the forest and lakes to understand that, whatever happened, the time would be rich in the intricacies of land, wildlife and sensory stimulation. Or else it would be cold and wet and horrible.

On that first morning, I hiked seven or eight kilometres east through the woods, up and down rock screes, through muddy soil and creek beds, along a trail that at times all but lost itself in dead ends or undergrowth. It led up and over a three-hundred-metre promontory, and eventually down into Rhyolite Cove, a beach from which billion-year-old boulders, some as big as Volkswagens, protrude from the sand.

There, in unseasonably pleasant sunshine, I spent four hours establishing a modest camp, reminded that in centuries past entire lifetimes were consumed in the excruciating business of merest survival—of hunting and fishing and gathering small fruit, and, particularly in winter, staying clothed and warm. If you couldn't make it happen, you were dead; if you could, you were only half-dead, from exhaustion. Without doubt, during my days at the cove, my appreciation deepened for those who had carved tools out of caribou bones, carried fire in clay pots, known the medicinal power of roots and bark and berries, and run down wounded deer for the meat and skins that were their only means of subsistence. Even my own light requirements demanded many hours of wood-gathering, of shelter and cooking arrangements—of a strategic self-reliance, in which my little bowsaw, my hatchet, my firewood, became items of almost talismanic power and appeal, the focus of my caring and affection.

I set my tiny green tent in a spruce grove a few metres back from the beach and, on that first afternoon, determined to have a "mother log" of sorts that would sustain my fire through the night, sawed off a ten-kilo chunk of root from a large stump of driftwood down the beach. Because my smallish bowsaw was inadequate for any piece of wood thicker than about twenty centimetres, and the root was half a metre thick, the chore took forty minutes with the saw and hatchet, leaving my arms and legs temporarily rubbery. From that point on, I would saw such a log every day, and, every morning, would stack a pile of dry spruce brush and another of driftwood, some of which I hauled from a kilometre or more down the beach.

On a walk after supper that first evening, I found a three-metre ring of stones piled knee high, apparently an old camp shelter of some sort. From it, I liberated a wide two-inch plank a couple of metres long, which I hauled back to camp to use as a cooking board by the fire—or, when necessary, as a shelter propped on poles and stones above the flames to keep out the rain. The fire quickly became a kind of paramour, and I tended it, pampered it, fed it the best dry driftwood and deadfall I could find—in fact, spent half an hour every morning rebuilding the ring of stones surrounding it, to prevent the day's winds from reaching it. I hated to see it losing life, and after establishing camp never once allowed it to go out. And it returned every favour, gave me warmth and hot food, light and companionship after dark. I would return from long walks down the beach, happy and stimulated to catch my first glimpse of its smoke, which, after several hours, was often reduced to a wisp, invisible from more than fifty metres away.

During those first few days, I surprised even myself with my decorum: I urinated well off down the beach; washed dishes after every meal; kept a tea towel on the flat rock that served as my table; cleaned up after even the most inconsequential spill; swept out the tent with a spruce-bough whisk; collected a little bouquet of late-blooming asters and put them in a can on my cooking board. I had brought along a small bottle of brandy that I consumed with the civility of a naval admiral, an ounce or two a day after dark, as I sat by my fire.

Early mornings were a version of paradise almost too basic for words: the woodsmoke, the sun, the breeze, the water, the coffee and toast and boiled eggs. One morning as I ate and read, I heard a rustling above and behind me, and glanced into a nearby balsam where a good-sized porcupine climbed slowly skyward to where he or she eventually nestled on a high branch. When I went over for a better look, I found perhaps a hundred kilos of porcupine dung, like piles of dog kibble, heaped around the bases of the neighbouring trees.

At night, the tent would warm gradually from body heat, and would grow moist from condensation and from the slow transpiration of the moisture in my lungs out into the trapped air. I did not lie long waiting for sleep, because on most nights I was exhausted from the perpetual cycle of walking, wood-gathering and water-getting. In full consciousness, then in half sleep, I would lie listening to the fire, able to tell after the third or fourth day what state it was in simply by the regularity and intensity of its crackling. I listened to the night animals—the skunks and mice and raccoons rustling at a distance through the underbrush, or sometimes close to the tent walls—and on windy nights, to the waves and the clicking of branches. Or to the rain when it came, popping against the tent fly, or spitting into the fire, each drop a decipherable hiss, those that hit rock differentiable, I thought, from those that went into the flame.

One moonlit night, and then on subsequent nights, I heard what was unmistakably the howl of wolves in the distance somewhere along the shore. Initially, the sounds brought my head off my pillow and left me holding my breath, waiting intently for—what? But as the days passed, even those sounds became a welcome connection—in the blackness, one of few connections—to the world beyond the tent door. For the most part, my dreams were rich and varied and confident. And yet even into the third or fourth night, I was still dealing, too, with fleeting trepidations and shadows, unable, as they crept across the threshold in the dark, to draw a line between those that were real and those that were imagined—assuming there was a line to draw.

I have been told that our terror of being hunted is vestigial and that, on some level, we carry the trauma of every fang and spear point that ever sliced through a jugular or rib cage and left a bloody trail and dying wheeze in the dust or snow. I have heard, too, that deer, for example, have no short-term memory, no sense of the danger of what they cannot see—so that the threat out of sight is no threat at all (in the sense that a child feels protected by covering his or her eyes). But I knew how a cougar could eat a person up, had read about it—and had spent enough time with big cats during travels with the circus to understand more than I needed to about their speed and instincts and blood lust. In the long night hours, in the absence of normal reassurances, despite my knowledge that cougars are more legendary than actual in these parts, I had trouble shaking the big cat, or even the lynx, as an image of the dark side. From time to time I would catch a glimpse of the slightly-too-small head in the thicket beyond the tent door, or in the trees just out of the firelight, sightings that too often metastasized into a range of old neuroses or nightmares—sweaty, chaotic affairs in which I was being chased, or tied up, or was unable to speak, or remember lines for a play, or answers for some torturous math exam, or was unable to hide from unnamed evils that crept in underground or came fast from behind like long-legged snakes.

I would awaken with a start from this chaos, casting off images of almost paralyzing power. During the warm afternoon of the third day, I eased myself into the frigid water and swam to where it was up to my neck. But here, too, forces unappeased by daylight or bright thoughts lurked in the sand bottom, prompting me to pull my legs up under me and get to shore.

———

I have heard it said of the nineteenth-century pioneers that they'd have been better off fearing their ignorance than fearing the certainty of what they thought they knew about danger—fearing blackflies and cold more than grizzlies and wolves. In the same sense, my own weird fears were better confirmed by what I couldn't see than what I could.

On the third night, for reasons I cannot explain, I sat upright in the tent, barely awake, recalling how, as a teenager, I had heard an Ontario park superintendent boast laughingly of how on a "sport" fishing trip he had caught a garpike and chopped off its snout before releasing it, bleeding and doomed, into the Severn River near Georgian Bay. The next morning, in a funk of sorts, I was unable to slip the memory of a student I had known at Trent University, who long ago told me that his method of dealing with bears was to smear a large pad of honey onto a rock, and then to sprinkle it with chips of broken glass, so that within hours an enticed bear would bleed to death internally. "You grimace and grin," said the writer Edward Hoagland, "to keep yourself from howling."

But by the fourth or fifth day, all of this had come to rest. On perhaps the fifth night, I awakened after several hours of sleep feeling so rested and optimistic that, when I emerged from the tent to tend the fire and had built it back up, I decided simply to huddle by it for the night, bulked up as I was in sweatshirts and fleece and thermal underwear. However, in the hours before dawn, I was startled to see what I took to be a flashlight coming toward me from perhaps a kilometre down the beach. I called out a salutary hello, but got no response. Thoughts of demented trappers, or even ghosts, played themselves out against images of lost children, downed pilots, shipwrecked sailors, wandering for days in the woods to come at last upon a distant fire and the soul who would save them. "Hello!" I hollered again—again to no reply. To be safe, I put a few extra sticks on the fire and retreated to a spot a hundred metres or so alongshore where I could see the fire but could not be seen from it. But when I got to my post and turned, the light, if there had been a light, had vanished. I questioned myself as the sun rose—had I really seen anything? And when I walked down the beach after breakfast to where the light might have been, I found no human footprints but discovered bear droppings and what were clearly moose tracks in the sand.

My daylight hours had themselves become dreamlike—stimulated not by apprehension but by a free-for-all of images from the planetary opera. One afternoon, for example, I noticed a small strip of orange on a sun-warmed rock at the top of the beach. A closer look revealed that it was a lineup of docile, faded ladybugs, more than twenty of them—doing what? Dying? Mating? Laying eggs that would hatch in spring? Within two days, there were *thousands* of them, fading in hecatombs, on sticks, on rocks, on chunks of driftwood and blades of grass. As I walked the beach one day, I came upon a monarch butterfly walking along the sand, apparently exhausted but determined to get somewhere, perhaps Mexico, before the birds or the winter got him. On another day yet, I saw hundreds of large grasshoppers ganged up and looking very much unlike themselves in a coating of orange dust. I saw an eagle spiralling above my camp, a pileated woodpecker bashing at an old pine, sunsets that reminded me of thick blue whales with pink bellies.

At times I felt rewarded, affirmed, capable in my humanity and choices. There is a romance to the wilds, but only as long as one has options. In this case the wilds were my option, and sometimes I caught a glimpse of myself for what I was—middle-aged, ignorant, ill-equipped to be where I was, as likely to put a literal axe into my leg as I was to suffer a figurative axe in the thicket that I had come from at my desk. The work I had spent twenty years obsessing over—words, sentences, pages—had no bearing at Rhyolite Cove. Here, as Eric Nesterenko once said of play in the National Hockey League, you couldn't "bullshit your way out."

On the subject of survival in the wilds and of so-called indigenous knowledge, one of Thunder Bay's most capable naturalists, Mike Jones, once said to me, "You could take some guy with a Ph.D. who'd studied the forest and its ways for thirty years, and put him out in the bush that he's supposed to know all about, and he wouldn't last six hours. Whereas you could send an uneducated, illiterate Cree or Dene or Mi'kmaq out into the woods and he'd have no trouble making a life for himself."

Was such thinking just another variation on the theme of the noble savage? I think not, although of the uneducated, illiterate Natives I have met, or even the geniuses, most, I have to think, would be as happy as I was to have with them the small burden of supplies and equipment I myself had brought along: a seven- or eight-day supply of canned tuna, bagged bread, eggs, peanut butter, margarine, canned milk, coffee, tea, almonds, apricots, rice, oatmeal, dried soup mixes, a tent, a sleeping bag, a Swiss Army knife, a can opener, a down vest, a change of clothes, a couple of rolls of toilet paper, a hatchet, a saw. At Matt's urging, I had an emergency pack that contained, among other items, snare wire, Band-Aids, antibiotics, a compass, a candle, some duct tape. He had put in a small mirror, which (bless his heart) he said I could use to signal an airplane if I was in trouble or lost. I had a suture needle and some sterile thread that I imagined I could use to stitch myself up if I split apart.

It is remarkable what a few days in the wilderness will do to refocus a man with a mortgage, a tax conundrum, a somewhat fragmented personal life, and fifty thousand dollars' worth of debt backed up on his credit cards and overdraft. In rare moments, there was an almost palpable drainage of the poisons—into the sand and soil and shallows; into sunsets and clouds (the waves along the horizon surged like a perpetual healing snake). I lay in my jockey shorts on the pebbles in the afternoon sun, and in the warm rain that came one morning while the sun shone in another part of the sky. I daydreamed of old basketball and hockey games, old travels, old loves and lusts; watched herons and terns and ravens; meditated and prayed. I stood on a high cliff overlooking Lake Superior in the wind, in a version of flight, but was unwilling to fly for the crimp it would put in my future.

And as always with time to myself, I appraised, unravelled, enumerated: friends, finances, property, gains and losses and liabilities, the sum of life's messes and miracles. There were times when I felt unspeakable waves of tenderness for my kids and loved ones—or surges of longing, accompanied by a gradual dissolution of old anger and frustration, long-stored resentments. The heart and ego let go—you don't need your defences out there, so remote from the world of getting and spending and ambition, from the endless onslaught of the quotidian. Things that had bothered me no end last week seemed remarkably trivial. Here the need was for contact, exchange, which, in the absence of people, was transferred onto animals and plants, sounds and sensory stimuli.

My connection to the planet had never been more direct, and in the altered context, my senses quickened at an almost aberrant pace. In the absence of distortion, life became a banquet for the eyes and ears and nose. The tiniest nuances of land, flora and fauna came to life. After a point, it was not simply that the leaves were turning, but that an individual birch leaf had begun to yellow overnight. New sounds identified themselves. Within a day or two, I was acutely aware of at least five different sounds that the waves made as they hit the beach, and by the end of a week had counted perhaps a dozen. There were those like the slap of a hand on a horse's back, or a door closing, others that came with a "plop" or the sort of "cluck" you can make with your tongue. One in particular caught my attention—a kind of thud or clunk, much like the sound a two-by-four would make if it were rapped against a tree. Others hissed and sizzled, or even crackled on the gravel up the beach.

Like any animal on the alert, my vision widened and sharpened to a point where I was picking up even the slightest of peripheral movements—of a bird or squirrel over my shoulder or, sometimes, it seemed (in the vastly increased corroboration of hearing and sight and intuition), behind me. At one point, I found myself inadvertently raising my snout to test the wind—could sniff a last live coal in the fire as easily as I could identify it by heat or smoke. I sniffed mosses and creek water and soil—and stones which, in their ancient mineralitic way, are as subtly fragrant, if not as varied, as fishes or trees or ferns.

One afternoon I cut the end off a faded piece of driftwood and was rewarded by the rich whiff of cedar that poured from the saw cut, preserved like a treasure across the years. On the same day, at dusk, as I drank my coffee, a toad hopped into my camp and sat basking, perhaps even hypnotized, in the orange glow of the fire. On one of the few occasions I actually spoke during nine days, I said to him that I hoped he wasn't thinking of a meltdown. "Don't you dare!" I ordered him as he inched toward the flame, at which point he uncoiled, landing with a hiss on a flaming chunk of driftwood, his eyes swelling grotesquely in his head, his skin baking into clefts and crust, and his limbs stiffening, before he melted and boiled.

I saw a bear and a moose, and what must have been a fisher or marten. However, when on my drive home a Wisconsin woman asked me in the restaurant at White River whether I had seen any wildlife, I mentioned not these but the thousands of ladybugs, causing her to look at me as if wondering who'd contaminated the wilds by letting loose such an obvious crackpot as me.

Using Bertrand Russell's prescription for saving the world, I learned to sit still. And to watch. And to move and watch. On walks deep into the woods, I would stop and shift a stone or two, lift a cushion of moss, tear the bark off a dead tree, or push aside the ground cover with whatever hiking stick I happened to have picked up. I found big brown mushrooms, and tiny orange ones, and purple ones half decayed—and one little specimen that resembled a flower with petals. I have never trusted myself to eat wild mushrooms that have not been identified by someone who knows more about them than I do. But I was sure enough of a big browny boletus-looking specimen that I picked it and took the tiniest fragment (as recommended by the experts) and placed it on my tongue to see whether I'd faint, or hallucinate, or begin to sweat. The risk was stirring, and when nothing happened, I swallowed the fragment and again waited to fall over. Eventually I cut the whole thing into a pot of soupy white rice, stirred it up with a little margarine and Tabasco, and wolfed it all down with gusto.

My only fresh produce was the handfuls of clintonia leaves, mature and somewhat leathery, that I found in the bush and consumed rolled like cigars (they taste like celery, and tend to clear the sluices), and the blueberries that were still around because of the moderating effect of Lake Superior, which, because of its immensity, tends to hold heat into the fall, making an artificially warm microclimate alongshore. In winter, before freeze-up, the temperature along Superior's north shore is often five or six degrees Celsius warmer than it is even a kilometre inland. In summer, the air is five or six degrees cooler, for which reason the lake is sometimes referred to as "the world's largest air conditioner."

And, again, I gathered firewood—cut it and stacked it and admired it. One day, I walked deep into the forest behind the beach, cut a dead spruce tree and worked two hours to haul it out to the beach, arriving scraped and enervated, believing less in myself than I had before I had left (if I were to choose a threshold point in my eventual decision to leave, I think it would be this one). That night, I fried four eggs, ate a can of cold tuna and drank what was left of my canned milk, subdued by the thought that I would now have no milk for my coffee in the morning. But a nap brought my spirits back up, and perhaps an hour before sunset I climbed back onto the promontory to the west. From there I could see out to Michipicoten Island and into the hills to the north, where the thermoclines had turned the leaves at the upper-most altitudes a deep orangy red atop a mountainside of yellow and green—in effect, a mile-wide sundae for the eye.

I poked around among the alpine flowers that thrive in sub-climates along Superior's north shore, nourishing an eerie little presentiment that I was going to see an animal. Whether such hunches are olfactory or auditory, or something more subliminal, I couldn't begin to say. But I have seen moose after such intima-tions, and in the Rockies, with Matt, saw an elk within minutes of announcing to him that I felt we were about to see some wildlife (actually, we saw a cow, and exploded laughing, a few sec-onds before we saw the elk). And sure enough, this time, just a few minutes after "animal" had registered on my subconscious, I saw a good-sized black bear across the bald rock outcrops atop the cliffs. He was drinking heartily from a stream that flows out of the hills and eventually over the cliffs. When I clapped my hands, he raised his head languorously, as if it were heavier than he'd remembered, tested the wind and stared at me for several seconds. My heart at this point was on full bongo, but any notion I had that there might be mutual trepidation, or even respect (as I have always read of relations between bears and humanity), was erased by the total indifference with which he lowered his head and con-tinued to slurp.

––––––––––

The purview widens, then shrinks again, then expands. Time, too, plays tricks—expands, then contracts to a point where, relative to billion-year-old rock, the postglacial forest and lakes, a mere ten thousand years old, seem as recent as the eleven-o'clock news. In the meantime, in the afternoon sun, my own measly life seemed infinite. And yet the daylight was short, the hours so full that nothing more could be wedged in. It was time without timepieces, and when I returned eventually to my van, and put the key in the ignition, I felt a surge of resentment to see the bright-green clock digits come up on the dashboard. Oh yeah, *that*, I thought.

––––––––––

I cannot say exactly why I left Rhyolite Cove when I did. I had run out of canned milk and tuna, and out of bread and eggs and tea. But I had rice and soup mix and margarine—and apricots and almonds. And a little hard block of Romano cheese that I had so far not touched. What's more, I had another huge boletus, and had picked three or four cups of blueberries, so was not about to starve. But when I woke up on the ninth day, the wind had shifted to the north, and the temperature had dropped. And as I nursed my fire into full heat, still wearing the black fleece gloves in which I had slept, I decided quite suddenly that it was time to go.

Within two hours, I had eaten, packed and walked down to the water for a last ritual cleansing of the face and hands.

On the hike out, I stopped at the ruins of an eighty-year-old stone house, perhaps a remnant of the old fishing village, high in the woods above the lake. I took off my pack, and as I poked around amidst the rubble, couldn't help but be impressed by the builders' obvious illusions of permanence, and by the equally obvious way the lake gales and winter and isolation had gradually subdued and then silenced them. I sat on the sun-warmed stones that were the base of the old hearth and took out my notebook, thinking that, before I returned to the city, I should record at least a few sentences in summary of my days on the shore.

––––––––––

But after twenty minutes, I was just another silenced inhabitant of the house, frustrated by the chicken scratchings before me, and, in a deeper sense, by even the idea of abstracting anything like a meaning or lesson—a specific meaning or lesson—from my days of water and woodcutting and fire. Was it any wonder, it occurred to me, that the tribes who had inhabited these wilds for millennia had been storytellers, not analysts, and that their stories, not their explanations or abstractions, had carried the meaning of their existence, along with so much else about them, forward from one generation to another? Somewhere down deep, I knew the meaning *was* the time in the wilds, and that if I had learned anything that could be construed as a lesson (conveyable to a culture obsessed with lessons that it never quite seems to learn) it was in the necessity, as the Luddites say, of *un*learning from time to time, of letting go. But even this was, for me, just a temporality, in that, soon, I would unlearn what I had unlearned, and would be back where I had begun, in need of another sojourn in the wilderness. Next time, I promised myself, I would not wait half a lifetime.

When I had my gear back up on my shoulders, and had buckled my pack in front, I had a momentary impulse to go back down to the beach for another night. But another part of me had already begun thinking about a warm bath, and, more enticingly, about a meal of gnocchi and Italian salad at Rosie & Josie's restaurant in Schreiber.

As the sun arced over into the west, throwing a ray or two straight down into the spruce trees, I hiked the last couple of kilometres down to Gargantua Harbour. There, under a toasty midday sun, I stretched out on my sleeping bag on the beach, and, for a few minutes, rested my head on the soft spot of my pack.

I awoke startled, perhaps two hours later, ravenous for food, and rattled by a bizarre and ambiguous dream in which I had somehow been granted the instincts of a wild animal, a predator, but without that animal's toughness or speed or defences. As I stalked through the underbrush behind the beach, in what now seems a ludicrous parody of my time in the wilds, I was snapped awake by a voice, and found myself staring up into the face of a young man in a wet-suit, who said to me for what I suspect was not the first time, "Are you all right, sir?"

Even in the fuzziness of the moment, it stung me that he would refer to me as "sir."

"Yeah, I'm fine!" I said, undoubtedly with more oomph than was necessary at close quarters. It took me a second to realize that I was not at Rhyolite Cove, and that a yellow kayak had been pulled onto the beach (a young woman was sculling just offshore in a second kayak).

"I called to you," the young man said, "and when you didn't answer, I came in to make sure you were okay."

"Yeah," I said, sitting up, "I'm okay. It was very good of you. Thanks very much."

"I'm outta here," he said, and within minues he and his partner, both of whom seemed now to be just another dream figment, were off out of sight beyond the next point.

Immediately, I rummaged in my pack for my notebook and, weirdly inspired by the dream, made several pages of notes.

Satisfied that I had caught the essence of things, I put my note-book away, pulled out my apricots and cheese, and bit off a mouthful of Romano. Then another one. When I had snacked to my satisfaction, I put on an extra sweatshirt and, having decided to stay another few hours, walked into the woods at the top of the beach and gathered up a knee-high stack of kindling. More than food, more than shelter, more than the aesthetics of land or of water, I was, after nine days alone in the woods, addicted to the presence of fire.

When I had scooped out a wide shallow pit in the sand, I laid down a heap of spruce scrub, most of it about the diameter of pencil lead. I covered it with a teepee of kindling, and added a good-sized chunk of driftwood. Then I got on my knees beside it—not exactly a supplicant at the altar, but not exactly not one either. Sheltering things as best I could from the wind, I brought my hands in close and struck a match.

Chapter Six

hile the idea is no less about cities than about landscapes or wilderness, I believe that when I tell another person where I come from—as opposed to something subjective or abstract about myself—I convey irreducible information about who I am and about the realities that have shaped me. Not long ago, a woman I'd been acquainted with for years surprised me by telling me she came from Deep River, Ontario, the eccentric little atomic-energy town where I myself lived for eight years as a boy, and which tended to shape people in ways that Toronto or Vancouver or, say, an agricultural or manufacturing community, never could. The gist of the town's identity was that an inordinate number of high-level scientists lived and worked there, imbuing the place with an exaggerated—at times, almost freakish—intellectuality. It was an identity that might have been dulled outside the typical urban or university setting, but it was in fact accentuated in the context of bushland, rock, river, mosquito infestations, forest fires, oppressively cold winters and relative social isolation. Whereas I had been happy in Deep River, the woman had been unhappy, intensely so. Nevertheless, the new, shared knowledge of one another's geographic and psychological testing grounds gave us a different perspective on one another, and created a base for a lengthy conversation that could not have happened otherwise.

On the same theme, I tell my writing classes that if they want to know the minds and biographies of their ancestors, they should concern themselves less with ledgers and official documents than with the landscapes and rooms in which these people contemplated marriage, or military enlistment, or watched the Depression dust pile up, or the first rain or snow, or gave birth to a son or daughter, or mourned a child dead of scarlet fever.

I know that to bring my own great-grandfather Scholey into focus, I have to go not to the one or two photos that exist of him (which are, essentially, a lie, in that they show him shaved and trimmed and all dressed up in a suit and tie) but to the hoary old Scholey farmstead outside Bracebridge, Ontario, with its humpy granite ridge, and the Muskoka River within sight of the front windows, and the boulder-strewn acres that were both the hope and the despair of what must have been an extraordinarily difficult life. His fields never produced enough grain to afford him a horse, which meant that four or five times a year during the late 1800s, he was obliged to walk fifty miles across the hills to the gristmill in Orillia, with a seventy-five-pound bag of wheat on his back, and then return the next day with a bag of flour. It is here—in the fields and on the granite, and on the trail to Orillia (I once walked about a dozen miles of it, with no weight on my back, before quitting)—that the crossable bridge exists between me and my ancestor, and I am able to locate a likeness of him that I can "read" and appreciate.

A friend, a Thunder Bay psychiatrist, Brian Frost, who has a long-standing interest in the First World War, recently toured that war's battlefields in Europe. Until then, the battles had been for him a collage of impressions garnered from maps, books, reminiscences and black-and-white photos. He told me that as he saw the trees, knolls and streams—saw them in colour for the first time—and got a sense of what the soldiers had actually been looking at as they waited or marched, and then fought, he was struck by an intense sense of connection to the men, many of whom died or spilled blood on these historic plots of ground at Vimy Ridge and Passchendaele and Flanders. He said, "As I walked around, figuring out where the troops had come from, how they'd engaged, what streams they'd crossed, where they might have taken cover, all of that, I was able to project myself into their experience in a way that, till then, I hadn't even imagined."

———————

Our contract with the planet extends from the broadest poetics to the most detailed sensory and scientific levels. In the same sense that the buffalo licked salt from the soil, we, too, consume the planet's tastes, nutrients and colours, and these become a reading, however subtle, of the earth's ecology and composition. As Canadians, we absorb a particular subset of these readings and associations. A roasted mallard, for example, tastes sweetly and distinctly of the tenderest water plants or field grain, while a goldeneye or spoonbill tastes of the pond bottom, and a scaup, of the fish that *feed* on the bottom. Snow geese coming down from the far north in fall have eaten so many cranberries and blueberries that they taste of them and, in fact, are a distinctly bluish colour beneath the skin. After a couple of weeks of fattening themselves on barley and corn, the blue is gone, replaced by yellowish fat, and the acid taste has become the sweet nutty flavour of the fresh grain. The white matsutake (or pine) mushrooms picked wild in the autumn in northern Manitoba are prized by the Japanese for the taste of the loamy, muskeggy soil, which cannot be duplicated in the commercial growers' barns.

There are thousands of similar examples that are no more Canadian than American, British or German. Butter, which these days is coloured uniformly with vegetable dye, was at one time a far

———————

brighter yellow during the summer than the winter, because the cows' summer diet included large infusions of buttercups. In the Bahamas, where the available "fresh" water is almost exclusively desalinated sea water, Coca-Cola tastes faintly of the sea. Now that Canadians have winced through the Walkerton depredations and inquiry, it is probably safe to say that most water in the country tastes more distinctly of skepticism, or even fear, than of any metal or salt. But the well water where my family and I once lived in Dundas, Ontario, tasted of the limestone in the local aquifer, whereas in Thunder Bay the water, at least by my reckoning, tastes of slate.

From the moment we're conceived, the planet enters us as fluids, smells, sounds, tastes, distastes; as images and dreamscapes, sometimes with soothing or satisfying effects, sometimes unsettling us for life. One of my lingering nightmares stems from an incident that took place when I was three, in the yard of a farmhouse my parents rented near Sydenham, Ontario, where my father taught English at the local school. One afternoon, the son of the farm's owner, a young man named Elwood Orser, beckoned me across the barnyard one afternoon, and invited me to watch while he squeezed a huge greyish slug, a creature as big and shiny as a Spanish olive, from a pea-sized red hole in the hide of one of his Holsteins. "Magic," he smiled as he placed the thing in his palm, and held it out to me.

Years later I would question my memory of the occurrence, because nobody I ever mentioned it to, including a university entomologist, had any awareness of what the creature might have been, or that such a thing could occur. Then one day, my brother-in-law, Nelson King, an immensely knowledgeable farmer, confirmed that, indeed, until the late 1950s, there had existed in Canada a species of large insect, a warble fly (now controlled by toxins), whose microscopic offspring could chew into the muscle tissue of a cow's leg, from where they would migrate through the flesh up onto the animal's back or side. There they would mature into larval slugs. To fulfill its life cycle, an individual slug would eat a hole in the hide, from where it would either emerge on its own or be squeezed forth by a diligent farmer who would explode it beneath the toe of his boot, as Elwood did after showing the thing to me.

More happily, I remember lying on my back on the dock at the family cabin at Torrance, Ontario, at the age of perhaps four, staring at the sky on a day when the clouds at different altitudes were moving at different speeds. Suddenly I sat up, feeling as close as I am likely to get to what Galileo must have felt when he realized the truth about the sun and earth. Within seconds I was in the cabin, revealing breathlessly to my mother that the clouds were *not attached to the sky*, were not a fixed part of the blue bowl, as I—and, I assumed, everybody else—had always imagined. I had seen them moving independently of it, and I would stand by this jewel of empirical revelation no matter who might refute it or call me a heretic.

I could swear that when my father threw me into the air in front of the Sydenham farmhouse, I rose well above the tops of the nearby maples and elms, providing me with my first experience of flight. And I recall how, at age five, in Deep River, after a long and exhausting winter that might as well have begun before I was born, I gained my first blessed awareness of the spring sun as I trudged down the hill on Parkdale Avenue on my way home from my weekly piano lesson.

Having had my tongue frozen hard to a steel post at age four, and having at age six come up under a diving raft while swimming in Clear Lake, unable to get to air (I was freed by my sister, Susan, who reached in and yanked me out), I am occasionally neurotic about the possibility that my own children will repeat my mistakes. But why spook them? Would it help them to know, for example, that my descent into any strange cellar is edged by my shocked discovery of an immense dead rat at the foot of the cellar stairs in Deep River when I was three or four? Or that when I wandered from the Sunday School picnic at Petawawa, I stumbled onto the maggot-infested carcass of a bear that, forty years later, I recall with fixated clarity?

It is perhaps as children, even infants, that we have our greatest natural affinity for the planet. Everybody has heard that a baby plunged directly from the womb into warm water will swim (although it has never been clear to me whether it will swim on the surface). Even in new shoes, my four- and six-year-old daughters will detour off high ground to slop through a mud puddle, or to wade into the shallows of a river or lake. As a kid, I could fiddle for hours on rafts or in rowboats, or at catching crayfish, or building forts, or cutting saplings for bows and arrows. My six-year-old, Georgia, will sit down to dinner with twigs in her hair and a gram of black clay under her fingernails.

As an eleven-year-old, fascinated by the idea that air and water could be united to propel a boat, I constructed a fourteen-foot sailboat out of a square-prowed punt that my grandfather Scholey had built in some prehistoric summer before my birth. The thing was as leaky as an orange crate and, in appearance, suggested the mating of river barge and garbage dumpster. My mast and booms were maple saplings, my sail an antique striped awning with a flappy, scalloped edge. I fixed sail to mast with roofing nails and propped the assemblage in a pail of sand on the floor of the punt. The sail, to quote Hemingway, "looked like the flag of permanent defeat."

But I was undefeated in my desire to sail—or by my ignorance of physics. I didn't know, for example, that you needed a centreboard or keel if you wanted a sailboat to go forward. Mine went sideways—all the way down Clear Lake to Camp Pinecrest. I knew about rudders, but a rudder would have been useless to me; my hands and energy were consumed entirely in keeping the mast from being toppled by the wind. My dad arrived on the weekend and showed me that by thrusting a paddle into the water amidships, in the manner of a centreboard or outrigger, you could make the boat follow its prow. With a little manipulation, you could steer with the same oar. One of us did. The other held the mast (guy lines were far too sophisticated). And thus we cruised Clear Lake.

The following summer, I was given a factory-made sailboat for my birthday. It came to the cottage on a truck, and since my dad was away, my Uncle Hunter and I unpacked and rigged it—blue nylon sail, pine mast and boom, moulded mahogany hull. It was made in Norway and according to its manufacturer was fully ocean-worthy, tested on the fjords of Scandinavia. All very impressive to a twelve-year-old.

I still have that boat, and treasure it. But its predecessor remains the foundation of my knowledge of that ancient form of transportation—of air pressure and vectors and aquadynamics, and the subtleties of waves and wind.

From infancy on, entire landscapes, not just their fragments, impress themselves upon us with lifelong effects. I have a friend who spent an unhappy childhood near Windsor, Ontario, and who, thirty years later, is still repulsed by the flatlands and vegetable farms around the city. By his own admission, he is paralyzed when it comes to getting any work done in the area. The same man is so exhilarated and at home when he gets to Montreal or into the Laurentian Mountains—where he spent a good deal of time during his university years at McGill—that he is unable to work there either.

I myself have never been much good in the area around Guelph or Kitchener, Ontario, where, on summer visits to my grandparents' home in Hespeler, at the age of seven or eight, I was lonesome, sometimes scared, in the upstairs front room by myself in the dark. Once, while I was there, I sat in the living room alone and watched a televised movie called *The Black Widow*, about a nasty woman who had murdered her husband. I came to associate the woman with that upstairs room, imagining in the darkness that she was hiding in the closet or coming down the hall or up from the basement with her stainless-steel ice pick or scalpel. I'd wake up in the middle of the night, longing for dawn, when the birds would begin to twitter in the big maple outside the window and I could breathe again.

My favourite line by the poet T. S. Eliot is not about April or cruelty or ashes—or hollow men (or women) measuring their lives by the spoonful—but is the simple truth that "in the mountains you feel free." Or in the desert, or on the prairies, or by the seashore . . . or in the garden, or (Hespeler excepted) in bed. In fact, bed, the anthropologists tell us, is a micro-version of a landscape we return to for respite and healing. When I am impossibly tangled in the here and now—as in, say, the miasmic perplexities of book-writing—I always know that a few hours of sleep, like a visit to the woods or seashore, will restore something of what has been lost.

Recently, a woman who'd been travelling in England told me that when she got to a certain part of a certain city—Leicester, I believe it was—she was "nailed," as she put it, by an overwhelming feeling of well-being, a sense that after decades in relative exile she had come home. I experienced a version of the feeling when I visited Wales in my early twenties. For days on end, I ranged happily across the rounded green hills, among farmers and villagers and sheep herders, and spent the better part of two days on a grass-topped cliff, gazing at the Isle of Anglesey and the North Sea, indulging what I took to be the same unnameable tie to the landscape that my acquaintance had discovered in Leicester.

I did learn later that a tributary of my forebears was Welsh. But our responses to the land are hardly that simply explained. When I visited Eric Nesterenko in Colorado—a man with no ancestral tie to the Arctic—he told me that, as a child, he had dreamed repeatedly of ice floes, icebergs and tundra, and had longed for such a landscape. At last, in his mid-forties, retired from hockey, he had journeyed into the far north, and had spent a couple of languorous summers driving a cat train, taking long walks in the midnight sun, and observing animals on the tundra that he was convinced had never seen a human being.

A Thunder Bay lawyer, Dan Newton, told me that one of his most treasured fragments of the universe was neither a landscape nor a lodestar but a single tree, a climbing tree, that had held a place in his heart as he was growing up outside Thunder Bay. He had recently visited the tree with his own children. As we spoke, I was nudged by the memory of another tree, in this case an alder with sharp-smelling reddish-brown bark that stood in a little grove of scrub across from our house on Parkdale Avenue in Deep River. I had not thought about it for decades, but could recall now exactly the positioning of the lower branches, and the feel of them, springy under the instep, and the association of risk and independence that went along with the climb.

It is evidence of the ease with which that tree could be climbed that one disastrous day, in perhaps 1954, I climbed it in skates. My mother had been determined to introduce me to the little outdoor rink in the clearing across the street. But because I had no skates of my own, I had been laced into an old pair of my sister's—white, with a fur ruff at the ankle. I did not know anything was amiss until we reached the rink, and I noticed that all the other boys were wearing black skates. In protest, I kicked my mother's leg, and watched as first the stocking, then the skin, peeled from her leg with a gush of red. As she lay crying in the snow, I headed for the safety of the tree.

Even Nature's smallest fragments carry potency and poignancy: the evening snow falling past the window, the ray of light angling into the room, the droop of an orange lily, the lapping of water beneath the dock.

As for drama, Nature is never at a loss. When I was a child, a wolf crashed through the basement window of a house owned by people we were vaguely acquainted with in the east end of Toronto (the story made the front page of *The Toronto Star*, and featured in my neuroses for weeks to come). On New Year's Eve 1986, as my wife and I drove from her home village of Lynn Lake, in northern Manitoba, to the town of Leaf Rapids, about a hundred kilometres away, a bull moose clambered out of the roadside snowdrifts, coming close to sending us off the highway in −40°C weather. While our hearts were still pounding, an immense green comet plummeted out of the eastern sky in front of the car, leaving a path of greeny yellow light from the high point of the heavens to the horizon, again sending us into planetary arrest. I have friends who, on weekends in November, race to their summer home on the cliffs of the Sibley Peninsula, where they can feel the bedrock-deep trembling of the storms that come in off Lake Superior at that time of year, and perhaps themselves enjoy a little trembling as the wind shakes their windows and tears at their eaves.

My own need for a fix is constant: out the window at sunset, across the lake, beyond the prow of the canoe, in the rear-view mirror. There is never a time when I am not happy to be out on the north shore of Lake Superior, with its beaches and palisades and old mountains—or on Lake Winnipeg or Lake Manitoba, with their deep dunes and grasses. Not long ago, I heard a woman say quite scornfully that men in this culture consider getting in a car and driving somewhere to be among the ultimate of life's experiences—the assumption seeming to be that the thrill is largely about cars. It isn't. It's about *going* (needless to say, women, too, have their escape fantasies). But it's also about *seeing*—forests, oceans, beaches, fields, mountains, deserts, rocks, rivers, wild animals.

The story of Western culture pretty much begins in a garden, with immediate highs and lows, proceeding eventually through to "green pastures" and "still waters"—and, in the end, to the imponderable "valley of the shadow."

We get what the planet dishes out, and see in its mysteries a vision as various and complex as ourselves (nature and human nature on the same long continuum). Or we get only what we bring to it in the way of vulnerability or imagination. When I go out to Silver Islet, a tiny historic community on the tip of the Sibley Peninsula in Lake Superior, I am impressed simultaneously by the certainty of billion-year-old rock, and by the uncertainty of the rather fragile dream that suffuses the place and is entirely untranslatable into the rigidities of basalt, science and civilization.

The fragility is partly a matter of scale, inasmuch as the community sits with its back to massive diabase cliffs, its front exposed to the rip-snorting winds and storms that regularly rage off the lake. Even on calm days in these parts, human settlement—humanity, period—tends to be dwarfed by the lake's vast and icy self-sufficiency. But the fragility is equally a matter of time and mortality, or perhaps of timelessness, in that just a kilometre offshore lies a forlorn little island from which the mainland community takes its name. One hundred and twenty-five years ago this tiny island was the site of the richest silver mine in the world—a glittering symbol of humanity's grandest plans. Today, there is no trace of what went on there, except for a few underwater timbers and two small black holes in the lake bed, the mine's shafts, eerily visible from a boat or low-flying plane. On a winter day just a couple of years after the community had established itself, the ferocity and frigidity of the lake simply swamped the mine and savaged the miners, too.

And so the paradox goes: grandeur addictive and inspiring to humanity, and yet capable in an hour of punishing its adherents—of humbling if not beating them into submission, and of sending them on their way.

PART THREE

Chapter Seven

ike all ship captains and navigators, Ken Strong has had scares and close shaves on the water—"ass tighteners," as the second mate, Serge Masse, referred to them. So when he began telling me one evening near Trois-Rivières about his "lowest moment as a navigator," I anticipated hearing about a storm or grounding or some dire navigational miscalculation. In fact, the captain was talking about a day on which he had sailed into the Saint-Lambert Lock in Montreal and had inadvertently forced a mother duck and four ducklings along in front of the vessel, until finally they were trapped in the twenty or thirty centimetres of space between the portside of the hull and the concrete lock wall.

"It was summer," he said. "Everyone and his grandmother was out to see the sights. There must have been 250 people along the lock wall. And, dammit, here was this family of ducks in plain view right in the lock, with everybody horrified that I was going to squash them." Ken knows what his ship is doing to within a centimetre or two one way or the other in any docking or lock situation. So when he said he did everything he could to avoid them, he meant everything. "People were screaming," he told me. "It was awful. We ended up killing the mother and one of the little ones. It was like a funeral along the wall. Oh, I felt awful. Geez, I felt awful. I felt just terrible."

———————

It is said of John Ringling, one of the five founding brothers of the Ringling Circus, that, during the early 1900s, when a hundred thousand miles of passenger rail criss-crossed America, he could recite by heart the rail route, complete with junctions, sidings and spurs, between any two points in America. It is also said that when he woke up at night on the train, he could look out the window anywhere in the United States and, at a glance, name the county through which he was passing. Ken Strong's knowledge of the vast surfaces and shorelines of the Great Lakes and St. Lawrence River—the waters and shores from the middle of the continent to the Atlantic—is every bit as compelling. He has made the trip from the Lakehead to the Gulf of St. Lawrence hundreds of times, has plotted it kilometre by kilometre on the charts and radar, and on the coloured screen of the Global Positioning System; has seen it in snow, in rain, in fog, under moonlight and halogen spots; and has taken bearings off a countless number of its lighthouses, islands, skyscrapers and communication towers. Ken's private template of the central and eastern continent is, in fact, not so much a map or chart as a vast internalized matrix of buoys, lighthouses, docks, depths, lock walls, treelines, skylines, bridges, shorelines, cottages, castles, beaches, cliffs, mountains, all seen across water, each fragment bearing its particular subset of private and professional values.

One day, on the St. Clair River, in my presence, Ken glanced out at a strip of sparsely wooded swamp that only a muskrat could have loved and said quietly, "There used to be a little poplar on that point; it made it easier to judge this bend." And when I asked about a barely perceptible smudge on the south horizon of Lake Superior, he said without looking, "It's the northern tip of the Keewenaw Peninsula." He can tell you without a chart the depth of any water you might happen to be sailing through, and what town, settlement or crossroads is represented by even the most distant hint of luminescence on the night horizon.

Certainly, one of the more fascinating aspects of my travels aboard the *M. V. Paterson* was that, for three weeks, I had unimpeded access to this veteran helmsman, widely acknowledged to be among the finest and most judicious ship handlers on the Great Lakes—which, by irrefutable logic, is to say one of the finest anywhere. It will surprise many Canadians to learn that the Great Lakes—not the North Atlantic, nor the Cape of Good Hope, nor the tight rocky passages of the Caribbean or Mediterranean—are the world's most exacting navigational challenge. Under anything less than ideal conditions, they can be an almost fiendish befuddlement of currents, tight passages, shallows, shoals, ice floes, tight lock walls, unpredictable weather and, during storms, waves that follow one another far more closely and treacherously than they do at sea. An ocean vessel, accustomed to dealing with one giant wave at a time, can on Lake Superior, for example, be faced with two or more storm swells in quick succession, sometimes two or three at a time. "If you're moving upwind, you tend to pound into them, instead of going up and over," the captain told me. "If you're taking them broadside, you roll quickly and violently."

Several career sailors, including a veteran Seaway pilot, confided to me that foreign captains come regularly, sometimes arrogantly, onto the Great Lakes, tacitly disdainful of the smaller waters, but that after experiencing a storm on Lake Superior or Lake Michigan they want nothing more than to get off the lakes and back out to the spaced swells and long, straight shipping lanes of the sea. Ken Strong told me that his father, a ship's officer during the 1920s who retired to work in the shipyards at Midland, Ontario, once took an old sea-vessel inspector from Halifax out on Georgian Bay in heavy weather to test-run a tugboat. "It wasn't long before they were taking waves right over the wheelhouse, and this guy was just howling a string of curses; if he ever got off that blankety-blank tug he was never, *ever* coming back onto these blankety-blank lakes."

As in the fictional era of Captain Bligh and Fletcher Christian, today's shipboard politics can be cranky and divisive, as they occasionally are aboard the *Paterson*. However, even those crewmen who feel no particular affection for Ken Strong are quite happy to acknowledge that he handles a ship as dexterously as any skipper they have ever seen. "I've worked with him for years," Don Wheeler said, "and I've never seen him make a false move at the helm. Some guys rant and rave, run around. He stays calm, just gets the job done."

The chief engineer, Ernie Oferi, told me the captain had "a mind like a pair of calipers." But from my own point of view, Ken Strong's genius is less a matter of mind than of eye and reflex and well-channelled confidence in his own abilities. He has an architect's sense of space, an athlete's anticipation and the nerve of a prize fighter. He is no scholar. On our first day out, he told me unselfconsciously that he had read six books in his life— one for every decade of his existence. He remembered each of them with almost photographic recall, and with an enthusiasm so far surpassing what the average reader might harbour for an old book that I wondered privately why he didn't try another one. He also told me that he loved poker and could play twenty-four hours a day. He has a perfectly shaped bald head, a prelate's fringe of hair, and a salt-and-pepper push-broom moustache. He has a preference for Docker-style khakis and wears those raffish-looking glasses that turn grey in sunlight and possess just a hint of the New Jersey mob.

One night Serge Masse got musing on the thousands of ways in which we greet and read the physical world—the geologist with his pick, the astronomer his telescope, the lumberman his axe or saw, the gardener his trowel, not to mention the eyes, ears, etc., which are of course each person's primary contact. But the sea captain, he felt, has drawn the toughest interpretation, in that he must read his element, the most capricious of all, with a probe that can weigh forty thousand tonnes and, in the *Paterson*'s case, is nearly a quarter of a kilometre long.

Even to a tire-kicker like me, the captain's talent was obvious—in particular, say, when he was bringing the ship into a lift lock, of which there are sixteen on the Seaway. The locks are barely wider than the vessels, and the standard manner of taking a vessel into one is to stop on the lock wall outside the actual enclosure and ease it in, as the captain normally did. But he also had the ability to take the boat in "on the fly," meaning to guide it into the lock without stopping and then bring it to a halt, without so much as brushing the lock walls. In this, Ken Strong is a kind of Tiger Woods among ship handlers—straight down the fairway, no drift.

The most dramatic and masterful example I saw of the captain's ship-handling came on the night of April 7 on the St. Lawrence River about a hundred kilometres west of Montreal, between Massena, New York, and Cornwall, Ontario. At about five that afternoon, as we'd come out of the locks at Iroquois, eastbound, it had begun to snow heavily. By dusk, visibility had been reduced to a ship length, and the federal Department of Transport was warning vessels to reduce speed and proceed with extreme caution. During cold weather, the heat from the grain in the holds will keep the deck temperature somewhat above the temperature of the air, and thereby free of snow and ice; but the wind was frigid, and snow settled quickly on deck and drifted into banks against the hatches and under the catwalks. The current on this part of the St. Lawrence is fast, because Cornwall Island, one of the largest islands in the river, acts as a plug in the channel, pinching the flow into two narrow, turbulent passages, making navigation tricky at the best of times. As we approached the Eisenhower Lock, there was talk of mooring at the lock wall for the night. The pilot of the *Olympic Mentor*, an Onassis-owned ship registered in Panama and upbound just below the lock, had already voiced uncertainty as to whether his vessel could continue into what was now a dense blizzard.

I had a quick dinner and, anticipating drama, went up into the wheelhouse. There, the captain was at the helm and, for the one and only time during my weeks aboard, all three mates were on the job—Terry Holt at the radar, Serge Masse at the chart table, and Dan MacDonald peering through binoculars into the snow, looking for the dim shape of the next navigation buoy (at times during the next three hours, all three mates would be on the bridge with binoculars). It is common practice for the wheelsman to repeat the captain's navigational commands—"gimme sixty-three," "hold 'er there," "hard to starboard," etc.—so that the captain knows he has been heard. Leigh Voutier, a young sailor from Cape Breton Island, was at the wheel that night, and was repeating Ken Strong's orders with apparent composure, although his blood must have been coursing as he steered blindly into the night.

The snow swirled out of the darkness into the huge halogen spotlights above the bridge, and suddenly the *Olympic Mentor*, black and rusted and nightmarish, appeared directly off our port bow, seven storeys high, plunging out of the storm as ghostly as the *Lusitania*, and eerily silent as it dieselled past with just metres to spare. Passing a ship at close quarters is more than just a test of nerves; it is one of the more delicate navigational chops, in that, on meeting, two massive vessels will, as their prows pass and their bow waves meet, push one another in opposite directions, sometimes quite violently, demanding immediate compensation from the wheelsman. But as they come alongside and extend their prows beyond one another's sterns, especially at speed, the effect of their displacement takes over, and quite abruptly they are sucked toward one another, demanding opposite compensation from the wheelsman. Leigh handled the pass flawlessly, and while I myself gaped, the officers barely glanced to port at the upbound ship—we hadn't collided, that was all.

A minute later, as we approached the wide concrete funnel that is the entryway to the Eisenhower Lock, Terry Holt bundled himself into his coat and scarf, left the wheelhouse and made his way forward on the slippery deck. From the port bow, he radioed back the distances from the angled wall—fifteen feet, five feet, two feet. At the centre window of the bridge, the captain, binoculars in his left hand, spotlight controls in his right, calmly gave Leigh his directions as, without stopping, we slipped blindly into the lock chamber and, for a few minutes of respite from the storm, came to rest.

———

When, in 1997, I travelled with the circus, I came to see in the inventiveness of its language a measure of the distinction and values of the community—a world of "gunsels," "bally broads," "candy butchers," "jackpotting," "ironjaw," "hotwagons," "grinders," "Georgia gangs," "grab joints" and "mud shows." The distinctiveness of life on water—its essential, radical departure from existence on land—is likewise represented in its working vocabulary. Not only are common nouns and verbs replaced by the ancient inventions of sea life, so, too, are words representing even the most fundamental spatial concepts and measurement, the directional abstractions on which humanity has come to depend for its safety and survival. It is a world of fathoms and knots and nautical miles—of fore and abaft, port and starboard. Early sailing ships, incidentally, always came into port on their left, or "port," sides, because the right side of a ship supported the steering board, or "starboard," which (until such devices were relocated astern during the eighteenth century) prevented the vessel from drawing close to the dock on the right. Otherwise, ships are a world of "spurling pipes," "hawse pipes," "snubbers," "soogying," "sheer lines," "coamings," "hoving to," "coming about," "monkey islands," "hawse holes," "poop decks," "plimsoll marks," "windlasses," "capstans," "galleys," "coxswains," "fo'c'sles," "chines," "bollards," "green water" and "fog dogs."

If a culture is distinguished by the specifics of its vocabulary, it is distinguished equally by what it does with that vocabulary—particularly in the line of storytelling. Anthropologists tell us that, over time, a tribe preserves and retells the tales that best embody its perspective and values. Get a few sailors around and, inevitably, the stories turn to storms, wrecks, fires, uncharted shoals, unheeded warnings, incompetent captains, freak waves, ghost ships, weird shadows on the radar, rotted hulls, men overboard; the crewman who "drowned" in the wheat of the hold; the whale that got carried from Labrador to Montreal on the prow of the ship; the woman who "died" aboard a Canadian vessel and was placed in the deep-freeze with no confirmation that her heart had stopped; the human remains so deeply entangled in the ship's propeller in New York Harbor that they were simply left there to shake loose on their own; and, of course, the *Edmund Fitzgerald*, the *Roy Jodrey*, the *Titanic*.

On some level, the sailors know well the underlying meaning of the tales they tell and, as the anthropologists explain, slowly codify that meaning into a cultural scripture. The themes are danger, uncertainty, dehumanization, aloneness, mortality, freedom, the ultimate indomitability of natural forces. Often, of course, there is exaggeration, especially as the tales are repeated by those unfamiliar with the realities of life on the water. A book on the Great Lakes by a revered Canadian writer cites a storm on Lake Superior that threw up "seven-storey-high waves." By even a conservative estimate, seven storeys would equal more than eighteen metres, on a lake where the most experienced sailors say they have never seen waves of more than eight or nine metres.

The stories are no less about the ambiguity of life on the water: the sense of simultaneous freedom and entrapment, pride and insecurity, detachment and connectedness. The sailor is quite literally connected everywhere—is linked navigationally to every sea and to all of the great rivers on earth. On the other hand, he is connected to no place in particular, and needs only stop to think of the last time he saw his family or sweetheart to send himself into pangs of self-doubt or depression. In the same ambiguous vein, his suspicion that those on land have somehow evolved a social superiority is accompanied by a persistent notion that the rest of the world is made up of ill-informed ciphers who have somehow missed out on the more intense, vital and knowing existence of the sea.

It occurred to me at a point that the absolute certainty of so much of daily life aboard—the rules, the punctuality, the union regulations, the endless succession of watches and the inviolable hierarchy of the command—is a centuries-old response to the often perilous *uncertainty* of the many forces that constantly threaten from just beyond the fragile membrane that is its hull.

The *Paterson*'s own developing mythology finds its apex in the frequently repeated tale of "the Michipicoten Storm"—a story I heard perhaps ten times while on board, and twice on my first day. During a deathly storm on Lake Superior in November 1998, the ship left Thunder Bay and made its way gingerly eastward in the lee of the lake's north shore, as far as Michipicoten Island, about halfway to the Soo. But at that point, rather than leave the shore's protection and head southeast across open water for Sault Ste. Marie, the captain on the trip, Larry Schmidt, decided to anchor— to "hove to"—in the shelter of Michipicoten Island. "We waited there for thirty-eight hours," Serge Masse told me. "Even out of the wind it was rough, waves maybe twelve, fourteen feet high, but it was okay, it was safe."

For reasons known only to himself, the captain decided quite suddenly at midnight of the second day to haul anchor and head toward Whitefish Bay, where the *Edmund Fitzgerald* had gone down in 1975. "My brother's ship was unloading ore in the Soo that night," said Ken Strong, "and when he heard the *Paterson* was out on the lake, he couldn't believe it—he said they'd have to have been crazy to be out there."

"We were the *only* ones on the lake," said Serge. "Dozens of other ships had taken shelter. We were taking the waves broadside, rolling thirty, thirty-five degrees each way—this went on for two days. We couldn't work, couldn't sleep, couldn't eat. Furniture was just flying—tables, filing cabinets, couches."

"The problem," Ken said, "is that in a situation like that you can't turn back—if you start making a big wide turn, taking those waves at a funny angle, there's a good chance you'll go over. Even just rolling, going straight, if your cargo shifts, you're cooked."

"The whole thing still pisses me right off," said one of the crewmen who had made the run. "Larry had no business taking us out there on a night like that, endangering our lives. We're all damn lucky we're still here."

The most dramatic story I heard during my weeks on board came from Maurice Arsenault, who, these days, is a well-fed galley porter on the *Paterson*, a prep man and dishwasher and mop jockey. But in 1984 he was a carefree young deckhand on a federally owned research and transport vessel called the *Arctic* (on which many of the *Paterson*'s crew have worked at one time or another). During the autumn of that year, the vessel was on a freight run to northern Europe from the Canadian port of Nanasivik in the east Arctic, when it came into a storm three hundred kilometres off the coast of Iceland.

"Twenty-metre waves had been coming over the decks and forecastle all day," Maurice told me. "Nobody was talking, nobody was sleeping, nobody was moving." During the late evening, an eight-tonne double-sided loading scoop—a "clam" in the argot of the trade—broke loose on the foredeck and was carried sixty metres sternwards to where it smashed partway through a hatch cover and lodged precariously. Fearing another wave would put it through the wall of the aft house and engine room, and sink the vessel, the captain turned the ship, at great peril in such a sea, and began to surf with the waves, so that the wind was coming from the stern and the waves would be far less likely to come over the bulwarks. "We hadn't taken a wave in half an hour," said Maurice, "so the captain figured we were stable and ordered the deckhands to go out and chain down this clam. I would have gone with them, except I had stitches in my hand—they would have been ripped open by the chains."

When the crewmen were perhaps twenty metres in front of the aft house, a rogue wave came over the stern, floating the three of them, and entirely submerging the deck. "We never saw two of them again," said Maurice. "They were just swept away. The third guy went straight up with the wave and came straight back down on deck."

After sixteen years, the details are as fresh for Maurice as if they had happened last week. "We threw out a dozen life buoys, twenty-five life jackets. We sent up dozens of flares. And we circled," he said. "By law you have to circle seven times when somebody goes overboard. Every time we went broadside to the waves, I was sure we were going over. When you can count three seconds at a thirty- or thirty-five-degree angle you've got problems."

It occurred to me to ask why the crewmen had not been wearing lifelines, as anybody on deck should have been doing in such a situation. "Because they didn't believe a wave would get them from behind," shrugged Maurice.

I wondered aloud how, after such a catastrophe, anybody involved would be able to regain his taste for deck life, and Maurice told me that when the boat returned from Europe to Nanasivik, twenty-one of the twenty-eight crew members quit. "I thought about it, too," he said. "It's natural at first. But if you like life at sea, you look at yourself and, in a case like mine, you say, Hey, I'm a survivor, destiny's on my side, maybe more so than the next guy, and here's the evidence. Maybe I belong out here."

Maurice reflected briefly, shrugged and said, "Water is powerful. Out here we're privileged to see that. People at home in their living room, or in their office, never do. But in exchange for the privilege, we face the dangers."

One of the sad ironies of the tale was that one of the lost sailors was not even supposed to be aboard. He was engaged to be married the following month, and had quit life at sea. However, the boat was short-staffed, and he had been persuaded to make one last crossing before he took permanently to life on land.

For Maurice, the vagaries of fate were accentuated on the day the vessel passed back over the spot where the men had been lost. "The sun was out," he said, "it was hot, and the water was dead calm. Even at twelve or thirteen knots, you could hardly tell we were moving." In anticipation of the ship's arrival at the spot, the captain had brought an enormous wreath of roses on board, which was being stored in the galley fridge. "When we got there," Maurice said, "they cut the engine, and everybody gathered on deck. The captain read a little funeral service, said a prayer and we threw the wreath on the water. And then we went back to work."

———

There were some tough sailors aboard the *M. V. Paterson*—some Popeyes and some Blutos, most of them as pliant and approachable as buttercups beneath the scars and tattoos and four-letter words. One of the thorniest and most intimidating was a massive, bearded engine-room mechanic named John Gadula, an intensely politicized scowler who wore grease-heavy coveralls and a black cotton skullcap. During my first week aboard, John reacted to my occasional modest greetings either with total indifference or with a grimace of the sort you might expect from someone who suspected you had poisoned his well, or at very least murdered his dog.

One evening, after listening in the background to a conversation I was having with another crewman, John tore into me over my presumed naïveté in thinking that there was even a shred of integrity in the shipping industry or in those who controlled it— or in the ships themselves, which he characterized as criminally unsafe rustbuckets kept intact by little more than emergency spot welds and, perhaps, duct tape. Most boats, he implied, would not even be licensed were it not for a system riven with graft, bribery and political corruption. The overall message seemed to be that, if I was too dumb to realize this, I probably didn't have the smarts to be writing about any of the rest of it either. I discovered only in retrospect that John's occasional outbursts were not so much of a literal as of a social intent, a kind of rough "Howdy" of the sort that, say, grizzlies practise when they swat one another's heads, even to the point of drawing blood, as a first phase of friendship.

I'd pretty much given up on any hope of compatibility when, a couple of days later, at the docks in Chicago, I spotted John standing with the third engineer, André Gill, in the lower gangway, a kind of half door that opens out of the engine room just above water level, and saw in the set-up the makings of a photo. I asked

John if he'd mind my taking one, expecting he'd reject the request outright or seize it as another pretext for some direct or implied put-down. But instead he just stood there like a slightly self-conscious schoolboy and, as I raised the camera, actually allowed himself a faint smile. Two nights later, in the crewman's lounge, I mentioned his black skullcap, and he told me, solemn-faced, that he'd sewn it himself, at which point one of the deckhands, Dave Hladysh, piped up that I should see John's paintings—oh, and yes, the "old-fashioned" Appalachian dolls that he made, with dried apples for heads, and hand-stitched clothing and accessories.

The day after returning to Thunder Bay, I took my daughters, Eden and Georgia, aged four and six, down to the ship for a meal and a tour. As we walked out along the pier of the Richardson Terminal, past the rat traps and rotted grain, who should come slouching down the pier toward us but big John Gadula, barely recognizable with his beard and hair combed, and in his all-too-respectable civvies. He was in his home port and was going out for the evening. I admit to having been mildly apprehensive as we approached one another along the narrow mooring wall. But when he was three or four metres away, a smile broke over his face, and when I addressed him, he knelt down in front of the girls and in a quiet, avuncular voice said, "Hi, girls—what are *your* names?"

"John makes dolls," I said to them, and watched a faint pink wash suffuse his cheeks. When they had chatted briefly, he told the girls he hoped they enjoyed their tour of the ship, and then shambled off down the pier for a night in the city that had made him.

Tough or tender, foreign- or Canadian-born, virtually every sailor on board possessed some atavistic story about his or her earliest roots as a seafarer and connection to the deep. Wheelsman Leigh Voutier recalled how, as a boy, he had chopped down an enormous wooden highway sign near home on Cape Breton, had carried it to the local pond and had floated it as a raft, because he just *had* to get out on the water. The second engineer, Andy Gourlay, recalled that, as a boy on the Firth of Forth, in Scotland, he had dreamed of a life at sea and, with a childhood friend, had cruised the Forth estuary, near the local naval yards, in a lifeboat salvaged from an old ship. At the age of nine or ten, the captain himself had listened to his older brothers' tales of life on the lake boats and what he called "the goings-on" in port, where the juke-boxes were loud and the partying hard. He had grown up near Midland, Ontario, had explored Georgian Bay on homemade rafts, and had written a grade-four composition on his certainty that he himself would eventually be a sailor and perhaps even a captain.

Deckhand Jimmy Anderson's father and grandfather had built ninety-foot wooden schooners at Cape Ray west of Port aux Basques, and had used them to carry coal between Port aux Basques and Sydney, Nova Scotia, or occasionally to haul salt cod between Newfoundland and Labrador. On Jimmy's first run with his father and uncle at age sixteen, their family-built vessel had been forced into an inlet near Sydney by a storm so heavy that Jimmy spent three days in bed, green with nausea, while the seas tossed up twenty-metre waves.

"When I was a girl," Marion Dorota told me, "my parents took us every weekend to visit friends who were loggers out on Gull Bay on Lake Superior, and we'd spend whole days out on the lake, fishing, or just exploring around in the boat." Marion's affinity for water is so deeply embedded that on the two occasions when she decided to take a break from shipping, she was drawn almost mag-netically back to water: the first time to the Gulf Coast of Florida, where she worked briefly in a seaside bar, the second time to the Georgia Strait, off Vancouver, where she worked on a British Columbia ferry.

As a kid in British Guyana, the third engineer, André Gill, dreamed of being a seafarer and meeting a beautiful girl in a foreign port and marrying her. "And that's what happened," he smiled, as we talked after dinner one night. At the age of seventeen, in 1963, he sailed on a Norwegian freighter from his home on the northeast coast of South America to Quebec City, where his ship was laid up for repairs. "I bought a second-hand black-and-white television—an Emerson!" he laughed, "and I would have spent the whole time in my cabin watching that little TV, I was so happy with it. But a friend on board who'd met a girl persuaded me to go ashore and meet the girl's friend."

At this point in his story, André got up from the table in the officers' dining room, left and returned holding a black-and-white photo of himself as a teenager, his arm around a dark-haired young beauty with a wide, innocent face—a girl whose possible misgivings over romance with a sailor (one of her eyebrows was arched in doubt) might have been justified had André not returned and married her within a couple of months of his departure.

André is as tough as snare wire but with a cheeky, good-natured presence. He is not above an occasional sarcastic goading of those whose sense of adventure does not quite match his own. "The old British fleet had ships of wood but men of iron," he said to me one day in the presence of a couple of Canadian crewmen. "The Canadian fleet has ships of iron and men of wood! Canadian sailors are pussies! They're more interested in their union contract than in sailing the planet. They get homesick!" he scoffed (registering perhaps the ultimate sailor insult).

On another evening, in the officers' lounge, André caught my attention by telling me I was the second writer he had sailed with and whom he had helped to research a book. I asked immediately about the first, assuming (as would any self-respecting *escritor*) that the writer in question must have been some plodding bacteriologist or climatologist unknown beyond the dusty, etc., etc. "The guy's name was Barry Lopez," André said, inspiring in me a gaping silence, then a kind of psychic version of the old movie gag in which some stark revelation causes the actor in the restaurant to spurt the coffee or cognac in his mouth halfway across the table.

"You've heard of him?" André said.

"He's one of the most famous writers in the world!" I said. "What book was he writing?"

"It's called *Arctic Dreams*," said André. "I'm in it twice."

Another spurt, inasmuch as the book is not merely a favourite of mine, but is one that, by remarkable coincidence, I had with me on the trip. I went immediately to my cabin and got it. Sure enough, there was André Gill, mentioned with great respect both in the acknowledgements and in a part of the text where Lopez is describing his Arctic voyage aboard an old Paterson vessel called the *Soodoc*, at a time when André had been the boat's second engineer.

"Heck," said André, "I gave Lopez the *title* for the book." He explained how one day when he and Lopez were on deck discussing the otherworldliness of the Beaufort Sea and its icebergs, he had said to the writer that it was "like a dream—an Arctic dream," and Lopez had mused on the phrase and, of course, had eventually immortalized it. Nowhere in the text, however, does Lopez acknowledge this particular contribution of André Gill's to world literature.

André is light-skinned but has, I believe, ancestral African blood, and at night he often huddled with the vessel's three other black crewmen, either in the officers' dining room or in the galley, where they'd laugh and kibitz and snack on the day's leftovers. I never got to know Albon Jackson, an engine-room mechanic, who had come originally from the Caribbean, but I was on good terms with both the cook, Sam Newton, and the chief engineer, Ernie Oferi.

About a week into our travels, Ernie took me down into the engine room, where the cataclysmic noise is by no means a simple amplification of the sound of, say, a car engine running. It is, rather, a relentless, keening roar that keeps the ironwork and decks trembling round the clock, and is so intense at close range that it could almost be imagined as a kind of prelude to one's own private Big Bang. I was, as they say, blown away by it—and by the breathtaking heat of the place, as well as by the scale of the machinery (the sixteen-cylinder engine is as big as a Greyhound bus, the spare pistons as wide as the columns of the Parthenon). The dimensions of the engine room are themselves vast, and are somewhat disorienting, inasmuch as the place rises nine or ten storeys, from way down at the level of the propeller shaft in the bottom of the keel, up through lattice after lattice of complicated steel mezzanine and catwalks, to the smokestack in the upper altitudes of the aft house—the result being that there is always some of this above and some below you, but you are never really on the floor.

Even in this bewildering and precarious environment, Ernie said he could identify with the water, feel its power and weight and rhythms, and absorb its comforts and stimulations.

Ernie was born in 1948, in Ghana, to an influential father who supported five wives at once and advised Ernie not to go to sea, because it was a life for drunks and street-fighters and womanizers (Ernie's reporting of this calls forth his most appreciative and seditious chuckle).

But clearly the life has not diminished Ernie, who is, at age fifty-two, a magnificent specimen—burnished, corpulent, self-possessed and, according to his fellow sailors, irresistible to the opposite sex. His almost heroic indifference to stress is an indispensable asset to him in a job that, at its most demanding, can be as hair-trigger and stressful as the captain's—sometimes more so. One of the subtle, hierarchical acknowledgements of the job's demands is that, of the ship's personnel, the chief engineer alone dines with the skipper in his dining room. And he is paid on a scale that, give or take a dollar, compares to a captain's pay, which is to say comfortably into six figures for seven or eight months of work.

I was eating dinner with Ernie one evening as we cruised eastbound down the St. Mary's River, on our way from Lake Superior into Lake Huron. At a certain point, as we talked, the vibrations that flow upward and outward from the engine to every corner of the ship (including up the dining-table legs and across the table, into the condiment jars and tableware) went suddenly still—or nearly still. Ernie, who was in the process of lifting a bite of tossed salad to his lips, brought his fork to a halt inches from his face, and for a moment sat motionless, fixated, like a robin listening for a worm. Almost immediately, the phone rang behind him. He snatched it from its cradle and, with no salutation, said softly, "What's going on?" Within seconds he was gone from the dining room down into the recesses of the vessel. Ten minutes later in the wheelhouse, I was told that a fuel line had broken, one of sixteen that supply fuel individually to the cylinders. It was not until I talked to Ernie the next morning that I learned the break had sent litres of steaming-hot fuel under immense pressure out onto the surrounding floor and ironwork, not to mention flooding in rivulets across the superheated engine. "Something like this is like a race-car crash," Ernie said. "You've got a very limited amount of time to do something, and if you don't do it there's a tremendous risk of a fire, or even explosion." While the obvious response to such a situation would be to shut the engine down, that, too, can be highly risky, in that a boat without an engine can easily run aground or, in confined waters, into another ship. "You're pretty much at the mercy of the current and wind if you don't have power," Ernie said. "When you're in a tight channel like we were, there's a good chance you'd be on the rocks even before you got your anchors down."

As it happened, the captain, aware of the evolving hazard in the engine room, was able to guide the vessel quickly into a part of the river where the engine could be stopped and the anchors dropped before a crisis developed. Ernie explained to me that, in an emergency, his priorities were for the safety and lives of the men in immediate proximity to the danger, for the safety of the ship and crew at large, and for the integrity of the environment. "The important thing is that you don't panic," he said. "If I panic, there's no hope of correcting things. Besides, if people see me panic, *they* panic, then we're all gone. Once I've done everything I can do, if there's still no way out . . . well," he said, with his low-volume chuckle, "that's what the Bayley suits and lifeboats are for."

Chapter Eight

t has occurred to me that, on some level, most of the sailors aboard the *Paterson* viewed the open water, and the life it afforded, as the world's last and perpetual frontier: unpopulated, unlegislated, and (unlike the continental frontier) untamable and incorruptible—if not environmentally, at least by commerce and politics. Open water is almost certainly as compelling to the free spirit today as was the Frontier West to nineteenth-century North Americans. At times, I looked at career sailors like Ernie or André or Serge, and wondered what life might be like for them without the water. And for more than a few of them, the prospects did not seem good. Ernie told me that, having experienced life at sea, he knew he could never again work at what he called a "normal job"—or at least work for anybody else, although he thought he *might* be able to run a business of his own, an operation in which he could feel free and in control. For a while, years ago, André Gill abandoned the water to work as a stationary engineer in a factory in Quebec City, so that he could be nearer his wife and home. But he couldn't take the tedium. Terry Holt told me he could never again do "straight work—shore work," while Serge Masse said that by the time of the spring breakup, after a winter on land, he was itching to get back on board—"dreaming about it," he said.

For some sailors, the risks of life aboard are a significant part of the attraction. "The only time I really get cranked up out here," I was told by wheelsman Clyde Moen, "is when the spray is just flying up over the forecastle, and there's green water washing right over the decks. I used to love the smaller boats, without so much freeboard, because they'd dip right down under the big waves, instead of riding on top. That was exciting."

The backside of life aboard is sleep deprivation, long hours, close quarters, the absence of friends, family, sex, leading frequently to broken marriages and domestic chaos. And to boredom. Terry Holt told me about a sailor friend who worked on a ship that, several years back, lost the use of its engine in a storm in the North Atlantic. "For three days," he said, "they were out there drifting, scared to death. Finally, they were so bored with being scared to death, they went to bed."

Marion Dorota said that she had "pretty much given up any sort of social life"—or taking courses, or going to concerts, or dance performances, all of which she had once loved doing. She fixed me with a look, and said, "I've missed having children—you can't have children if you're on a boat eight months a year." Was it too late? I asked, and she said that, given the karma she'd been dealt, it probably always *had* been too late.

———

Beyond privation, the very real dangers of life on board need no recapitulation. The hazards are not what they were in the 1600s, or even the 1800s, when, despite advances in shipping, many of the hundreds of thousands of sailors who left port either on the lakes or seas were never seen again. And yet echoes of the lawless past persisted even into the 1960s and early 1970s, when shipping on the Great Lakes could still be both perilous and unhealthy. A number of sailors on the *M. V. Paterson* worked during the Seaway's early years for the now-defunct Westdale Shipping Company, a lakes shipper whose specialty was buying up derelict vessels, mostly American, some as old as sixty years, and running them unreconstructed on the lower lakes until, as John Gadula put it, "the paint on them had worn too thin to hold them together."

"Paint!" hooted Kevin Coleman, when he heard John's assessment. "No Westdale boat I ever worked on had any paint holding *anything* together!" As a young sailor, Kevin had been a deckhand for the company, and now seemed almost to revel in the remembered risk and squalor of those years. "A lot of these tubs," he told me, "were so rotten that in colder weather, when you got the ice and storms, they were prohibited by law from travelling further north than Sarnia on the St. Clair River, or further east than Montreal. If they ran into a piece of ice, it was liable to go right through the hull. In a storm, they would have broken in half!"

Most of Westdale's vessels were driven by steam turbine engines, massive roaring contraptions that threw dense soot and coal dust twenty-four hours a day. "You'd get out of bed in the morning," said John Gadula, "and your face would be black! Even your teeth and tongue! God only knows what your lungs looked like." Sailors slept four or five to a cabin in temperatures that often hit 100 degrees Fahrenheit. *"Smell!"* winced Kevin Coleman. "We'd sling hammocks out on deck and sleep there to keep from suffocating. And even then the soot would get to you."

The sailors' foremost defence on such vessels was booze. At the time, drinking was legal not just on ocean-going ships (which still have bars) but on lake vessels, where drinking is no longer allowed. "Conditions were so bad, you *had* to drink," Kevin told me. "I've been on board when everybody was blind drunk except the wheelsman—from the captain right down to the galley porter. A lotta drugs, too—and *fights!* Most of the time, the only thing that saved the loser in these scraps was that the winner was too drunk to kill the guy. I remember once I was drunk for twenty-four hours straight. When I sobered up, the deckhands told me I'd worked a whole watch down in the hold—I didn't remember a minute of it. It's a miracle I wasn't killed. You can fall forty feet onto steel down there."

It is an understatement of almost gasping proportions to say that the hard-living vessels of the era were a less-than-ideal environment for naive young women interested in trying their luck as sailors. The details of Marion Dorota's initiation into the seafaring life suggest the script from some particularly black Mel Brooks comedy. "When we were kids growing up in the East End of Thunder Bay," she told me, "the ships would come up the Kam River to the elevators, and we'd all go running over to the river. It was a game—the first one there could claim the ship. But for years that was my only real awareness of the big boats."

Then one day in 1977, when Marion was twenty-two and had quit her job at the psychiatric hospital in Thunder Bay, her mother, whose friend was a ship's cook, urged her to apply for such work. "She figured if this woman could do it, anybody could," Marion said. "So I went down to the union hall on Simpson Street and asked about a summer job, and it turned out they needed help."

The following day, by coincidence, Marion was out on a charity cruise on Thunder Bay Harbour when she spotted "a horrible, rusty old scow, a real sea-bag," at one of the city's grain elevators. "It was called the *Judith M. Pearson*, built in 1906, and when I saw it my heart kinda sank. I told my brother-in-law that, with my luck, I'd probably end up working on something like that. He said, 'Oh heavens, no, Marion, they'd never start you out on an old wreck.'"

That night, Marion prayed that she would not end up on the vessel, and the next day got a call to report immediately to the *Judith M. Pearson*.

"I was scared to death," she said. "So my father and brother-in-law went down to the ship with me. This was totally unheard of, and of course, everybody looked at us and said, 'Oh, yeah, here's a greenhorn for sure.' We went to the captain's quarters, and he sent me back to the galley to talk to the woman I was replacing. I'll tell ya, she was no debutante; she was a rough, tough gal, with a very nasty nickname, and when I asked what the job entailed, she said right off, 'Do you ————?' and she used a common four-letter word meaning—well, you know—to have sex.

"I said, 'What?'

"She said, 'You heard me!'

"I started stammering. She said, 'If you want any overtime on this ship, you have to do it—with the first mate.'

"By this time I was more or less in shock. Finally, I got up the courage to say I didn't think I wanted this job. She said, 'Oh no, honey, you've got this job. You took it. You threw your card in at the union hall.'

"By the time my brother-in-law and father got back to the galley, I was shuddering. I said to them, 'I can't do this.' And I explained to my brother-in-law what had happened. I couldn't tell my father or he'd never have let me on *any* ship."

As it turned out, Marion did sail the following day aboard the *Judith M. Pearson*—but only with the captain's sworn assurances that he would watch out for her, and under her brother-in-law's strict injunction that if anything went wrong she was to stay locked in her room and get off at the first place she could, the Welland Canal, in three days (a crew member on a Canadian vessel cannot jump ship at the locks in Sault Ste. Marie, because the locks are in American waters).

"I shared a tiny little cabin with the only other woman on board, a porter named Ruthy, twice my age, and a serious alcoholic," Marion said. "Our cabin was tiny, and our washroom was an even tinier little cubbyhole in the engine room alley—it was always just black with soot. You had to wash it all out before you could wash yourself."

While Marion managed to dodge the alleged sexual expectations of the first mate, she points out that, generally, there was far more sexual harassment on vessels of that era than there is today.

"And of course there was no recourse, no process for complaint. You just took it. During that first week, all I did basically was work in the galley and sit on my bunk reading, mostly my Bible, while Ruthy and the cook and a few others sat on the bottom bunk getting plastered."

One day, when Marion had been on board a week, and Ruthy and the cook had drained a forty-ounce bottle of liquor during the early afternoon, a barbaric fight erupted between Ruthy and the cook. It began in Marion and Ruthy's cabin in the forward part of the vessel, and migrated back to the aft house and galley, where dinner was to be prepared. "Oh, it was awful—they were throwing things, dumping water on one another, the cook's head was cut. I thought they were going to go after one another with knives. I tried to calm them down, and Ruthy started chasing *me* around the galley with a broom, hollering that I was a Bible-thumping virgin and that she was going to throw me overboard. We'd go out one galley door onto the deck, and I'd run across the deck and go in the other galley door—it was like a Marx Brothers movie. What we didn't realize was that we were being watched by the captain from the rear windows of the wheelhouse up front."

The upshot of it all was that Ruthy and the cook were fired. "I was allowed to stay," said Marion, "although the next cook made things worse than ever for me. He was always asking me when I was going to have sex with him, and I'd say 'Never,' and he'd send me into the walk-in refrigerator for something and lock the door behind me. I'd be pounding away, and every once in a while he'd come over and open the door and say, 'Are you ready to come across yet?' and I'd say, 'Never,' and he'd shove me back inside."

One afternoon, Marion was called into the deckhand's lounge where a number of crewmen invited her to join them for a drink. "I told them I didn't want a drink," she said, "and when they kept urging me, this kindly old watchman named Snoopy jumped up and told me to follow him, he'd fix me up. So, to get out of there, I went with him. He was a little bald guy, with thick glasses, a big bulbous nose, a Newfoundlander—his accent was so thick you hardly knew he was speaking English. We got to his cabin, and he gave me a glass and, even as I was telling him I didn't want any, he poured three or four ounces of whisky into it. His door opened outside onto the deck, and no sooner did I have this liquor in my hand than there was a knock, and someone called for Snoopy. 'Oh, me darlin',' he whispered, 'it's the captain. Here, you have to hide.' Well, hide, sure—but where? The cabin was about four feet by eight feet! 'Here, get behind the door,' he whispered. So I got behind it just as the captain slammed it open, right into my face. The captain says, 'Snoopy, where have you been? I've been looking for you.' And Snoopy says, 'I've been tidyin' up me room, Cap— keepin' it shipshape!' Meanwhile, the captain looks down and sees my girly shoes sticking out under the door. He rips back the door, and hollers, 'Marion! What are you doing here?'"

Without waiting for an explanation, the captain ordered Marion to his office and stomped off, calling over his shoulder that she had better have a good excuse, or she could expect to be fired.

"Of course, I'm freaked. I said, 'Oh, Snoopy, what am I going to do?' And Snoopy says, 'Well, me darlin', you mustn't panic . . . uh, lemme see . . . uh . . . oh, oh, yeah, yeah . . . you just tell him you were here to borrow some books—you tell him that. Cap believes in education.'

"I went up there, and the captain was in a *very* stern mood. He said, 'Now, Marion, I'm supposed to be watching out for you, and I've told you before you can't be in the men's cabins! What's going on?' I said, 'Well, Cap, I just went to Snoopy's to borrow some books that I wanted to read.' And he gets this skeptical look on his face, and he says, 'Are you by any chance lying to me, Marion?' And I said, 'Why would I be lying?' And he said, 'Well, Marion, I don't mean to be impertinent, but you might be interested in knowing that Snoopy *has* no books. Snoopy can't read!'"

If the sea was occasionally hard on the sailors in that unfettered era, the sailors were equally hard on the sea. "When I think of some of the things we did on these boats even up into the seventies and early eighties, it just makes me cringe," Ernie Oferi told me one day. Until perhaps sixteen or seventeen years ago, he said, ships routinely dumped massive amounts of fuel sludge—sometimes as much as fifteen tonnes at one time—into the Great Lakes and Gulf of St. Lawrence. The thick, tar-like sludge is a by-product of the process by which the heavy fuel oil carried on the vessels (far less expensive than fully refined fuel) is heated and purified for use. Today, lake vessels empty their sludge tanks ashore, rather than into Lake Superior or Huron, where, in the old days, the sludge made life miserable for fish and waterfowl, and eventually washed up as "beach tar" on rocks and in the sand along the shores of the Great Lakes. Sewage, too, was pumped by the ton directly into the water, and garbage was simply pushed over the rail of the poop deck, either loose or in bags. "It may have looked pretty to have fifty or sixty seagulls flying along behind," said Marion Dorota, "but I assure you, they weren't there for the aesthetics."

A veteran ship's officer told me that, even today, many foreign vessels, rather than pay the cost of having their sludge tanks pumped, or their garbage or sewage carted off while in port, wait until they are free of the Seaway and the scrutiny of the coast guard, as well as other government vessels and aircraft, and then simply dump their waste into the Gulf of St. Lawrence. Serge Masse told me that, during the late 1980s, a ship on which he was working spent fifty-eight days anchored in a South American harbour, and produced so much garbage that, every few days, the crew would compact several hundred kilos of it into steel drums, cap the drums with cement, then puncture them and throw them overboard. Serge said, "It's all small potatoes compared to the City of New York hauling barges of its garbage out to sea and dumping them, rats and all, in international waters."

The very existence of the Seaway has been insidiously destructive to the integrity of fish and plant populations in the Great
Lakes. Of the roughly 140 alien species that have entered the lakes
since 1800—many of them unchecked predators—more than half
are a direct result of the opening of the Seaway in 1959. Zebra
mussels, for example, came into the lakes either on the hulls or in
the ballast water of vessels that had come from the Caspian Sea.
Prior to the Seaway, such vessels would never have reached the
lakes, because they were unable to come up the St. Lawrence further than Montreal, where they had to transfer their cargoes to
smaller lake vessels.

Anyone who has seen the zebra mussels beneath the surface of
Lake Erie, like broad swaths of nubbly black chain mail, will have
no trouble accepting that up to six-hundred thousand of them can
cling to a square metre of rock or metal—or that just one of the
little shell-dwellers can lay up to a million eggs a year. The mussels
are not predators, but destroy by eating vast quantities of tiny,
often single-celled, plant life, leaving many of their fellow lake-
dwellers with no food at all. Lake Erie, once greeny-grey from the
floating plant life, is now as colourless as Perrier water. Beyond
their impact on the food chain, the mussels have made life
extremely difficult for fish such as walleye and sauger, whose preference is for the cool shadows afforded by the old opacity.

Sea lampreys, whose access to the upper lakes was once
blocked by their inability to get past Niagara Falls, entered the
lakes through the modern Welland Canal when it was opened in
1932. By 1937, the eels had infested lakes Superior and Michigan,
and by the mid-1950s, had all but destroyed the vast population
of resident lake trout, not to mention the multi-million-dollar
lake-trout fishery.

An unprepossessing little fish called the alewife, or sawbelly—
a bony, silver-coloured ocean-dweller that grows to a length of
twenty or twenty-five centimetres—came into the lakes through
the Welland Canal during the mid-twentieth century and ate up
so much zooplankton that it all but eliminated other species

competing for the same sustenance. By the late 1960s, alewives comprised 90 percent by weight of the fish in Lake Michigan.

My friend Peter Colby, a Michigan-born biologist, studied Lake Michigan's alewives during the years of their greatest dominance and became the foremost authority on their invasion of North America. "What disturbed me almost as much as the prevalence of the fish," Peter told me recently, "was that, when we'd get out in the shipping lanes dragging our nets to catch them, we'd pull up endless numbers of disintegrating green plastic bags that the ships had thrown overboard full of garbage. I bet if you could photograph the lake bed from a satellite, you'd see a mile-wide trail of green plastic running right down the middle of Lake Michigan. God alone knows what that plastic's going to do to the water as it breaks down—and that's not to mention the garbage."

Peter told me in passing that government agencies, including the U.S. Army Corps of Engineers (responsible for the integrity of much of America's inland water), once thought nothing of dumping steel drums of toxic chemicals into the Great Lakes, just to get rid of them. "We figure those drums rust through in forty to fifty years," he said. "A lot of that dumping took place in the forties, fifties and sixties, so it won't be long before there may be a lot more down there than just garbage."

———

On the evening of April 14, as the *M. V. Paterson* unloaded grain at Port Cartier on the Gulf of St. Lawrence, Ernie Oferi and I walked forward along the deck, glancing into the open hatches and holds, where the ship's vast tonnage of wheat was slowly disappearing. As we stood at the rail in the cool evening air, Ernie mentioned that, just five years ago, it was possible to hang a fishing line over the edge of the ship within metres of the loading docks and catch a good-sized cod within minutes. "At Pointe Noire," he said, "we'd put six or seven hooks on a line before dinner, and come up with sole, halibut, mackerel, anything. It's as if someone took a huge net, dragged it through the bay, and took every living thing out of here. Forever!" He reflected for a moment, divested himself of a rather rueful chuckle, and said, "Which I guess is approximately what happened."

The point is perhaps as much figurative as literal, but according to Ernie, "The only thing you can catch now around here are those ugly fish that look like toads." Various crew members described to me how whales and seals used to come right into the bay at Port Cartier, where they could easily catch the abundant herring. "The seals would be right behind the fish," said Leigh Voutier. "Now, with nothing for them to eat, you don't see a single whale or seal."

Only recently have scientists realized that ships themselves— their physical presence, as opposed to their effluents or dumping —can subtly destroy fish and water mammals. West Coast biologists reported in 1999 that a vessel's noise and vibrations put stress on a fish's sensory and guidance systems, to the point where some species' mating and spawning patterns are disturbed, and their reproductive rates drop. For a fish or mammal, the underwater sound of a ship passing is said to be the equivalent, atmospherically, of an intense rumble of thunder at close range.

Whales are not thought to be significantly influenced by ship sounds, although they are occasionally injured or even killed in collisions with ships. "I've had grey whales dive right under the prow," Ken Strong told me. "I'm sure we must have hit some of them." Other crew members told me they had seen whales bearing what were clearly keel or propeller scars on their backs and sides. The first mate, Dan MacDonald, mentioned a ship that had inadvertently caught a grey whale in the vertical notch between its upper prow and the underwater extension of the hull, which is referred to as the "bulbous bow." The ship, he said, carried the whale, unknowingly, from the Gulf of St. Lawrence nearly a thousand kilometres upstream to Montreal. In September 2000, the Montreal Port Authority confirmed that in "perhaps 1997 or 1998," a whale had indeed turned up in Montreal Harbour, where, for several days, it had floated, rotting and covered with seagulls. It is not clear whether the coast guard or the federal Department of the Environment took action—or perhaps some other agency—but the whale was eventually tethered by its flukes to a tugboat and was hauled back out to the Gulf.

———————

The fish populations are irredeemably scrambled, toxin bombs lie waiting on the lake beds, and much of the water is polluted. And yet on the morning of April 18, in the wheelhouse of the *Paterson*, I was treated to a happy little revelation that made it obvious there is still hope for the Great Lakes. I had been examining charts of Lake Ontario and Lake Superior, and on each of them had noticed a tiny pencil-drawn circle accompanied by the words "water hole."

"What does this mean?" I said to Ken Strong, who happened to be passing the chart table on his way between the coffee maker and the controls.

"That's where we take on water," he said.

"Ballast water?"

"No, water for the ship."

"What kind of water for the ship?"

"Every kind of water."

"Drinking water?"

"Yeah, and other water."

I straightened up and looked at him, still thinking I had somehow misunderstood. I said, "The ship gets its drinking water out of the lakes?"

"Right!" he said. "There are lots of places on the lakes where you can drink the water."

"But you treat it," I said.

"No," he said. "We just filter it, take out any junk—otherwise, it tests as clean as the water in most city water systems."

I asked if all ships drew from the same holes, and he told me every captain has his favourite. "Here's mine," he said and he pressed his finger onto a tiny pencilled circle near Cariboo Island in Lake Superior. "The water's beautiful here—there must be springs around. But if we need water when we're on Lake Ontario, we'll get it there, too. We've never had a problem."

———

The water holes were by no means the showiest evidence of Nature's irrepressibility. The Calumet River in south Chicago is one of the most contaminated rivers on earth, and for years was considered an unlivable habitat for fish or for any other form of life. And yet on Easter Sunday morning, at the docks of the Acme steel mill, on the most industrial part of the Calumet, the river was alive with mallards, Canada geese and ring-bill gulls. Later, a flock of cormorants, as black and scrawny as Halloween spectres, cruised around the ship, diving with abandon for whatever small fry were down there nourishing themselves on sludge and PCBs. A tattered version of the Jolly Roger flew from the steel mill's unloading crane, and all day iridescent grey pigeons strutted over the ore piles on shore, pecking up kernels of wheat that had come out of the hold with the ore pellets. As I left the ship that afternoon and walked down the pier, I came across a pair of oily-looking frogs that, as I approached, leaped into the river and disappeared beneath its surface.

As I returned to the ship a couple of hours later, I saw two men in a big Arkansas bass boat, tossing out lures within sight of the steel mill. A soot-covered ore digger told me that if I thought the river was dirty now, I should have seen it ten years ago when it was "pure black," as opposed to its present pure fecal brown. "Sometimes, it shines real good," he told me without skepticism. He said his co-workers often fished off the docks and fried up their catch on the wood stove in their crumbling brick shack in the lane behind the ore piles.

"What do they catch?" I asked.

"Fish," he said solemnly.

"I mean what kind?"

"Bazz," he said.

In the meantime, his friend had come down the pier and was standing beside us. He said, "Some people say you could drink this water."

"Maybe upstream," said the other man. "I dunno. It's a nice river. Specially when the leaves is out in summer."

"Yeah, that's when it's nice—that's when it's pretty."

Even in this relative hellhole, I felt I understood their pride of place. When I lived with my family outside Dundas, Ontario, near Hamilton, during the late 1980s, I developed the same sort of feeling for some of the worst parts of Hamilton—in fact, would often take out-of-town guests to the shore of Lake Ontario and up onto the Burlington Skyway Bridge, from where they could look down on Hamilton's filthy and fascinating Stelco and Dofasco steel mills. I would also take them out along the Bruce Trail, which ran in front of the house, through the thick deciduous forests of the Niagara Escarpment, where they were afforded a more gracious impression of the region. The mills, though, were a more telling image—for me, a weirdly attractive image—of the meaning of the vicinity during the late twentieth century. At times, I could get quite defensive about Hamilton, and grew to resent Torontonians who more or less ritualistically slagged Hamilton as a kind of treadmill for lesser specimens, notwithstanding that the Toronto people had usually come out to see us in cars made from Hamilton steel, on roads held together with Hamilton reinforcing rod, worked in buildings made from Hamilton girders, used appliances made in Hamilton fabricating plants, etc.

My retributive assessment of it all was that Steeltowners had a better sense of themselves relative to the earth—to the escarpment and lake and surrounding orchards, even to the slag heaps—than did Torontonians. Many of the latter, it seemed then, related to the planet largely through their prim yards and patios and, during this particular period of the late 1980s, their consuming fascination with real estate prices, a disease that never hit Hamilton.

I am not in denial. I know that a city such as Toronto can impart a sense of place and identity every bit as vivid as any mountain or seashore. Even so, when I'd stand on Hamilton Mountain, looking across Lake Ontario to Toronto (Could any Canadian city other than Hamilton turn a seventy-metre escarpment into a "mountain"?), Toronto invariably seemed flat and vague, its only physical distinction at that distance the teensy CN Tower, a distant toothpick onto which someone appeared to have jammed a pickled onion.

As we left the Calumet River on the evening of April 20 and headed north up Lake Michigan, I went up on the bridge and watched the skyscrapers of Chicago against a magnificent lilac-coloured sunset. By eleven o'clock, the wind was up, the sky overcast, and in the west we could see the silvery glow of Milwaukee, projected like an immense display of northern lights onto the fast-shifting cloud cover. Shipping is in many ways a slow-moving old barque of an industry. During my weeks on the water it had become abundantly clear to me that, despite advances in navigation and technology, the trade is practised today much as it was by the ancient Babylonians: load up a ship and take it to sea, reload it in a foreign port and bring it home. Today's sailors are as fascinated and appalled by big water and big waves as they were five thousand years ago, and are, in some ways, as much at the whim of hierarchical discipline as were their counterparts under the command of Jacques Cartier or Christopher Columbus or Hernando Cortés. Sea routes have barely changed in four hundred years, and sailors are only marginally less vulnerable than they ever were in, say, the North Atlantic, or on Lake Superior during a November gale. Native traders travelled today's Seaway routes anywhere up to four or five thousand years ago, when canoes loaded with furs, copper goods and pottery plied every metre of water between the Lakehead and the Gulf of St. Lawrence. Even the Seaway—arguably the engineering marvel of the continent—could not exist without lift locks whose ingenious low-tech design was invented during the sixteenth century by Leonardo da Vinci. Moreover, the locks are built of a high-density, dry-mix concrete invented by the Romans and first used in Rome's famous aqueducts well before the birth of Christ. A storm at sea can still tear a vessel in half, and a shoal can leave it high and helpless, or in pieces. What's more, there are still pirates out there to plunder the cargo of a wrecked or grounded vessel, or simply to board it and carry off what they can.

But much, too, has changed in the industry—to the point where the working Canadian sailor, with his extraordinary knowledge and skills, and his affinity for the lakes, is an all-but-endangered species. The sad truth is that, right now, he or she has fewer opportunities for work than at any time in the history of Canadian shipping. With the coming of the Seaway, the hundreds of small cargo boats that once plied the lakes—many with capacities of just two or three thousand tonnes—were replaced by a vastly reduced number of much larger vessels such as the *M. V. Paterson*, with cargo capacities of up to thirty thousand tonnes. The jobs were lost because the large vessels can be operated by crews that are barely bigger than those that were required to operate the old steam-powered canal vessels.

Whereas the Canadian lake fleet once numbered six or seven hundred ships, it is today down to just forty or fifty, owned by just five shipping companies. The entire Great Lakes fleet—Canadian and U.S. vessels—is in fact just eighty ships (the majority of boats on the lake at a given time being foreign owned). The Paterson fleet alone once consisted of forty-two ships, some seafaring, others confined to the Great Lakes. Eight of those vessels were torpedoed during the Second World War, and eighty-six men were lost. Today, N. M. Paterson and Sons in Thunder Bay owns seven ships, of which four or fewer are operating at any one time. But the capacity of those four is approximately the capacity of forty of the old lakers. It is vividly indicative of the shrinking of the Canadian fleet that the *M. V. Paterson* was the last ship built for the Great Lakes, in 1985, the last year the Canadian government offered subsidies for ship construction.

Jobs for Canadian sailors were further restricted when, during the late 1980s, Canadian vessels offshore began employing foreign crews, often Filipino, who work for a fraction of what a Canadian crew costs an owner. Canadian vessels working on the lakes—the *M. V. Paterson* among them—must, by law, employ Canadians. There are rumours, however, that the law may change, allowing foreign crews to work on inshore vessels as well. Plus, there are suspicions that foreign vessels (with their foreign crews) will one day be able to operate fully in our waters, whereas today they are limited to bringing in a single load of foreign cargo (often European steel) and taking out a single load (usually wheat) bound for a foreign port. With the Canadian fleet aging and shrinking, such suspicions may one day be realized. And Canadian sailors don't like it.

Many such sailors harbour a particular grievance toward the current Canadian minister of finance, Paul Martin, whose family has long owned Canada's largest shipping company, Canada Steamship Lines. Despite Martin's public endorsements of job creation for Canadians, CSL has been responsible for putting hundreds of Canadian seamen out of work by replacing them with foreign crews on its offshore vessels.

Opportunities for sailors are further limited by a reduction in the size of crews on most lake vessels (had the *Edmund Fitgerald* gone down in the year 2000, rather than 1975, it is likely that only twenty-two sailors, not twenty-nine, would have been lost). What's more, fewer *boats* are needed, because wheat, which has always been a mainstay of Seaway shipping, is not being shipped in the quantities it was twenty years ago. Countries such as Russia, for example, are growing wheat of their own, and need less of ours. At the same time, much of what *is* shipped is going out through the Port of Vancouver (often on foreign vessels), as opposed to through Thunder Bay and the Seaway. And trucks are doing more of the work that ships used to do. "Right now," Ken Strong told me, "there are just too many ships waiting in too few ports for too few cargoes."

One of the more insidious erosions of seafaring tradition is the degree to which old-style navigation, with its dependence on an officer's knowledge and awareness of the earth, is gradually being sacrificed to the automated navigation systems that, today, are aboard every Canadian vessel. (Many foreign vessels do not have such systems, as witnessed when an Asian-registered freighter wrecked on a shoal off Vancouver Island recently, and was discovered to be missing not just high-tech navigation equipment but any computerization whatsoever, and even a functional gyrocompass.)

On the *M. V. Paterson*, the computerized navigation unit is referred to unofficially as "the Wizard." Its official dub is an acronym, ECDIS, or Electronic Chart Display Information System. The on-board part of the apparatus is a colour video-display unit that, with incontestable precision, shows those in the wheelhouse where they are on the planet at any moment. The positioning data are gathered from sixteen satellites, and the ship itself is symbolized on the screen by a neon-green, boat-shaped bullet against a backlit chart of the surrounding water and land. The machine is seldom turned off, even when the ship is at anchor or in port, and the electronic charts can be viewed at any scale the navigator punches in—from charts showing, for example, the whole of Lake Ontario or Lake Huron, or indeed the entire Great Lakes and St. Lawrence, down to those confined to, say, the docking area at a single grain elevator in Thunder Bay or Port Cartier.

There is something almost scriptural about the processes and imagery of navigation. But of the *Paterson*'s four certified helmsmen during my weeks aboard, only one, the first mate, Dan MacDonald, a taciturn, middle-aged bachelor, possessed even a faintly ecclesiastical aura to go with his navigational responsibilities. And this was perhaps more a function of his hooded eyes and somewhat closed posture than his actual habit of mind.

One night in my presence, Dan unfolded a gentle and thoughtful disquisition, in many ways a lament, over the way contemporary navigation—in effect, virtual navigation—has contaminated the long-standing link between those in the wheelhouse and the water and land that surround them. From the time of the Phoenicians, he explained, early sailors navigated by their knowledge of the physical universe—of islands, of mountains, of stars and sun. In later centuries, they had primitive charts. "If they were near land that was familiar to them," he said, "I imagine they used the same sorts of cues we use on the lakes. And, of course, being under sail, they would have had knowledge of wind and waves and currents—probably even global winds and currents." But mainly, Dan enthused, the ancients possessed what he called "this fantastic knowledge of the heavens—the sun, the night sky, all the motion and mathematics, and so on. That's really how they got around! And all they used in terms of machinery were some very basic navigational tools—astrolabes, sextants, that sort of thing."

Dan admitted somewhat sheepishly that he didn't have a clue how a sextant worked and, what's more, that he didn't know a soul who did. Moreover, he didn't know anybody who even knew the stars or constellations—the sort of knowledge that was once taught routinely in Canadian elementary schools. "Most people these days can't even name the planets," he shrugged. "Even people who are fixated on astrology don't seem to know anything about the night sky." I told Dan that the captain had mentioned a sailor who, as an experiment, had tried celestial navigation on one of the captain's boats and had managed to fix the ship's position within about a dozen miles of where it was. Dan responded that he was sure early sailors did much better than that with the same equipment, allowing that, in the eighteenth century, in the middle of the Atlantic, ten- or twelve-mile margins might have been tolerable.

Before the advent of global positioning systems such as ECDIS, twentieth-century sailors navigated by identifying a point on the shoreline, and then fixing the point visually through a device called a pelorus or (since radar became common) identifying it on the radar screen in order to get a bearing relative to the position of the ship. Then they transferred it all to their charts—to longitude and latitude. In a broad sense, this meant that a navigator was constantly studying his surroundings—subliminally calculating distances and angles, establishing whether he was looking at an island or a peninsula, a distant town at night or a well-lit oil refinery. Dan said, "You had to be familiar with your surroundings—literally thousands of miles of shoreline."

With a system such as ECDIS, the ship's position and the navigational chart appear together on the screen, the position precalculated, so that there is no actual navigating to do. "No need at all to look out the window," said Dan. "At the schools, they drill the trainees on the old ways, but in practice the kids don't want to bother—too much effort. Plus it's more fun to play with the electronic stuff. You've got a colour screen almost like a video game. You've got controls, variables, gizmos. We push these people to practise looking at the land and to hone their observational skills, but a lot of them just can't see any value in it when it can all be done quicker electronically."

Officers such as Dan MacDonald, Serge Masse and Terry Holt—and Ken Strong, too—might be inclined these days to take the same shortcuts used by the cadets. The difference is that they are entirely comfortable with the older method of navigating, and are pretty much perpetually aware of the ship in the context of its surroundings. "If you're not seeing it relative to its surroundings," Serge told me, "you're not 'handling' the ship, you're just aiming it—aiming it across unidentified stretches of water toward unidentified points of land. You know yourself that you can't just aim a car and put the accelerator down. If you're going to drive, you've got to be aware of what's going on around you and respond to it."

"The functional trouble with ECDIS," said Dan, "is that computer systems are fallible. When they shut down, you have to use traditional navigating. If the kids coming out of training schools have no practice in it, and have no knowledge of the water or land, God help us, the ship could end up anywhere. The charts can show you where the rocks are, but if you don't know where you are on the chart, it's pretty hard to stay off those rocks."

Serge said that he had recently asked a couple of trainees on the *Paterson* to find their position on the ship's charts without reference to the Wizard. "They couldn't do it," he said. "One of them plotted us twenty miles off course. They're TV watchers! They're video-game players! They don't want contact with real water or land! Mind you, they're not alone. I know people who turn on the weather channel to see what it's like out, rather than looking out the window or opening the door."

Several years ago, an executive at Canada Steamship Lines said the company's aim was to make navigation so automated and easy that shipowners would eventually be able to paint over the windows of the bridge. "I mean, it's just so ludicrous," Dan said. "It sends all the wrong messages to young officers. A hundred years from now, a good ship handler is still going to need a good feel for the water and land. Actually, the guy who mentioned painting the windows has since been fired by CSL, which isn't too surprising."

One afternoon on Lake Erie, when the captain had described to me how heavy rain, even more than heavy snow, could mess up a ship's radar, I asked him what would happen if both the Wizard and the radar shut down at once. "When everything else is gone," he said quite cheerfully, "you go by dead reckoning"—in other words, establishing a position on your chart by using speed, elapsed time, a compass reading, and the last known point of longitude and latitude. "If for some reason you can't calculate these things, you get out your binoculars, and use the best instincts you have to keep the ship on course."

After the briefest of pauses, he looked at me across the instrument panel, and said, "And you pray."

Chapter Nine

uring the weeks after my trip aboard the *Paterson*, I was reminded occasionally of Dan MacDonald's observation that no one these days knew anything about the night sky. I assumed my book would be enhanced by a chapter on someone who did. However, I didn't pursue any such person, and no one presented him- or herself as a subject. Then one evening in early summer, at a dinner gathering, I met a middle-aged Toronto man—a portly, charming, ruddy-faced engineer—who told me the planet was, for him, both an earthly base and a stage for his broader fascination with the universe. Not sure immediately whether I was talking to a NASA scientist or an L. Ron Hubbard disciple—or perhaps a *Star Trek* or science-fiction enthusiast—I gave him my most inquisitive "tell me more" look, and he said, "I watch stars."

"Fantastic," I said. "What's it like out there?"

"Fantastic," he said.

Which is why, on an evening in mid-August, just after 9 P.M.,

I found myself racing east out of Toronto on the Macdonald-Cartier Freeway, with Winston Books in the van beside me, and with Winston's big Newtonian telescope in carefully padded quarantine behind.

Winston admits to being "a bit of a clean freak." When he is handling his telescope at home, he washes his hands every few minutes, and asks others who are handling it to do likewise. When the time came to load the telescope into the van—a virtual landfill site of food wrappers and crayon stubs and dog hair—he gazed into the tailgate and, diplomatically appalled, asked if I'd be insulted if he were to clean out the interior with his Shop-Vac. When he'd finished, he spread laundry-fresh towels on the seats and floor, and we began loading the big black "hat boxes" that are the shell of the disassembled instrument.

Our viewing place that night was familiar territory for Winston, who had discovered it a couple of years earlier with the help of the U.S. Department of Defense. That agency produces a glorious "night illumination" map of North America—in effect, a satellite picture showing the extent and intensity of every blotch and speck of electric lighting on the continent. Not surprisingly, the bright spots are many—especially in, say, Florida, California and the New York area, and around the lower Great Lakes. But the black spots are rare, particularly in areas such as southern Ontario, where the population is dense.

"It's no problem finding a dark spot if you want to drive two hundred kilometres north," said Winston. "But I needed something close enough that I could get to it in an hour, get set up, use my telescope for several hours, take it all down, get home and get a few hours' sleep before going to work."

As he was examining the illumination map one day, he noticed an area just north of Lake Ontario, near Bowmanville, that looked surprisingly light-free. "I went out to check it one night," Winston said, "and it was remarkable. Except for a little haze back toward Toronto, it was dark. Really dark."

And so it was that we turned north off the Macdonald-Cartier

Freeway at a well-known tourist spot called The Big Apple—a twenty-metre-high McIntosh that exists as a promo and sales site for everything that can be made from the region's best-known and tastiest agricultural product. We took a series of ever-narrowing roads that led finally into a fragrant upland pasture overgrown with grasses and wildflowers and young sumac.

Winston's midnight operation is so unobtrusive that the farmer across the road has never known that his unused buttercup pasture doubles as a staging platform for the wonders of the universe. And when a group of screaming teenagers roared past on an adjacent side road on all-terrain three-wheelers, it apparently never occurred to them that anything as rarefied as astronomy was being practised right there in a field on their own concession line. Had they caught wind of us and decided to investigate, who can say what occult depredations might have been suspected of a pair of middle-aged men on a cave-black night, in an untilled field, in possession of a stepladder and a capacious black tube? Oh, and a van full of towels.

On the one occasion during the night that I opened the van door, allowing five or six candle-power of light to escape (I was desperate to retrieve a muffin I had bought in an Oshawa-area Tim Hortons), Winston informed me amiably that if I had pulled such a stunt on an official Royal Astronomical Society outing, I would not have been invited back—the reason being that once the eyes of Society astronomers adjust to the darkness, not even a man starving for a Tim Hortons muffin messes with the dilation of their pupils.

My lesson in telescope use and etiquette included the more or less solemn counsel that I should not "talk into the eyepiece," inasmuch as it would create warmth around it, which would in turn create condensation on the lens. When later, I cautioned Winston good-naturedly for "talking into the eyepiece," he paused momentarily and said, "Excuse me," and carried on in his attempt to locate a particularly elusive stellar nursery, in effect a gas cloud out of which anywhere up to several thousand stars will eventually take shape.

Winston is a cultural anomaly, a brilliant and genial eccentric who owns neither a car nor a telephone, "or anything else I don't need," he says. "I grew up as one of seven kids, didn't have much, and eventually just decided I'd go with that, make a virtue out of necessity." He does own two bicycles, two cats, a stereo, a mixed bag of simple furniture and, of course, his telescopes, two of them which occupy his living room in the way a pair of high-pedigree borzois might occupy their master's boudoir—no one else need apply for occupancy.

"I'm not a purist about cars," Winston told me. "When I want to go out and see stars, I rent one." In fact, Winston's grand new telescope—by far the larger of the two—was meticulously designed so that its pieces, disassembled, would fit conveniently into the back seat and trunk of a mid-sized rental sedan.

The story of Winston's love affair with the heavens possesses something of the character of a Steven Spielberg film—lots of plot twists, stirring highs, heart-wrenching lows. It began on a night of galactic blackness in the winter of 1962, when, as an eleven-year-old, he stood alone in the backyard of the family's home in the northern Canadian city of Sault Ste. Marie. The snowdrifts were high, and in the east, above the treetops, the new moon was as delicate and silvery as shaved steel.

"As I stood there gazing at the stars, I had a kind of satori, an almost visceral response to these mysterious distant bodies," Winston told me. "And right there and then, I made a decision that I was going to find out more about what was out there."

The following week at school he located the address of the Royal Astronomical Society of Canada, which was soon sending him pamphlets, books and star charts.

Winston is a natural teacher with a gift both for clarity and for patience. And as he described his own development as an astronomer, he made every effort to provide me with a parallel working base, from which I, too, might develop an interest in the stars. "Every star in the sky," he said, "is either a direct part of a constellation or is within the boundaries of a constellation. And before you can do anything, you have to learn those constellations."

It took young Winston the better part of two years to learn them, and to learn the thousands of visible stars that are encompassed by them. By the time he got to grade eight, he knew, as he puts it, "every pinprick up there," and how to describe and locate it.

At Christmas, during his thirteenth year, Winston's parents gave him a ten-power telescope that he now describes as "a toy, a spyglass," considerably less efficient than a pair of binoculars. "But it was what they could afford," he says, "and when you're twelve and have been studying the heavens daily for two years without a magnified glimpse, even a little spyglass can look like the Hubble Telescope by comparison. I was awfully glad to have it."

He was even happier two years later, in grade ten, to get a telescope with a sixty-millimetre front lens, several eyepieces, and the capacity to magnify the heavens by a power of one hundred. "Now I could really see stuff," he said. "I used to have my friends over, but instead of putting on music or something I'd take them out in the backyard, set up the telescope and show them the planets and stars."

In the second of his basic astronomy lessons, Winston explained to me that there are two main types of telescopes: the refraction telescope, like those the old seamen carried, with a front (or objective) lens, an eyepiece and, generally, a collapsible tube in-between. The second type, the reflector, comes in many variations, all of them rooted in the eighteenth-century design of Sir Isaac Newton, whose invention featured a parabolic mirror to collect and concentrate light from the object being watched, and an eyepiece to magnify and focus the image.

"What happens after working with a telescope for a while," said Winston, "is that you want to go bigger; you want to go deeper into space. The extreme form of this is called aperture fever."

Winston suffered his first significant dose of the fever a few months after getting his second telescope—a dose that, before it got better, took a terrible turn for the worse, leaving him humbled, discouraged and severely astronomically debilitated.

"I'd won a hundred dollars in a local high school science fair," he told me, "and I used it to order the parts for a Newtonian telescope with a six-inch parabolic mirror." The telescope, he assumed, would take him as deep into the night sky as any fifteen-year-old could wish to go. The difficulty was that the kit required him to grind his own mirror. By hand. "They send you two inch-thick circles of glass, six inches in diameter. One is mirrored, one is not. You put the plain one on the bottom—the 'blank,' they call it— put a little grit and water on it, and start rubbing the mirrored plate back and forth across it in strokes that extend exactly halfway out over the edges of the bottom piece. At the same time, you rotate your plate *exactly* so many degrees after exactly so many strokes—on and on for weeks." If all this is done perfectly, Winston explained, the top piece will eventually "hollow out" and become the telescope's parabolic mirror.

"At the time," Winston said, "I didn't realize that even Newton didn't make his own parabolic mirrors. It was so difficult to get them just right, he farmed the chore out to optical specialists, who ground them with machines. And of course the company that makes these kits doesn't *tell* you that even the slightest variation in the procedure will create irregularities in the mirror that will ruin your telescope. If you're a millionth of an inch out, it can cause distortions. It's a job that no kid should ever be encouraged to do. I was always gouging the mirror a little, or getting it off-centre, or something. Once in a long while, amazingly, I'd get it to where it *seemed* to be coming into an almost perfect figure— but inevitably somehow, *always*, I'd go a little past the point of perfection, and would then have to start regrinding the entire rest of the mirror to compensate."

Simple tests to gauge the shape of the parabola as it was being ground invariably horrified and frustrated the teenager.

"After more than two years of ongoing exasperation," Winston said, "I had the mirror as close to being right as I was ever going to get it—or so I thought, in my frustration. So, I decided just to assemble it all and try it out."

On a dark clear night during the summer of 1969, Winston took the instrument into the same backyard where he had achieved his satori seven years earlier, aimed it at the North Star, Polaris, and bent for a look.

At this point in his story, I interrupted and asked Winston to assess what had been going through his head as he'd approached the moment of truth. "Oh, I was quite optimistic," he brightened. "I could imagine a clear image of the pole star, no haze, no double vision. I've never been a pessimist by nature."

His disappointment at the reality of what he saw is detectable in his voice after thirty-one years. "It was awful," he said quietly. "It was a mess. It was fuzzy. You couldn't see properly. It wasn't all the mirror's fault, though. I didn't have the telescope tuned right." The problem was that, at that point in his career, Winston didn't know what telescope-tuning was.

The following year, Winston was off to the University of Toronto to study math and physics—but decidedly not astronomy. "I guess I figured I knew it all," he said. "Although I've wondered about that since, and think now that part of my reluctance was simply that I was heartbroken about my telescope; it really turned me off. Certainly, I didn't want the thing in Toronto. I told myself it wouldn't be dark enough there to see any stars. But I'm sure at heart I just wanted to be rid of it."

The small miracle was that, despite his disappointment, Winston maintained his fascination with the night sky. "I kept up on celestial events, kept reading about the stars, always watched them when I could. I just didn't have any interest in telescopes. They were the enemy."

Winston has always had a special affinity for the planets. "In astronomical terms," he told me, "they're the neighbourhood. They're so bright and close, you can see them in downtown Toronto." In 1971, Mars came into favourable opposition to Earth, an occurrence that happens once every seventeen years. "What

that means," Winston explained, "is that Mars and Earth were passing close to one another. It was the big event of the season, and
I just had to see what was happening on Mars."

Winston's independence is clearly one of his strengths as an
astronomer. It has allowed him to forge ahead in the absence of
teachers or a mentor, or even a friend who might have shared in his
ambition or despair. But it has also been his weakness, in that when
advice might have been available—as it surely would have been
during the Mars opposition—he kept typically to himself. "Mars,"
he told me categorically, "was my telescope's last big chance. And I
actually had it functioning pretty well. I'd learned some things
about tuning, had managed to bury some of my disenchantment,
and was quite looking forward to this new possibility."

The difficulty this time was that, in his isolation, Winston had no
idea that Mars was experiencing massive dust storms, which made it
impossible to see with any clarity. "When finally I got to look at it,
it was just a big fuzzy dot," he said. "It wasn't red, it wasn't mountainous, it wasn't Mars. As far as I was concerned, that was it."

As a last measure of disengagement, Winston took the deficient
telescope to his brother Joe's home on Long Lake outside Sudbury.
"They had four kids, and Joe thought one of them might take an
interest in it. I knew it was an extreme long shot, because they
didn't know how to use it any better than I did—or even as well."

And so ended what Winston described as his "muddled and
agonizing coexistence with telescopes."

Well, not quite ended.

Fast-forward seventeen years to the summer of 1988. On a visit
to his brother's, Winston remembered the old telescope, retrieved
it from storage and, almost out of nostalgia, began cleaning it and
tuning it for yet another last chance.

"I was nearly twice as old as when I'd last seen the thing," he
said. "I was more patient, and I was more knowledgeable. I'd studied university physics and math, and by this time had spent a dozen
years or more working on fairly complex engineering problems. I
guess it's possible, as well, that I didn't have such exaggerated

expectations as I'd had as a kid. Anyway, I'd always maintained my fascination with the sky, and when we took the telescope out behind the house that night I was amazed at how much better it was than I'd remembered. My brother said to me, 'We could never see anything with it.' Which, of course, was because they didn't know where to look in a night sky that's literally billions of miles across. Casting around randomly is pretty much the equivalent of pointing binoculars into the daytime sky and expecting to see, say, a meadowlark or a heron. The chances are like winning the lottery. But when I showed them the planets Saturn and Jupiter, it blew them away—in fact, it blew me away, too, after such a long absence."

As, indeed, it blew *me* away on the night Winston hosted my own introduction to the heavens. There is something breathtaking and lush—and indisputably alien—about the sight of Jupiter through a sixteen-inch Newtonian telescope. What to a neophyte like myself is, on any other night, undifferentiable from the rest of the bright specks in the sky, is suddenly a soft and radiant green ball, as cool as krypton, and surrounded by glassy blue moons. The lot of it ascends huge and dramatic in the east, and so close to the end of the telescope you could reach out and give it a twirl while it's in the neighbourhood. Saturn is big and pale, a silvery orb and halo—"the queen of the night sky," as it is sometimes called. Like the galaxies, it is a kind of child's idea of what a heavenly body might look like—a fixture both defined and obscured by its rings, which are made of ice particles, some as small as snowflakes, others as big as Mount Everest.

During Winston's seventeen years without a telescope, much had changed in the world of amateur astronomy. "For one thing," he said, "charts became available, showing the location of thousands of non-stellar objects—by which I mean anything that isn't a simple star: a galaxy, a star cluster, an exploded star or supernova remnant, planets, stellar nurseries, which are basically big clouds of gas that are stars in formation." During the late 1700s, the French comet hunter Charles Messier numbered and catalogued 110 of these non-stellar objects. They still bear his initial—M-1, M-2 and so on, right up to M-110. "When I started as a kid, nobody thought amateurs could see these things," Winston said. "And the reason they couldn't see them was that they weren't properly charted. Suddenly, here was all this wonderful stuff!"

Winston caught my attention by explaining that, for the most part, recreational astronomers—and many pros, too—use the visible stars only as a kind of road map for locating these more picturesque non-stellar treats.

If you want to find, for example, the Veil Supernova—a million-mile swoosh of white mist, once a solid star that exploded—you look just off Star 52 in the constellation Cygnus. Likewise, the Whirlpool Galaxy can be found in Ursa Major, and the Androm-eda Galaxy in the constellation Andromeda.

The galaxies are a smile-inducing surprise, in that they look like the heavenly bodies we remember from our childhood comic books. Andromeda—billions of years old and 2.5 million light years away—is the proverbial flying saucer, as simple as a pie plate, except with a tennis ball lodged in its centre. The Whirlpool Galaxy might have been modelled on a child's plastic pinwheel.

As I stared into the eyepiece at a cluster of galaxies—in particu-lar, the "A" cluster in Perseus—Winston said, "The light you're seeing now left home about five hundred million years ago and ended its journey tonight on your retina." I took the opportunity to ask if Winston thought there could be intelligent life in other parts of the universe. After joking that he wasn't sure there was intelligent life on Earth, he said, "Let's say there *were* other beings on some planet, circling a star in some distant galaxy. If they set off to discover a civilization like ours, it might take them five hundred million years just to get here—that's if they could travel at the speed of light and knew exactly where they were going. So they'd have to be not only very intelligent—way more intelligent than earthlings, to figure out where they were going—they'd have to have almost infinitely long lives, unless they reproduced on the way and carried on with successive generations.

"The truth," he said finally, "is that if there's a civilization similar to ours out there somewhere, we'll probably never know."

───────────

Winston's emotional responses to the skies are not obvious—in fact, tend to be guarded, as if out of an awareness that others might not share his rather unusual taste in entertainment. Only on occasion did I detect some obvious excitement at having focused on an object that clearly enthused him. "Ohhh, that's *nice*," he said, as he brought a planetary nebula known as "the Ring" into focus for me.

The planetary nebulae are stars that are undergoing what Winston referred to as "a catastrophic but not fatal change." They are late in their lives, and because of internal heat and pressure are throwing off vast shells of coloured gases, which, relative to their diameter, get well out into space before they are halted in their spread and pulled into a kind of stasis by the stars' gravitational field. The Ring is a gorgeous thing, like a great oily pool seen under infrared light, and I was heartened to see it not going gently into either the good night or the wispy grave that awaits it fifty thousand years or so down the line.

One of the more subtle pleasures of a spell on the end of a telescope is simply hearing the names of the constellations and stars. The verbal exotica of *Star Wars* and *Star Trek* and *2001: A Space Odyssey* are suddenly the commonplaces of a night bundled up under the heavens. There are many more constellations than we might be led to believe by our overexposure to the Horoscopic Twelve, the Dirty Dozen, which have somehow escaped metaphor and myth to become a cut-rate affirmation for the faint (or the great) of hope. There are in fact eighty-eight constellations in the northern sky, the largest being Hydra, the Water Snake, and Virgo, the Maiden, the smallest being Crux, the Cross, and Equuleus, the Little Horse. Between these is a magnificent serial metaphor linking Cassiopeia, the Queen, Aquila, the Eagle, Cetus, the Whale, Draco, the Dragon and, among others, Monoceros, the Unicorn, and Vulpecula, the Fox.

───────────

The stars, mostly named by the Arabs of the first millennium, are an equally integral part of the sky's poetry. Bellatrix, Betelgeuse, Rigel, and Mintaka, for example, can all be found in the constellation Orion.

Winston said, "People sometimes ask me what mysteries I unlock when I come out here in the dark, and I have to tell them that sometimes the greatest unsolved mystery is just to find what it is you want to look at. These things don't have signs on them. They don't have addresses. Sometimes it's impossible even to pick the right night to go. You get it all planned, and a cloud cover sneaks in. Or you get ground fog and can't see a thing. Or the telescope acts up. Even when things go perfectly, you don't solve mysteries—you just kind of keep moving on to the next unanswered question."

———

Winston is no advocate of telescope building. "It takes too much time," he says. "It's time you could be spending out there looking at the sky. I lost two whole seasons building my first telescope. Besides, it just about did me in."

I reminded Winston that he had lost two seasons plus seventeen more.

"Yes," he said, "plus seventeen."

So it was with marshalled ambiguity that he considered a return to the builders' art in mid-1996. His itchy old nemesis, aperture fever, had gotten into the water, and he had caught it. He wanted, as he put it, "to go deeper."

One thing he didn't want, couldn't stand the thought of, was grinding another mirror. "This time I was going to buy one," he told me. "A big one."

Nor did he want a big, heavy telescope that he couldn't carry around. He said, "It had to be light and it had to be transportable." The problem was that the only powerful commercial telescopes that are light are what astronomers call "open" models—instruments in which the mirror and inner structure are not enclosed in a tube. "One of their shortcomings," he told me, "is that thermal currents flow right across the unprotected optical parts. Even the warmth from your body sends currents through the viewing space and breaks up the image. I wanted mine enclosed, and yet I couldn't get anybody to build me a closed model that was light enough and convenient enough to carry around."

The only answer was to build it himself.

While today Winston works for a company called Bristol Babcock, where he designs and oversees the installation of municipal water-purification systems (without ever having been there, he told me in a trice exactly what had happened at Walkerton), he once worked on defence systems for a company whose products he characterizes as "really nasty." But as a result, he is familiar with the defence industry's "system engineering" approach to design, and is adept, as he put it, at "getting everything about a design integrated"—budgets, aesthetics, materials, mechanical and thermal properties, overall durability and so on.

For two years he considered every facet of his hypothetical telescope, made drawings, made computer simulations, took measurements of the space capacities of rental cars. "I considered everything about ten different ways," he said, "then took about two months to make my choices."

For lightness he chose wafer-thin birch plywood for the telescope's 2.5-metre octagonal enclosure tube. For transportability he built it in three detachable sections, simple and quick to assemble for maximum viewing time on a given night.

Lastly, he told me, it had to be "totally beautiful."

While Winston's standards of total beauty might not conform to everyone's, the telescope is, in fact, totally beautiful in a sculpturally functional sort of way. It took six months to build, and took us roughly half an hour to set up in the one-time cow pasture northwest of Bowmanville. As we worked, a whiff of freshly mown alfalfa drifted softly in from another field.

When I climbed the stepladder to the telescope for the first time, and eased up to the eyepiece, Winston withheld any comment until it was clear I was fixed on M-13, a tight, spherical cluster of perhaps several thousand stars within the constellation Hercules. When elapsed time and the formation's impact on me pretty much compelled me to say something—in fact, when I was about to open my mouth—Winston said quietly, "The pupil of your eye is now sixteen inches in diameter." His words had the double advantage of personalizing the process for me, of placing it not just within me, as opposed to "out there" somewhere, but of placing it at the centre of the most delicate and treasured part of my anatomy, my eyes. It also neatly dispelled whatever gawkish inanity I myself might have been about to utter. Beyond that, it roundly and elegantly articulated the difference between the planetary knownothing who had climbed the ladder and the wondering fool who stood appreciatively on the threshold of the universe.

For everything we looked at, Winston brought the object into view for me, and urged me to track it as it moved and to focus the eyepiece to my own specifications. Locating an image in a highpowered telescope is anything but easy. For one thing, because the telescope operates with a parabolic mirror, the viewer has to move it in exactly the opposite direction to the motion of the object being tracked. Up becomes down, left becomes right (think of watching a baseball game, behind you, in the reflecting bowl of a spoon). The result, for me, was that when I let the telescope stray even a fraction off, say, a nebula or galaxy cluster, I could seldom relocate it.

The reason, of course, is that in space as in life, *everything is always moving*. Astronomy through a telescope is a non-stop reminder that the earth rotates and revolves, that moons revolve, too, and that even stars are born and grow old and turn to vapour.

Our sun itself is gradually burning out, although it is by no means just another star. Because of its relatively small size, it will never achieve great heat or internal pressure. As a consequence, it will burn long and gently, and never start throwing off great shells of gas or simply blow up—"go supernova," as they say—and turn to dust, as the largest stars will after a hundred million years or so. "Which is like *nothing* in astronomical time," Winston said. "Our sun is leading a nice quiet life, and is expected to keep doing so for a long time. Which of course is what makes planets like ours and the life on it possible. I guess if you're a Creationist, you believe we're here because it was a perfect place for God to put us, and if you're an evolutionist you believe we evolved perfectly to suit the conditions. Whatever anyone believes, we couldn't be here if the conditions weren't stable and quiet. We're basically in a quiet little corner of the universe, away off in the middle of nowhere."

For all of Winston's exactitude and reserve in discussing his life with the stars, there is at least an element in him of star-struck sentimentality. At a point in the evening when he had paused to tune the telescope to the North Star, he said to me, "Hold your hand up to the eyepiece." I did, and a bright white dot of light appeared on my palm. "There," he said, in subdued gratification. "You've got a handful of starlight. Not many people can say they've had one."

When in the van on the way home I asked what it all meant to him, he said, "I think about it in the way you might think about a very fascinating place you'd been, and intended to return to. There tends to be an impression among people who have never done it that you just go out into a meadow some starry night, lie back and soak up all these distant wonders—when nothing could be further from the truth. There's nothing passive about it. You really have to work, first just to develop skills and patience. You have to be ingenious and determined and sensitive and hard-nosed. You're always working to tease these secrets out of the universe, to get it to reveal just the tiniest bit of itself. For the most part, it doesn't co-operate. So when you do find something way off in some other part of the universe, there can be an incredible sense of accomplishment and satisfaction."

As opposed to being intimidated by the vastness of space, Winston said it made him feel significant, even powerful. "It can't hide from me," he said. "I'm as big as it is. I'm an undeniable part of it. No matter how mighty it may be, I can go and get it."

While Winston did his best to play down the emotional components of his relationship with the sky, he did say at one point that when he was personally down or depressed, it did him good, raised his spirits, to get out under the sky with his telescope and visit what he called his "old friends." He said, however, that the heavens were not comforting or nurturing in the usual sensual way. "You're not basking in the warm glow of the sun, or in someone's loving care or embrace. It's you and it, millions of miles apart, playing this kind of tag. Mind you, it can be incredibly sensual visually. I love the feel of the sun and the glow of the moon. I know what these thing are physically—have perhaps a special attachment to them that others might not have."

Winston submitted that, on a given night, having spent several hours "in space," he could return to the city free of the burdens of the day or week and fuelled for whatever lay ahead. "Where the mysteries and teasing are concerned," he said, "I love the thought that I can put my eye up to the telescope and, with effort and ingenuity, go as deep into the universe as I want to go."

Chapter Ten

Toward the end of my mother's life, in perhaps 1987, when the Alzheimer's that killed her had reached a point where she could barely speak a comprehensible sentence, I drove her one July day to the rocky uplands south of Bala, Ontario. It was a place where she had wandered and picnicked as a girl, had gathered blueberries all her life, and which, in her private way, she loved as much as any place on earth. I guided her gingerly across the mosses and rocks, holding tight at times so the wind wouldn't blow her over. As I sat with her under a tree, having picked her some berries, a remarkable thing happened. So powerful was her sense of identification with the local rocks and vegetation—and the sounds and smells of the berry patch—that, for a few minutes, the combined effects of these almost totally dispelled the ravages of her disease, and we were able to converse quite normally, as we hadn't done for many months.

For her, the blueberry patch was a place rich in the rewards of summer—and of family life, too, even though as kids on picking expeditions we often squabbled and bellyached. She prized not just the berries but the sensory vocabulary of the patch: the granite, the lichens, the snapping of the cook fire and the redeeming cool of the lake. Once as a child, I came over a ridge of rock, not far from where we sat that day reminiscing, to find her staring down a rattlesnake, which eventually turned under her gaze and slithered off.

Even within days of her death, when she was all but comatose, I could rouse her by asking if she remembered Bala or Torrance, or nearby Bracebridge, where she was born. "I do," she'd say out of her chaos.

"Do you remember the blueberry patch?" I'd ask, and she'd whisper, "Yes, I remember it."

A year or so ago, my son came running upstairs to where I was working in our home in Thunder Bay and said, "You'd better come down, a crazy lady's here." I went down and found my wife talking to a gentle elderly woman in the front hall of the house. The woman was clearly confused, probably by Alzheimer's, and was wearing an admission bracelet from St. Joseph's Hospital five or six blocks away. But she was upbeat and curious, and was anxious to find her mother, whom she said would be in the kitchen. We phoned the hospital and learned she was in chronic care, and fifteen minutes later the woman's daughter arrived to fetch her. It turned out that the woman—Joan was her name—had lived in our house as a girl, nearly eighty years ago. Such was the power and clarity of this once-important place in her life that it had reeled her back at a time when, according to her daughter, she could not be relied on to find her way from the bedroom to the bathroom. What's more, it had left her looking not just for her mother but for herself, or at least a childhood version of herself. "Is Joan here? Are you Joan?" she had asked my daughter Georgia at one point.

"No, I'm Georgia," Georgia had told her, both perplexed and

impressed by this obvious disturbance in the normal order of things.

"*There's* my mother!" Joan said emotionally when her daughter arrived at the door. If it was a middle-aged woman at 108 Prospect, it was clearly her mother, just as she remembered her.

Mental clutter notwithstanding, we are stretched across the decades by even the simplest stimulations of the planet. The fragrances of my boyhood summers in Muskoka, for example, are a kind of olfactory rubbing of that time and territory. And I can summon those years through the remembered smells of, say, the pine cones that we gathered to ignite the wood stove, or the chunks of green apple that my mother would occasionally toss onto the stove-top to sweeten the air—or through the smells of fresh-split hemlock, balsam or maple, all of which I could identify at a whiff, having split cords of it for the woodpile by the time I was twelve or thirteen. The lighting of the stove is itself a flight path for the memory, beginning at the woodbox with the organic mustiness of old bark, followed by the surprise assault of a struck wooden match, the flash flame of newsprint and kindling, then the woodsmoke proper, overbearing when it leaks into the cabin, but an irresistible opiate when you step outside and catch it adrift on a morning breeze off the lake (the word perfume comes from the Latin noun *fumus*, meaning smoke).

My memories of summers in Muskoka are so deeply associated with the land and the life it supported that, years later, when I moved out west, I could hardly stand a summer spent in the wind and dust of the southern Manitoba prairie. *It just wasn't summer*, and my sense of the season could only be fully revived by getting back to the rocks and lakes and evergreens.

Faced with the fact that in recent years large tracts of Muskoka have been turned into a hogswallow of opportunism, and the dance of the hour is the non-stop real estate shuffle, I am obliged to remind myself at times that it was at one time paradise, and in a sense always will be, at least for me.

All of us are linked, of course, to places that offer comfort or inspiration, or in one way or another represent the deepest of our longings or connections to ourselves. On a wider arc, people have from the beginning identified places of power and meaning, and have made of those places a kind of billeting grounds for their spirits and gods. Here at the Lakehead, the early tribes acknowledged the surpassing power and mystery of Lake Superior by naming it Chigaming or Gitchee Gumi, both of which refer to the expansive spirit and dimensions of the lake. Tribes further to the east named Manitoulin Island for the Great Spirit, Manitou.

Viewed from Thunder Bay and the Trans-Canada Highway, the Sibley Peninsula resembles a vast supine figure some ten kilometres in length and well known in these parts as the Sleeping Giant. According to Ojibwa legend, this colossal figure—Nanabijou to the Aboriginals—is, like the lake itself, an embodiment of the Creator. There are several protracted stories about why Nanabijou should be lying sleeping on his (or her) back, turned to stone, twenty kilometres out in Lake Superior—tales involving silver, storms, betrayal and greedy white men. But the stories are not particularly absorbing or enlightening, taken even on the level of bedtime folk tales. A Native anthropologist once told me that the Giant stories collectively are "a lotta crap. They're white men's stories," he said. "They contain nothing of the spirit of the land or of the imagination of the tribe." He told me the Giant had possessed meaning and power for the early tribes, but that because most of the old stories had been lost, there was no way to know how that meaning or power might have been expressed.

I asked if he had heard any such stories, and urging me not to quote him (there is apparently a protocol for disseminating such tales), he described one told by a local elder, in which the Giant was believed to have power to transform those who "prayed or meditated" in its presence. He believed the story derived from what he called "the Giant's many looks and moods."

Certainly, any of us who live in Thunder Bay are aware of that spectrum of looks—under snow, under cloud, under overhead sun, at dawn, at sunset, in fog, in summer haze, spring green, autumn yellow, half moon, full moon. One day last winter when I looked out from the desk at which I write, long vertical slashes of new snow against the Giant's basalt flanks gave the whole thing the appearance of zebra stripes, which became tiger stripes as the sun swung yellowish into the west, and then a kind of High Vegas gartered effect as the sunset threw a hot-pink glow onto the snow and ice. The anthropologist suspected that the tribes interpreted these transformations as "some sort of spirit lesson on the human capability for growth." It is perhaps symptomatic of the fate of the sacrosanct in the twenty-first century that a significant number of area businesses are registered under the name "Sleeping Giant." One of the more vivid examples is a scaffolding company that calls itself Sleeping Giant Erections—sacred site as brand name, as sexual innuendo, as widget pitch.

A Minnesota journalist told me recently about a tribe of southwestern Native Americans—I believe Navajo or Hopi—who objected to being moved off land they had occupied for thousands of years in southern Arizona so that the land could be used for industrial development. Part of their plea was that the land included sites that they considered culturally and spiritually sacred. On their behalf, the state government called on that judicious and respected arbiter of North American Native culture, the Vatican, to assess whether or not the sites in question were indeed holy ground and had any spiritual significance. Representatives from Rome visited the places in the absence of tribal elders and, without further consultation, announced that they were not sacred, couldn't be, because no temples or places of worship had ever been constructed on them. Bring on the bulldozers—and consider, alternatively, that the land-inspired Navajo and Hopi would almost certainly have rendered a similar judgement on the Vatican; it could not truly be a holy place, because it *is* cluttered with ecclesiastical bric-a-brac, making it a decidedly unsuitable dwelling place for the Spirit.

The further back you look into North American prehistory,

the more mystical were the connections between the people and the earth. It is a comprehensible irony—and, I think, quite beautiful—that the connections were simultaneously more practical as well. Most Native North American tribes believed that the spirit world existed in every tree, every rock, every bird, animal and stream. On a utilitarian level, they built their homes of these same trees and animals (in the form of bark and skins); ate berries, roots, fish, fowl; drank berry juices and Labrador tea; made their medicines of plants and roots, their tools out of rock and bone. They made music of tree trunks and animal skins. In recent years, there has been a revival of interest in early Native medicines, to the point where at least one large pharmaceutical firm is plying the jungles of South America in an attempt to preserve fading knowledge of, for instance, natural antibiotics, analgesics and painkillers, as the biological sources of these ancient curatives are consumed by industry.

It is probably safe to say that, in their earliest stages, Western or Oriental cultures were as reverential as were Native North Americans in their sensitivities to the world around them. And perhaps still are. Not long ago, a Native elder told me that "many Indians these days" have no interest at all in their traditional ties to the land. We have come to expect it of Caucasians. A woman who had lived in Thunder Bay for thirty years told me recently that the day her husband retired, he and she were going to be out of here pronto—that they just didn't care about nature or the outdoors.

Even Nature's ingrates are of course redeemed by the planet's faithful and irreducible interest in *them*. Acknowledge it or not, they thrive on its sunshine, breathe its air, eat its foods, drink its water and wines. They dress in its fabrics, write on its paper, eat off its silver and crockery, wear its diamonds and pearls, place its rubber and steel between their bottoms and the highway. They thrive on its sounds. The music of the spheres is no mere metaphor. In her book *A Natural History of the Senses*, Diane Ackerman mentions a group of Buddhist monks north of Bangkok who believe that music "falls out of the earth's rocks and roots, its trees and rain." In support of that belief, one of them has recorded the electrical emanations of the planet, and has found that when he transcribes these into standard musical notation, they correspond precisely to traditional eighteen-bar Thai music.

One of my closest friends, the Winnipeg poet and fiddler George Morrissette, described in a recent letter how fish and other sea creatures have, for billions of years, been able not just to hear but to communicate via submarine sounds. He went on to explain that when the sound from a vibrating violin string has become so faint that it is no longer communicating any audible wavelength, it continues to send out ultrasonic waves, in effect echoes of those primitive sea sounds. This inaudible resonance appears to be both recognizable and comforting to the ancient marine awareness of the human ear. "Music created on electronic instruments or synthesizers," George wrote, "cannot diminish to such faint echoes— my point being that we are the first generation whose music has cut us off from sounds that go back two or three billion years."

A local wilderness outfitter named Bruce Hyer told me that when he came to Canada from Connecticut during the Vietnam War, he wanted a place in the boreal woods, and believed that if he took the CN train across Northern Ontario and watched as the forest rolled by, the right piece of land would somehow speak to him, make itself known, and he would thereby locate his site. And that is what he did—stood out on the tiny deck between cars, until eventually an idyllic lake gave him the word, and he signalled the engineer to stop the train and let him off with his supplies and axe and ambitions. As it turned out, the land spoke with authority, because thirty years later, he still runs his resort and outfitting business from the site near Armstrong, Ontario.

Any grade-twelve biology student is aware that, in both body and mind, we are in more or less perfect synchronicity with our planet—with its electrical and magnetic fields, its gravitational field, its air supply, its atmospheric pressure, its light and radiation, its natural bacteria. There are times when we must make adjustments—for instance, as the ozone layer is depleted, or water or air is contaminated, or the land becomes incapable of producing required food. But for the most part, our bodies' electrical coding, blood pressure and tissue density, our skeletons and muscles and brain circuitry, are flawlessly adapted to the surroundings in which they have evolved. Light (or its absence) triggers hormonal activity and influences our circadian rhythms. During the months of shortest daylight, particularly in northern Canada, psychoses intensify, alcohol and drug consumption increases, and suicide rates climb.

In some areas, suicides increase as light *returns* to the land in spring. The dark joke up here on the north shore of Superior, where the Finns have historically shown a higher than normal suicide rate, especially in spring, is that "spring has come and the Finns are hanging in the trees." Winter depression, or seasonal affective disorder, is virtually epidemic in these parts during the short days of January and February. In many cases, such depression can be alleviated with increased exposure to natural light, or even intense daily doses of artificial light. The human pineal gland, which controls testosterone production, functions partly in response to light, one result of which is that men's testosterone levels are highest in October, specifically during the early to mid-afternoon. Nature's evolutionary wisdom is that a baby conceived in October will be born in summer when, in millennia past, the newborn would have had its best chance of survival. In a parallel vein, white-tailed deer from the boreal forest to southern Texas hit the peak of their rut on exactly the same day in mid-November— and likewise send their young into the world under optimal conditions in late spring. Ravens hatch in early spring, well ahead of their competitors, when their chances are optimal, in large part because winter-kill deer and the like—a banquet for corvid scavengers—are beginning to thaw and become edible.

One of the more readable of our physiolgical links to the planet is the synchronicity of the twenty-eight-day menstrual cycle with the twenty-eight-day cycle of the moon. Most connections are more difficult to decipher. According to Dr. Ruth Carson, a Seattle-area biologist, a late-millennial shift in the earth's axis has perceptibly influenced what she calls "the energy fields" that we generate around and within ourselves. A local reflexologist told me that, for many people, this has disrupted the electrical impulses that control physical and mental well-being. The shift has affected not just human physiology but, for example, that of whales, whose migration patterns have been altered to the degree that many beached themselves on the shores of the Pacific over a relatively short time in 1998.

Humanity's long-evolved adaptation to regional bacteria has been increasingly tested with the proliferation of global travel. For thousands of years, Native North Americans treated their infections and sicknesses with natural cures. But germs brought by the Europeans, including venereal diseases, were untouchable by centuries-old treatments such as burdock extract (to purify blood), juniper root (for kidney problems) or pearly everlasting (the leaves and blossoms of which were smoked to treat respiratory ailments and paralysis).

Similarly, children who grow up in apartment towers, attend day-care on the seventh floor of the YWCA, get driven to dance lessons, and vacation at the West Edmonton Mall have been found to lack immunity to common bacteria, such as those in garden or farm soil. They have not had sufficient exposure to build up tolerance, and as a consequence, are apt to get sick during their first trip to summer camp, or even to their cousin's sandbox in the suburbs.

For a reverse view of the ways in which body and planet co-depend, consider a list of the maladies that befall the human body in the altered environment of outer space. Bone mass shrinks; red blood cells disappear; spinal discs expand; the heart enlarges, then shrinks; the muscles and immune system weaken; sleep patterns are altered. What's more, a person's normal defences against solar and galactic radiation disappear in the absence of the earth's protective atmosphere and magnetic field.

———————

During my occasional forays into teaching, I have asked university-level classes to write a few introductory sentences about themselves.

The exercise generates mostly uninspired abstractions about their feelings and philosophies. But when I ask them to write about a landscape or neigbourhood from their past, they are quickly, almost invariably, producing textured, concrete sentences, even anecdotes, not just about places but about themselves.

The link between land and lives is acknowledged tacitly by one of my favourite American writers, Harry Crews, who subtitled his memoir of growing up in Bacon County, Georgia, *The Biography of a Place*. The book reveals how profoundly Crews was shaped by the farms, attitudes, language and people of his particular part of the rural American South. Think of almost any Canadian writer, and their places come to mind as readily as their plots: Margaret Laurence's Manitoba prairie; Mordecai Richler's Montreal; Alice Munro's southwestern Ontario; Jack Hodgins' Vancouver Island; Wayne Johnson's Newfoundland. For me, the settings of movies —*Barry Lyndon, The Deerhunter, Paris, Texas, Highway 61*—generally remain vivid long after I've forgotten most other things about the films. A novice writer who once took a class from me attempted a detective novel set in Miami, a city she had visited once and barely knew. The characters were as dull as dishwater, had no idea where or who they were. The woman rewrote the novel set in Vancouver, a place she knew well, and her people snapped to life in relation to the mountains, cityscape and climate.

It is hardly surprising that so many books begin with an evocation of the land, or at least of place: John Steinbeck's *The Grapes of Wrath*, Ken Kesey's *Sometimes a Great Notion*, Margaret Laurence's *The Diviners*, Jim Harrison's *Wolf*, Sandra Birdsell's *The Missing Child*, Gabriel García Márquez's *The Autumn of the Patriarch*, Edward Hoagland's *Notes from the Century Before*, Clark Blaise's *Lunar Attractions*.

"Here was the lowest common denominator of nature," begins W. O. Mitchell's *Who Has Seen the Wind*, "the skeleton requirements simply, of land and sky—Saskatchewan prairie. It lay wide around the town, stretching tan to the far line of the sky, shimmering under the June sun and waiting for the unfailing visitation of wind."

CHARLES WILKINS

Annie Dillard's *An American Childhood* starts with a rhapsodic projection into the last hours, or perhaps minutes, of her own life, a time when all rational knowledge has dissolved—including the names of presidents, relatives, neighbourhoods—and her only remaining intimations are of the landscape and rivers and forests, "the dreaming memory of land as it lay this way and that . . . the city rolling down the mountain valleys like slag . . . forested mountains and hills, and the way the rivers lay flat, and the blunt mountains rose in darkness from the rivers' banks . . ."

Language itself is a geographic variable, homogenized these days by radio and television, but not to the point where the legendary Southern drawl, or Cajun "French," or Ottawa Valley twang—or any of hundreds of the Gaelic remnants of the Canadian East Coast—has been significantly diminished. One of the deckhands on the *M. V. Paterson*, a Newfoundlander named Don Scott, told me that at a recent wedding back home, he had been in the company of outport relatives who spoke English with such a violent twist—including "thees," "thous" and "thines"—that, for the most part, he didn't know what they were talking about.

I was intrigued to learn recently that even crime has its regional valences. Like the rest of us, criminals are so grounded in their locales that Detective Kim Rossmo, who spent seventeen years with the Vancouver Police Department, has been able to develop a finely layered computer program that can identify a criminal's home neighbourhood—sometimes to within a few houses of his actual address—by assessing the vectors and variables of his criminal activities. One American forensic anthropologist possesses such an encyclopedic knowledge of geology and botany that by examining a murderer's car, for example—by removing microscopic layers of soil and road dust from the wheel wells, or, say, tiny seeds and stones that have lodged in weather stripping and tire treads—he can retrace the car's travels sometimes over thousands of miles through remote backwaters, each of which bears a distinctive geographical thumbprint.

The land-life interdependence has been acknowledged by any number of popular musicians, from Woody Guthrie down a long line of performers that includes Canadians Neil Young, Robbie Robertson, Leonard Cohen, Bruce Cockburn, Connie Kaldor, Heather Bishop, Murray McLauchlan, Stan Rogers, Ian Tyson, Sylvia Tyson, k. d. lang, Robert Charlebois, Hank Snow, Stompin' Tom Connors, Susan Aglukark, Kashtin and, only slightly less directly, instrumentalists such as Ashley MacIsaac and Natalie Mac-Master. Joni Mitchell's lyrics are a rolling profusion of "whisker wheat," "meadow grass," "river skating," "woodlands and grass-lands and badlands," "the geese in chevron flight racing on before the snow." Just a single ensemble by Gordon Lightfoot, "The Canadian Railroad Trilogy," gathers images of land and water from virtually every geographic region of the country.

The link is expressed equally in visual art ranging from that of the Dutch Masters to the Impressionists to the Group of Seven—to an extensive group of more avant-garde Canadian practition-ers, which includes Winnipeggers Ann Smith, Ivan Eyre, Wanda Koop, the late Kelly Clark, Esther Warkov, Eleanor Bond and Don Proch. Proch has, with painstaking delicacy, incorporated the likes of bird bones and snare wire into his sculptures, and has etched geese, spruce trees and plough furrows onto the faces of his sculptural masks.

I have seen real faces and hands on which the soil and rock cliffs and forests seem to have been scribed or carved, but in this era of mega-tattooing on all quarters of the human hide, I had not until recently seen a tattoo that did justice to the deep pictorial and psy-chological connections that exist between our selves and our land-scapes and cities. Then one day last August, as I was walking west along King Street in Toronto, I saw a young man perhaps twenty metres ahead of me, naked from the waist up, apparently with some sort of landscape tattooed on his back. I closed in for a better look, impressed to realize that his back was covered with a baroque collage of pine trees and shoreline and rockscape, the lot of it interspersed with bits of foliage and sea life, and drawn with Dürer-like precision. I followed him for maybe twenty-five metres, then, curious beyond containment, stepped up beside him as we approached University Avenue and said, "I like your tattoo."

"Oh," he said. "Thanks."

I asked what place had inspired it, and he asked if I'd ever heard of Blacks Harbour, New Brunswick. "That's what it is," he said. "That's where I come from."

We exchanged comments on that part of New Brunswick (where the province and the state of Maine meet at the west end of the Bay of Fundy), and he told me that the tattoo had started small, on one of his shoulders, when he'd begun art school in the Maritimes at the age of nineteen. "It just sort of grew," he said, adding that, in total, it had cost eighteen thousand dollars and that, once, drunk, he had considered extending it up his neck and onto his shaved head. He told me it was the work of several "talented, expensive" tattooists, but that the original drawings were his, so that a continuity had been maintained.

I remarked idly that he had nothing on his front, and he said he'd done drawings for the front but wasn't sure he wanted what he called "the same freakin' landscape" all over him. He surprised me by saying that no one in Blacks Harbour had ever seen his tattoo, and that he'd recently had an offer from a travel company that wanted to make a poster of it. Five thousand dollars they had offered him. "I told them it'd cost them ten times that. Besides," he said, "they just wanted a pictorial—me standing looking out to sea or something. I wanted something like the tattooist working on my back while I sat working on the drawings—you know, facing the sea near the town or something. To most people it's just pretty pictures," he shrugged. "To me—you know, it's me! It's my art, it's my place, it's my skin!"

By this time we had reached the intersection at University Avenue. As he turned north, I said, "Nice talking to you."

"Okay!" he responded, and by the time he had taken ten steps up University, he was being loosely trailed by a new gallery of perhaps half a dozen people, each of them fixated, as I had been, on the broad-backed young man whose art and place and skin were Blacks Harbour, New Brunswick.

Chapter Eleven

here is no shortage of evidence, either statistical or anecdotal, that we move faster, further and more often than any culture in history. But it has little to do with an adventurous spirit. The tracks on which we move are as predictable as the rails that our forebears spiked into place during the late nineteenth century. And the Xs on which we settle are as inarguably located as the stops on a game board. But unlike the millions of us who settle in an area because we grew up there and never got out, or got that far and no further on our way to somewhere else, or were drawn by romance or education, or the promise of work, or these days, by the old folks' home, or a better climate in which to age . . . unlike the millions of us on the tracks and on the Xs, Steve Lawson chose the wild west coast of Vancouver Island because, incontestably, it is where he knows he is "supposed to be."

When as a ten-year-old boy, in 1959, Steve saw Long Beach on the island's outer shore for the first time, the area was still a kind of

paradise, accessible only by boat and inhabited largely by the remnants of Native tribes and by villages of local loggers all too willing
to begin selling paradise to the sawmills and pulp factories.

A dozen years later, Long Beach would be transformed into a
national park, replete with parking lots, public washrooms and
interpretive displays. But in the late fifties, it was loosely populated
by tenters and cabin dwellers who were either squatting on bits of
the Crown-owned beach or forest, or owned patches of untaxed
land that they had picked up here or there for a few hundred dollars. One of them, a middle-aged woman, who kept cabins for
rent, befriended Steve that summer, and became what he describes
as "a friend for life." When he returned to the beach in subsequent
summers, he did odd jobs for her, and when he quit school at age
fifteen he lived in one of her cabins for a portion of each of the
next four or five years.

However, when the inhabitants of Long Beach were expropri-
ated for the national park in 1971, Steve did not move with them
up or down the coast. For, by this time, he had cut and planed
thousands of board feet of cedar and fir; he had bought an inboard
engine, a quarter tonne of marine hardware and, having taught
himself boat building, had constructed a fifty-four-foot sailing vessel, the equal of anything its size that ever came out of the building
sheds at Vancouver or Lunenburg. For the next decade, the boat
would be not just his home and transportation, but his social life,
inasmuch as three or four people, including his female mate of that
period, often lived on board with him. What's more, it was his
place of business, in that he fished both for food and for market.
"But fishing," he told me, "was really just an excuse to own a boat,
and to travel and explore. We'd stay anywhere on the coast of
North America—we'd be in the harbours and ports during the
rough months, and in the summers we'd be offshore."

Steve's message to the world has always been a kind of eco-lyric
poem, an unwritten opus cobbled out of storytelling and spindrift
and intuitions about nature and its balance. And always at the base
of it, there has been his extraordinary affinity for the sea. "We talk

about Mother Earth," he says, "and the ocean is the same, a great mother, a life-giving thing—it's a feminine energy, and I have no qualms about saying that I feel loved by the ocean, and that I love it in return."

Nor does Steve have any qualms about attributing to the sea a magnanimous living spirit—spirit not merely as a metaphor for the sea's energy and fecundity, but an actual persona, "a will," says Steve, whose affection for the ocean is not without ironies. He admits, for example, to being afraid of the water, and having been so since he was little. Moreover, he has never had an urge to get beneath the sea's surface, to dive or explore—in fact, has never learned properly to swim. "I guess I'd have to say that as much as I love the ocean, it's the relationship between the ocean and the land that really affects me. Nowhere in my life have I ever seen more life per square inch than there is in the intertidal zone where the ocean meets the northwest coast of North America."

Certainly, to take a stroll along any stretch of beach or through the shoreline outcrops south of Tofino is to encounter a teeming inventory of sea anemones, hermit crabs, sand crabs, clams, starfish, sandpipers, gulls, terns, sea urchins, horsetails, kelp, minnows, mussels, plus any variety of beached jellyfish and *Coelenterata*, everything feeding on something, or if not feeding being fed upon. An occasional large sea bass or rock cod washes ashore and is gone within hours if it is in any way edible.

The power of the ocean is another of Steve's ongoing inspirations. "Some of the winter storms around here send up seas that shake our whole island," he said. "I'm talking about a literal trembling coming right up through the rock." Such fury has never been a problem for the family, except inasmuch as it can keep them island-bound for a week or more at a time between mid-autumn and early spring. If anything, the Lawsons' problem during the winter of 1999–2000 was that there were too *few* storms on Wickininnish Island. "Normally, we get maybe twenty a year," Steve said. "And I'm talking big ones—so powerful that even the fish often can't survive them. We have no *idea* what goes on out there underwater during one of these cataclysms, but we get big ten-pound fish washing in here, no scales on them, alive, but totally incapable of functioning because they've been battered so hard."

It is difficult to think of an equivalent effect on land-based animals, except perhaps by imagining a storm that would leave, say, bears or wolves naked of fur, or birds plucked of their feathers, and lying helpless to die.

The Pacific Rim, according to geologists, is the most volatile earthquake zone in the world. "The good thing about these storms," Steve said, "is that they're a kind of check on earthquakes, in that they tend to give a shake to the planet's tectonic plates and ease them across one another gently, so that we get ongoing small tremors, rather than having the pressure build so that a big quake occurs when they let go. This past year, we only got two smallish storms, in November and then in May, so you can see why this would make me a little nervous. Somewhere out there, there's just too much pressure building."

One of the pleasures of being around Steve is listening to how his oftentimes rhapsodic commentary tends to elevate even commonplace detail to unexpected levels of eloquence and meaning. He recalls standing on Long Beach as a young man after a three-day blow of 150-kilometre-an-hour winds and twenty-metre waves. "The seas were still incredibly huge. The power was just unimaginable, and yet, in spite of this, what struck me was that the ocean, the tide, continued to come in a certain precise distance twice a day, and go out a certain distance, always the same amount. And there I was standing on this ribbon of beach, on the edge of North America, looking out across thousands of square miles of water curving over the face of the earth—registering for the first time in my life an awareness that one relatively slight shift in the forces that rule the planet would inundate not just me and the beach and half a dozen huge cities but thousands of square miles of land, and that it was entirely by divine will and grace that those forces of land and water stay in such perfect balance, and have allowed hundreds of generations of us to live as we do."

At more or less the time of this satori, when Steve was perhaps twenty and was at work building his boat, he walked into a bar in Comox and had yet another of his illuminating experiences. "One thing a person needs if they're to follow their path in life is a name," he explained, "and at that point I was dissatisfied with mine—'Steven' doesn't really have any significance for me, and I wanted a name that meant something." Steve had never been in the bar in his life, and has never been in since—he is pretty much a teetotaller—but, by chance, inside (or by fate, as a fatalist would see it), he met a hereditary Ojibwa chief, a Canadian Air Force captain, who, when they had talked for a while, said to Steve, "You need a name, and I'm going to give you one."

"And he gave me the name Matahil," said Steve, "which in Ojibwa means sailor with a long blue toque. And for ten years I lived that name and that life of the sailor in the toque. And at about the time I sold my boat, in the late seventies, my own son was born, and I passed the name on to him, which it turns out is what the tribes did in the old days."

Understandably, many things happened between the building of the boat and its sale nearly a decade later. For one thing, Steve met his lifelong match and love in Suzanne Hare, who was in her early twenties at the time and was living at Wreck Beach further south along the coast.

In 1972, a year after expropriations for the national park, Steve and Suzanne and eight others headed up the coast in what Steve calls "a flotilla of boats," looking for a place to start a community. The group chose a spot nearly two hundred kilometres north of Tofino at Cape Cook on the Brooks Peninsula, an area so intractable and isolated that, historically, not even Native tribes had attempted to stay there, except briefly in their travels up and down the coast.

But the homesteading did not work out, and within months, four of the settlers, including Steve and Suzanne, had returned to the Tofino area. "By this time I had recognized that my place was not to be away out in the wilds totally out of touch with the mainstream," Steve told me. "I felt I had to be separate from society, but to have access to it—there had to be a bridge between those worlds, and my life was to be that bridge."

By the mid-1970s, Steve and Suzanne had established themselves on Wickininnish Island and had begun building the home in which the family lives today. The island is named for Chief Wickininnish, a legendary tribal potentate who greeted the English Captain Meares when he arrived in the area during the late 1700s, and traded him fifty sea-otter pelts for a pair of copper kettles. At the time the Clayoquots numbered about four thousand in the area (by the beginning of the twentieth century, they were down to five hundred, and are now just scattered remnants). While initial relations between the Natives and the colonists were warm, they soured quickly, and the Natives turned combative. The result was that the English began calling them the "Clayoquot," a name from their own tongue meaning "people different from what they were." The name, of course, has redoubled meaning today, in that many of the Sound's late-twentieth-century inhabitants—people once submissive to the interests of government and industry—have been radicalized politically and environmentally and are again "different from what they were."

By 1979, Steve and Suzanne had begun openly to oppose those whom they perceived as politically or ecologically delinquent, whether hunters, loggers, miners or government agencies. They have always had a profound empathy for wildlife. One of their deepest concerns about logging, for example, was not simply that it destroyed irreplaceable rain forest but that it reduced habitat for mammals and birds and reptiles, and ruined spawning beds for salmon and other fish.

If there was a galvanizing episode in their public stand against abuses of wild animals, it came on a morning in mid-May 1988, when they were preparing to travel up Clayoquot Sound to Sulphur Pass, where a logging dispute was developing. The family was in the bakery in Tofino buying bread for the trip when a friend

informed them that thirteen bears had been killed in the area during the previous two weeks. "I don't remember how our friend
had found out," Steve said, "but within fifteen minutes we had five
boats with thirty-five people heading up the Sound to try to find
out what was going on with these bears."

The Lawsons and the rest of the fleet eventually located a boat
of guided hunters, who had been "sport" hunting bears along the
shorelines for several days. "The guide was from the north end of
Vancouver Island, and the outfitter was from Port Alberni," said
Steve. "We didn't know either of them, and nobody in the boat
would speak to us. So all we could do was keep getting in the way
of their shooting access to the shore. It was pretty nerve-racking,
with these big rifles. We'd position our boats directly in their line
of fire, until, finally, they got frustrated with our tactics and headed
back to the boat ramp in the national park at Long Beach. It
turned out the hunters were Americans, and it seemed one or two
boatloads had killed all thirteen bears, although we didn't know
details at this point."

As Steve and the rest followed the hunters to the boat ramp and
their boat trailer, Steve called the police on his radio phone. "It
was an obvious thing to do after an angry confrontation involving
guns," he said, "and at that point we assumed what they were
doing was illegal, and that there might be action taken against
these guys."

At the ramp, one of the two hunters began a protracted tirade
against those who had spoiled the hunt. "He'd already killed his
bear," said Steve. "He had his trophy, and he was full of piss and
vitriol. The other guy hadn't had a chance to shoot his bear,
because we'd shown up, and this was their last day of hunting. So,
this guy was just disconsolate. He was literally in tears, because he
wasn't going to get to kill a bear—in his mind a trophy, a decora-
tion for his rec room, in ours a beautiful, innocent wild animal in
the prime of its life, and of course a functional part of the ecology
of the planet. What I saw in both those guys was little boys about
eight years old trying to live up to some image that was probably

imposed on them by their fathers—to be real men, to have power, to lay waste."

One of the aspects of this sort of butchery that particularly rankles Steve is the way it is often rationalized culturally and morally by the notion that humanity should "have dominion" over the animals, as stated in the first chapter of the Book of Genesis, in the King James translation of the Bible. "I don't know how that got there," he bristles. "It shouldn't be there. Maybe it's a mis-translation of the Hebrew—maybe an intentional mistranslation. Humanity's responsibility is to care for the animals. I mean, why do other cultures' divine teachings about our relationship with animals stress protection and responsibility, and Judaism and Chris-tianity stress this dominion thing?"

I wondered aloud if maybe apologists for wildlife destruction were simply carrying the idea of dominion too far.

"Oh, they're carrying it too far all right!" Steve laughed.

I said, "Even if you accepted the idea of dominion or authority, authority over something wouldn't typically mean the right to destroy it."

"Well," Steve said ruefully, "the way our provincial government sees things, it obviously does include the right to destroy it. Because it turned out everything those guys were doing was legal. They were killing the bears either from boats or onshore, then skinning them. They'd take the hides, the heads, the paws, plus a few inner organs to sell into the Asian medicine market—which for the most part isn't medicine at all, but just sex stuff, aphrodisiacs—and they'd leave these big, skinless carcasses lying on the beach. It may have been legal, but needless to say, it wasn't right. It was obscene."

Obscenity notwithstanding, the Lawsons and their friends returned home after that first confrontation in what Steve called "a kind of celebratory mood," having made a significant, albeit dark, discovery.

The next day, Steve phoned every newspaper and broadcast journalist he knew. "I thought maybe we'd get a bit of publicity," he said, "and damned if the story didn't take off! The newspapers wanted photos, and within a few days lots of them had run it on their front pages. Friends saw it later in Quebec. My cousins in Ontario heard a radio interview about it from Detroit."

The reports were accompanied by embarrassed mutterings from the B. C. Ministry of the Environment, which called such hunting practices legal but distasteful. "I'm sure it had been going on for years," Steve said, "and probably hundreds, if not thousands, of bears had been slaughtered. We just happened to come across it. Suzanne and I believe issues are presented to us for a reason, so when we're given the opportunity on something like this, we act."

From that point forward, the Lawsons and others concerned about the issue were up at dawn, patrolling the Sound, the inlets, confronting hunters when they came across them. "If you saw a strange boat, you went over and found out what they were doing, made a nuisance of yourself on behalf of the bears," said Steve. "We'd explain to strangers in their boats what we were doing, and most of them were shocked at what was going on and were totally sympathetic—to the point where, gradually, it began to change people. The guide-outfitter himself changed. We always felt he had a good heart—he'd talk to us. Eventually, he didn't want to be in it any more, and he sold out."

At one point, Steve and others were charged with obstructing a legal hunt—in fact, were charged three times for the same incident. Steve was found guilty on all three charges, and was fined five times the highest penalty ever meted out for such an offence. "Which didn't really matter," said Steve, "because I had no intention of paying anyway. I wasn't going to put money representing my time and energy into their effort. The way I saw it, it was they who owed us."

The most dramatic episode in the battle came on a day more than a year after the discovery of the hunt, when friends of the Lawsons happened upon hunters who had killed a bear, and pursued them to the boat launch, where several other protesters also gathered. "These friends saw a fresh bearskin in one of the hunters' boats," Steve said, "and they angled alongside, and one of these guys grabbed the skin, which, because it was fresh, was massively heavy—great big male black bear; it was supposed to be a record size, and probably was. My friend said, 'You so-and-sos may have shot that poor bear, but you're not keeping his hide!' And they backed away in their high-speed Zodiac, and headed out into the inlets, while these hunters stood there with their mouths open. There went the champion trophy that had cost them thousands and thousands of dollars and days of time to acquire."

The Lawsons, as it happened, had been out in their own boat, and were just returning home when they saw their friends converging on the moorage at Wickininnish. "They were very excited," said Steve. "They told us this story, and I told them, 'Well, bring the hide ashore.' I wasn't sure what we'd do with it, but we'd do something."

A few moments later, other acquaintances of the Lawsons who had been protesting the hunt at the boat launch pulled up and demanded the hide. "They thought that somehow the guys who'd taken it had gone too far, had transgressed, probably criminally," Steve said, "and they were there to take the hide back to the hunters. I told them out of the blue, 'Well, the hide's on the island now—it was brought to us freely, it's in our possession, and we're not giving it to you.' It was kinda funny, because we had our laundry in a bag on the beach, and at this point one of these acquaintances marched up and grabbed it, thinking it was the hide, and said, 'I'm taking this back.' I said, 'Oh no, you're not.' And I went and took it from him. And he said, 'What are we going to tell the police?' And I said, 'You tell them that a medicine person is going to do a ceremony with the bear hide, to try to bring all this chaos and absurdity back into balance.' The strange thing was, this was a couple of years before I realized I actually *had* these unexplored roots as a medicine person. I said, 'That's what we're going to do.' And after a lot of hand-wringing and anxiety, they took off, and we went ahead and inadvertently did what people in the old times did when a bear was killed. They honoured it, and held a feast for it."

This was the second time in a little more than a day that Steve had reported unknowingly enacting rituals that had been part of the ways of the ancient Native tribes. I mentioned it to him, and he said that such untutored emulations just reinforced for him that the medicine powers that had come down to him were "right in the DNA, right in the blood." How else, he asked, could it be explained that he had even an inkling of any such rituals?

"We put the bear hide on a sheet of plywood," he said, "and kinda solemnly carried it up to the house, right on inside, and laid it out on the dining room table. And you could tell from the energy coming off it that the spirit of this bear was as angry as hell. Oh, he was testy. There was torment here. In the meantime, we laid out eight place settings, including a setting for the bear, and we all went to work preparing a feast—our family and the two guys who'd brought the hide in. All kinds of food: fruit, rice, salmon, vegetables, nuts, grains, juices, special spices and sauces, preserves. I mean, bears love all foods. And through the whole thing, we expected the RCMP to come busting in and arrest us. But they stayed away, and by the end of it I'll tell you, there was a big, *big* difference in the energy coming off that bear. He was at peace."

At dawn, the Lawsons and their guests put the bear's remains back in the guests' Zodiac, with its twin 200-horsepower outboards, and sped him on his last, fast journey to a secret cave that Steve had discovered years earlier, in the area where the bear had been shot. "It was a place where Native people had obviously done ceremonies with bear skulls and remains—there were bones around," said Steve, "and we put the bear in there where he could be at peace with his ancestors."

———

During the months to come, the Lawsons and others founded what they called "Bear Watch," an ecological and educational tourist service whereby visitors to the area could, for a price, take knowledgeably guided tours up Clayoquot Sound and observe bears in their habitat, in the same way tourists have for years been able to take guided whale-watching tours. "At the same time, we lobbied hard for a change to the laws," said Steve. "So far it's still legal to hunt bears, although the activity has tailed right off in our area, because of our efforts. There's a lot less tolerance for it than there was."

Steve told me that in subsequent months and years, during travels to various parts of Canada, the United States and Mexico (it was in Mexico that I met the Lawsons, in 1996), information and stories about bears would reach the family almost uncannily, virtually everywhere they went. What they learned was that almost all Aboriginal cultures recognize the bear spirit as the protector and healer of the North American continent. "On a spiritual level, that gives a lot more scope to what we're trying to do locally," Steve said. "We're protecting the bears, yes, but also functioning as a kind of locus, one of many, for a deeper sort of healing."

The Lawsons eventually gave up their central role in Bear Watch, for the simple reason that their wireless telephone link with the mainland was not reliable enough for the rising demands of the business. Fortunately, other outfitters in Tofino have taken the business on, so that it continues to operate in conjunction with a variety of whale-watching and eco-tourist operations.

In broader perspective, the Lawsons' concern for the bears has vastly expanded their voice in the environmental dialogue. The First Nations Environmental Network (FNEN), for example, approached Steve and Suzanne in 1995 for their support on issues relating to bears. "We attended a meeting," says Steve, "and found a wonderful group from all across the country—real grassroots, down-to-earth, spiritually connected people who were fighting for environmental issues the same as we were." Today, Steve and Suzanne are FNEN's representatives on the steering committee of the Canadian Environmental Network. "This latter group came to me and asked if I'd represent our Native group," Steve explained. "I said I would as long as Sue and I could go together. We've come to recognize that we work best together, as a unit, and that's important to us. The balance between the male and female entities is out of whack on this planet, has been for some time, and although a lot of work has been done to bring it back into balance—and it's come a long way—there's still a long way to go before things really start to change."

In Steve's cosmology, Earth is an essentially female planet. "Most cultures have tended to think of our planet—and of individual nations, too—as female. During its time of worst imbalance, Germany referred to itself as the Fatherland," he said. "But to everybody else it's always been Mother Earth, Mother Nature, the Motherland. In, say, French and Spanish, Earth is a female noun. Unfortunately, our various cultures have pretty well paved over that essential femaleness, and instead imposed a male character on the planet. Which is very sad, because when the male and female energies are working together, there can be magic, something greater than the sum of the parts. Anyway, I wouldn't have taken this work on—or any work really—without Suzanne."

In their official role, the two travel to Ottawa and further abroad to act as group spokespersons on a range of environmental issues. They have represented FNEN at the United Nations in New York and at other U.S. environmental conclaves, and will represent them at the International Forum on Forestry, in Puerto Rico, and at the United Nations Workshops on Forestry later this year.

"What we're working on," says Steve, "is making a place, clearing space, for traditional Native knowledge to be brought into the discussion of how human beings relate both to one another and to the planet—to bring that lineage of knowledge into play in such a way that it's going to be properly heard and not just tokenized or exploited or ignored."

Steve says the gist of the traditional message is "the importance of balance and dignity in our relationships regarding all things physical and spiritual—the forests, the water, one another, the spirits, including the Great Spirit, everything right up to and including life itself and the striving to walk a good path. If I wanted to help someone understand this," Steve said, "I might use the example of the balance between the hunter and the prey. Few Native elders are going to tell you, don't hunt—they'll say, hunt, but hunt in balance. The best hunters are dreamers, and traditionally the hunter dreams the hunt. Then in the morning, he goes to the place where the dream took place, and the prey is there, waiting, respectful of the hunter and willing to give up its life to feed him and his family, and to clothe them. And the hunter respects the prey even though he takes its life, never looks down on it, never wastes an ounce of it. It's totally balanced. All of which was missing, say, in this pointless slaughter of bears back in the late eighties—or is missing with the elimination of the old forests. Where's the balance?"

As for our human relationships, Steve says, "We trade energy there, too. And again balance is the key. A three-word exchange on the street can leave one person drained and depressed and another uplifted and full of energy. That's imbalance. It's destructive. New energy can be created, but it can come only through the Great Spirit, and only into the heart. That's where we can access it, not through the mind or through logic. Which is why so many people's solutions to the problems we're facing fail—because they address these problems through the rational faculties exclusively."

I asked Steve how bureaucrats and others in Ottawa responded to his and Suzanne's message, and he said, "A lot of it we don't even mention. Essentially, we're bringing a First Nations perspective into the lives and thinking of non-Natives. The Canadian Environmental Network's core funding comes from Environment Canada, so they're always watching over it, and we deal with bureaucrats who pay lip service to us. But the communication of a healthy relationship isn't there yet. That's what we want to make a base for, so the elders and medicine people who we represent, particularly those who have something to bring to the global society, can eventually bring their knowledge, their gift, can bring their part of the equation, and know that it'll be accepted and respected, and that the time is right for it. We believe a time and a place for it will come. We may not be the ones who achieve what we'd like to see happen. That may be left to another generation. But we're preparing the way. For now, it's just terribly important to realize that the knowledge of the old cultures, most of which went underground at a point, is not gone. It's alive, and it's accessible."

The dimensions of Steve's own unique spiritual connection are something he does not claim to fully understand. He has been told and shown that he is connected to a bloodline of medicine people, people with a special gift for healing or wisdom, granted by, and connecting them to, the elemental spirit. "The concept of a medicine person is extremely broad-based," Steve told me. "Old cultures in many parts of the world knew and were guided by such people but had quite different conceptions of who and what they were. Even in different North American Native tribes, medicine people acquired, and acquire, the medicine powers by different means. In a sense, every person has the potential to be a medicine person, has a gift, and it's our life's work to find out what that gift is."

On our second day at Wickininnish, Steve was scheduled to pilot a fourteen-seater Zodiac of tourists up Clayoquot Sound on a five-hour whale-watching expedition, which would include a stop at Hot Springs Cove in Maquinna Provincial Park. A Zodiac is an open motorboat, invented originally for naval use, and constructed essentially of a waist-high inflatable tube that forms the perimeter of the hull. Such boats have a steel or aluminum floor, and, because they are virtually untippable, are often used in tourist transport.

Early in the morning, Oren woke Matt to see if he wanted to go along. At the last minute, after Steve had called the tour company to find out how much room there might be in the boat, I, too, was invited to go, the eighteenth person in a boat designed more or less for sixteen (fourteen passengers, a driver and perhaps a guide). Suzanne opened a quart sealer of the family's private stock of home-canned salmon and quickly made up four or five fat sandwiches on homemade bread. We added chocolate bars and juice at the docks in Tofino, where we picked up both the boat and the tourists—and off we went, each of us in a hooded orange splash suit (awkward but not a tenth as stiff or unruly as the Bayley Survival Suits on the *M. V. Paterson*).

Steve has been bucking the sea on one boat or another since he was a kid, and is recognized as an expert navigator and driver. Even so, in the gusting west wind, we took an occasional spanking and, at the point where we swung out of the protection of the Sound onto the open Pacific, were soaked by two or three sheets of spray that rose off the bow like Saran Wrap and came straight back onto our heads.

As we passed Vargas Island, Steve told me above the roar of the outboards that I should look out for wolves along the beaches. "We've seen quite a few there recently," he called. But on that day, none showed up. Later, he recounted how on a recent visit to the island, he, Suzanne and Oren had been approached by a pair of wolves that had emerged from the woods and had spent several hours in peaceful contact with the family. On yet another occasion, the Lawsons had taken an Ontario family, Dave and Jane Schneider and their children, to Vargas to meet the wolves. The rendezvous had evolved more or less as anticipated, inasmuch as a trio of black and grey wolves, a male and two females, had emerged from the forest, and for an hour or more had mingled with the adults and children in what any observer might have taken for an update on "The Peaceable Kingdom"—people and animals at ease with one another, as if the enormous animals in the mix were kittens or bunnies, rather than the powerful carnivore *Canis lupus*.

Dave Schneider is an experienced woodsman himself, and, perhaps contrary to appearances, admitted later that he had been nervous about the wolves when they had come out of the forest, and had been particularly hesitant about them approaching his children. He said, "I kept thinking, there are my kids, here are these big timber wolves—I'd feel a lot better if my kids were behind me. I figured anything could happen. But it didn't! It was just the most amazing thing to see how placid the wolves were, and how Suzanne and Steve just sat around on the beach totally relaxed."

Suzanne and Steve announced eventually that they had to return to Wickininnish because of a meeting in Tofino that night. "This had been one of the most amazing experiences of my life," Dave said later. "I honestly didn't feel I'd had enough of it at that point, so I told everybody else to start back to the boat—I just wanted to hang around these wolves for a few more minutes."

Suzanne and Steve and the rest went up around the point to where the boat was moored, away from the heavier surf, and were just out of sight when the behaviour of the wolves changed. "Immediately they started pacing," Dave said. "There was an anxiety to it. I thought, Well, you weren't doing that thirty seconds ago. I figured, okay, I'll just get out of here, and I started walking away from them. I'd taken maybe two or three steps when, out of the corner of my eye, I caught just a bit of movement, and I turned. The females had their heads down by this time in a stalking posture. I'd barely started walking again when the big male came right at me, just kind of hip-checked me from behind, hit me pretty hard. Fortunately, I didn't go down, or I figure they would have been all over me. This big guy was growling, oh, he had his fangs bared, and I was yelling at him to calm down, settle down, back off." Within seconds, Steve reappeared around the rocks, immediately restoring the wolves' passivity. "I wouldn't have believed it if I hadn't seen it," Dave said. "But Steve's effect on this big male was to completely reverse his aggressive behaviour. I just walked away with Steve, left the wolves slinking back into the woods."

It is a sad footnote to the story that, during the summer of 2000, several of the wolves on Vargas Island, which is, in fact, a provincial preserve, were shot by officials of the B. C. Ministry of Natural Resources, because of their unpredictable behaviour in the presence of sea kayakers who stay periodically on the island's shores. At the time, I was unable to reach Steve and Suzanne to discuss the wolves' deaths. But I spoke to our mutual friend Anne Gardner about it, and she told me more or less what I had expected to hear: that the Lawsons had been angered and offended by the killings. "Oh, it was sad," Anne said. "And of course it played right into Steve and Suzanne's belief that these wildlife officers aren't there for the nurturing of the wildlife but simply to eliminate it if it becomes an inconvenience."

At the provincial docks at Hot Springs Cove, Steve stayed with the boat, while Oren, Matt and I hiked through the rain forest to the springs, which pool in the mouth of a mountain stream on the precipitous outer shore of the point that forms the local harbour. The hot springs are umbrellaed by mist and send delicate scarves of vapour into the crowns of the surrounding cedars and firs. They must have been an exotic resource for the early tribes— possibly a holy or healing place, certainly a hot bath—even though the water is far too sulphurous and mineral-laden to drink, except maybe in medicinal doses.

I left Oren and Matt stewing playfully in the hot fountains with a boatload of foreign-speaking tourists and, mildly unnerved by a sign warning of cougars, returned alone to the boat through a kilometre or so of rain forest. I found Steve lying on the dock in the sun, his head propped on the mooring rail, gazing at the sky and treetops, where eight or ten bald eagles rode the air currents without moving a wing muscle.

As we lay there in a low-level euphoria induced by sun and air and sound—not to mention the broader freedoms of the after-noon—Steve told me, among other things, that, several years ear-lier, he had been involved in an international conference on the environment, near Tofino. Having wandered onto the beach one day for a break, he had thrown his head back, thrown his arms wide and, in his words, "asked the Great Spirit simply to use me in whatever way he might have in store. When I opened my eyes," he said, "there were no eagles in view, but a single eagle's feather, from an immature eagle, was fluttering down out of the sky." Steve picked it up feeling that, in some way, it represented not only his spirit connection to the species but his yet-unformulated role as a person of medicine and healing.

One of the last things Steve told me before the return of the tourists was that, over the years, along with the eagle, the killer whale had been a significant part of his spirit guide. Against the muted lapping of the Pacific, he described a twenty-year-old dream in which he had envisioned himself sitting on a hillside overlooking the sea, where five or six killer whales were up on their tails, in a line, their bodies out of the water, dancing to a beguiling, mantra-like drum beat. One of Steve's graces is his capability to be sincere without being sanctimonious about even those things that mean most to him. So when I told him that what he was describing sounded like a conga line, he just laughed and said, "something like that," and proceeded to explain that, as the dream had unfolded, he had had an increasing sense of the importance of his learning the cadence. "I still know the beat perfectly after twenty years," he said, and he began to tap it out with his fingers on the dock. "I was up on the hillside happily imitating what the whales were doing, kinda moving from side to side, but it was clear, too, that I had a responsibility to do something with this knowledge I was receiving."

Before the dream ended, Steve said, he looked behind and realized there were hundreds of people on the hill above him, and that all of them were picking up the rhythm from his own interpretation of it. He said, "It wasn't until we went up against the government at Meares Island that I could see the significance of the dream."

As recorded in an earlier part of this book, Steve confronted the government not only at Meares Island but at Sulphur Pass and Strathcona Park, and at numerous other showdowns and negotiations, and was inspirational in the drive to preserve the whole of Clayoquot Sound. A taxi-boat driver at Tofino told me that Steve is one of the most respected people in the West Coast environmental movement and, on the strength of his commitment, one of the most feared.

Steve said, "The whole effort at Meares was extremely demanding, and necessitated us breaking through what had seemed an impenetrable barrier—pushing past industry and government, through public apathy and fear, to bring a higher value both to the people and to the land."

In the wake of that first standoff, Steve realized that on a spiritual level his dream had been a kind of "power source" for him, and that the drum beat signalled his connection to the spirit. "The dream as a whole showed me that I was to lead," he said, "that I was to take my connection to the spirit and spread it to those around me. I guess you could say it gave me the courage and strength to do what needed to be done."

Chapter Twelve

t about the same time Steve Lawson was dreaming of killer whales on the west coast of Vancouver Island, a southern Ontario tavern owner named Murray Monk, a man of approximately Steve's age, was experiencing an epochal wilderness dream of his own.

Like Steve's dream, Murray Monk's would influence his course for years to come. "I woke up one day," Murray told me, "and I knew that if my life was going to work out, if I was going to survive, I had to move north—had to have a different life."

While the two dreamers' respective oracles have, in the years since, led them in radically different philosophic directions, they have also at times led them onto paths of apparent common ground.

On a day in 1982, Murray acted on his dream by divesting himself of life in the most populous part of the country and moving 1500 kilometres to the north shore of Lake Superior, at Nipigon, Ontario.

Seven years later, he took his dream a step further, cut every tie that bound him, including his $72,000-a-year job as a northern millwright and union man, and devoted himself exclusively to Canada's most ancient industrial endeavour.

In the years since, he has transformed himself into one of the most knowledgeable and influential trappers in Canada.

———

One day in late March 2000, I drove out to Nipigon to spend a day with Murray in his skinning shed—to discover, if I could, something of the state of the culture's longest-standing tie to the land and its life forms. The shed sits within thirty metres of the Trans-Canada Highway on Nipigon's northernmost fringe and is an almost Smithsonian collection of the implements, images and (if the pun can be endured) trappings of the contemporary fur trade. On its walls and floor—and hanging from its rafters—are, among other things, snare wire, fur stretchers, skinning beams, traps, culinary supplies, survival garments, plus a collection of knives that look as if they had been liberated from an eighteenth-century surgical ward. There are stubby little "skinners," and double-handled "fleshers" and vicious-looking "pelters"—plus Murray's all-time favourite, a kind of hybrid of switchblade and straight razor with a five-hundred-dollar surgical steel blade that he can open and close with his right hand without having to free his left.

The shed's smell is a quite pleasant mix of wood-stove and tobacco smoke, cut with the heavy, gamy musk that is the olfactory signature of skinning and of the prepared hides of wolf, lynx, marten, mink, fisher, weasel, fox, muskrat and squirrel, all of which sway, tails down, from overhead racks to the right of the door as you go in. Further in are waist-high stacks of perfectly oval beaver pelts, as yet untanned and as stiff as the plywood on which they were shaped and dried.

An array of sub-fragrances emanate from, say, the hanging sheaves of tobacco that Murray grows to stoke his eighty-cigarette-a-day habit; and the pile of split birch by the wood stove; and the clusters of what appear to be dried figs above the work bench, but are in fact bunches of the sweet-smelling castor gland of the beaver. The gland is a rear-located sac of dischargeable fragrance, which, in the highly territorial world of the beaver, is used by the animal to "paint" a border around its territory, beyond which only a very foolish or very brave beaver will dare trespass. For hundreds of years, castor glands were a valuable market commodity, prized especially by the perfume trade, most recently at more than fifty dollars a pound. But they have been worthless since the perfumeries turned to other sources, most of them synthetic, in response to lobbying from the anti-fur movement.

Murray calls the glands "beaver bags" or "beaver nuts" and, for my benefit, pulled one down, twisted it open and gave me a whiff of the latex-like orangy-yellow taffy inside. The material smells sweetly of distilled birch and poplar—is in fact so fragrant and appealing, you could quite happily stuff a "bag" in your coat pocket for future reference, or even hang it on a cord around your neck. Murray said, "One old trapper I knew used to cut a piece off every morning and chew it with his chewing tobacco. And he'd throw a piece in the stew, too. Used to say we'd all live forever if we did it."

On the shed's plywood walls, there are perhaps half a dozen fur-industry promotional posters, two of them showing apparently naked young women lounging in voluminous lynx and fisher "Northern Supreme" coats, either of which, Murray said, would set a buyer back approximately the price of a high-end import car.

Within minutes of my arrival, Murray guided me though his hanging thicket of furs, explaining which was a mink, which a fisher, which an otter or marten. He told me among other things that it takes seventy marten to make a full-length coat, and that by the time the garment reaches the fur salons of Bloor Street or Fifth Avenue, it has been artfully reinvented as "sable." A mink coat requires seventy-five pelts, and while the coat might sell for

$30,000 or $40,000, the trapper gets no more than $2,500 for the raw furs. Murray told me that a squirrel skin is worth $1.50, a muskrat $3, and a weasel $5.75, although weasel skins have at times fetched as much as $17 or as little as seventy-five cents. "The Queen of England," he said, "is the only person in the world with a full-length weasel coat."

A fridge in the middle of the shed held a large bottle of Clamato juice, a 130-ounce can of "barbecue" baked beans, several cans of beer, and, chockablock with everything else, a dozen or more dewy-looking, rough-skinned beaver pelts, rolled about the size of footballs, awaiting their fine skinning.

At about 11 A.M., Murray took a pelt out of the refrigerator, unfurled it like a prayer rug, and spread it, inside out, across a torpedo-shaped poplar "beam." He put on a full-length black rubber coroner's apron and, over top, a cloth apron deeply embedded with old blood and grease, the better to grip the pelt as he held it against the beam with his abdomen. He then picked up his double-handled "flesher," tested its edge against a hair on his forearm, and, looking increasingly like something out of an Inquisitional nightmare, went to work.

In no time, an unbroken veil of translucent flesh and fat was cascading down off the interior of the hide. "A good beaver pelt is worth fifty-five dollars," Murray told me as he worked. "A poor one that's all scarred up might be worth eight or ten." The world of the beaver, as Murray puts it, is "pretty much a constant war over territory," and whereas some beaver will fight other beaver to the death, some run at the first sign of a battle. "I can always tell the character of the beaver I'm skinning," Murray said. "The aggressor has his scars up front on his shoulders; the wuss is all bit up on the backside. This one's a yellow-belly," he said pointing to three or four lumpish scars where the chisel-like teeth of a dominant foe had penetrated to the interior of the hide. "Sometimes I'll see a bear-claw scar in a pelt," he said. "Beaver are food for bears— they're slow-moving, very vulnerable when they go up on land to cut a tree. That's why they build dams, to move water to the trees.

It's both easier and safer to move a tree through water. A beaver's almost like a fish in water—with that powerful tail, it has a big advantage over any animal, including a bear or a human being. It just comes up underneath, sinks its teeth into the animal's groin and takes it down."

———

Murray is perhaps six foot four, with a thick head of reddish-brown hair, and an equally thick beard stained with nicotine and, at times, flecked with tobacco. His "smoking" fingers are the colour of Pears soap, and his fingernails are impacted with the inevitable residue of the trade. When I asked about his past, he declared, as if reciting lines from a script, that he was born on the last day of the Second World War near Hanover, Ontario, and that when he was six days old, his mother stood up smiling to greet his dad, who had entered the room where she lay in bed, and fell dead of a blood clot. "At school," he said, "it was as if my teachers wanted to kill everything in me I loved best: geography, geology, history, biology, all that sort of thing."

During the sixties and seventies, Murray served what he called "a six-year sentence" as a junior executive for Eaton's of Canada. When he paroled himself in 1972, he bought into a tavern in Bradford, Ontario, and operated it with a partner for ten years.

Murray is an almost mythically diligent ladies' man, if not husband, and along the way he acquired both girlfriends and wives, or let us say "wives"—at latest count, two officially, three minus the ring (with the stats in either category showing no signs of stabilizing). On the day I visited him, he was morosely between partners, and commented several times on his loneliness and what he called "the need in the world for love." All of which is not to say that he is by nature unfaithful or promiscuous. "I'd say I lost four women because I gave too much to trapping. I stayed away too long. We grew apart, or someone moved in while I was gone."

To pay the bills when he came north in 1982, Murray took a job in the Domtar pulp mill at Red Rock, near Nipigon, and, before long, had seriously injured his legs in a mill accident. Today, his knees are so bad—"bone on bone," as he puts it—that he cannot bend to tie his shoelaces and, as a consequence, wears children's coiled elastic laces, glitter-coated, in his "skinning" Nikes.

He became a union rep at the mill, then a national rep, and began touring the country, organizing locals, writing first contracts and working an occasional week in the mill back home. He rigged his work schedule so that he got sixty days off every fall to accommodate his burgeoning love of trapping.

But he was not happy. "By 1989," he said, "almost everything I earned was being swallowed up by my ex-wives, who, as far as I could see, were doing a hell of a lot better than I was." He was stressed. He was in heavy physical pain. There were days when he smoked a hundred cigarettes and, by his own acknowledgement, didn't care whether he lived or died.

It was on exactly such a day during the winter of 1989 that he made the life-saving decision to quit everything and to return to the land.

By spring, he was trapping and skinning full-time. In the name of self-sufficiency, he quadrupled the size of his garden, began raising chickens, grew tobacco, cut firewood, and reduced costs in a variety of quietly subversive ways. He points out, for example, that of the five buildings on his property, three were built at less than one hundred square feet of floor space, so that they did not require building permits and thus did not have to conform to costly building codes. On the day I visited him, he traded a load of firewood for necessary repairs on his septic system. "A guy gave me a pig a while back," he told me. "I gave him some muskrats to eat and cleaned some skins for him."

Murray recycles almost unto parody, going so far as to use his Kleenex tissues twice—once to blow, once to soak up whatever needs soaking up on his skinning-shed floor. He built his entire skinning shed out of four dollars' worth of scrap lumber, much of it from the local plywood mill. But his personal economies and professional ethics perhaps best coalesce in his scrupulous recycling of animal carcasses. He seldom leaves one for the ravens. Because of its oiliness and superior olfactory appeal, beaver meat is a highly effective trap bait, so that much of what Murray traps goes back out on the line. He also boils dozens of carcasses a year for dog and cat food, and cooks a few for himself. He has eaten numerous varieties of wild animal flesh and says, for example, that lynx tastes like chicken, while muskrat, which I too have eaten, is like wild duck, in that the animal's diet of tender pond shoots is pretty much identical to that of, say, a mallard.

As we pondered these things, I told Murray that my late father-in-law, Bill Carpick, a lifelong trapper in northern Manitoba, had at times used Chanel No. 5 perfume for trap bait, and had at other times used soiled "feminine hygiene" products (his cache of which he showed me once, stored in a Ziploc bag). Murray knew about "perfume and Tampax," and said the former was good for lynx and the latter for bears, which he said were "crazy" for the smell of menstrual discharge. He told me that during his days as a tavern-owner, he had known a bear wrestler, whose "pet" bear once broke into the wrestler's house while his wife was menstruating, and "ate up most of her mid-section," killing her before the wrestler arrived and shot him.

"The irony of all this," Murray reported, "is that I grew to love trapping so much, got so close and committed to it, that I ended up getting distracted away from it—I couldn't help it." Indeed, it seems inevitable that a man of Murray's inclinations—much talk, much passion—should eventually have been drawn into the fulminating politics of fur. He had been trapping full-time for barely four years when he was elected president of the Ontario Fur Managers Federation. Two years ago he was elected president of the Canadian Trappers Alliance, which represents tens of thousands of Canada's registered trappers. As a result, he has spent much of the past two years on the road—in Europe and all over North America—dealing with trappers' issues, protecting their rights, promoting trapping and the fur trade, and working directly with trappers to advise them on both safety and productivity. One of Murray's colleagues told me that, as a result of his work, Murray has for several years been "the most powerful and best-known man in Canadian trapping."

Murray has the uncanny ability while smoking to talk, work, inhale, exhale, relight, perhaps even eat, without ever removing the cigarette from his mouth. But he removed it now, wrenched himself to full height, and said, "I've succeeded in the politics of fur because I tell it like it is. I'm not afraid of the risks, and I can't be bought. Last year, my cousin Fred said to me, 'Murray, some of the family scorn you for your marriages and divorces and your whore's life. Everybody knows you loved fast and loved many, and nobody would believe what you are in the north today by the way you grew up. But you know as well as I do that all your kicks in the nuts, the school of hard knocks, everything, has made you what you are and has put you up on the podium and sent you around the world fighting the battles.' "

Like the beaver, the fur industry itself is in a war over territory these days. And for the most part, that territory is shrinking. "One damn country after another goes anti on us," said Murray, "cuts us right off at the knees." On this spring day, it bugged Murray greatly that Holland, Canada's long-time friend from the Second World War, had officially outlawed Canadian furs—and, what's more, had become a front-line global proponent of the anti-fur lobby. "Canadian soldiers are lying dead in their graveyards," he protested, "and they have the audacity to prevent our trappers from making a living."

But Murray's argument with the Dutch was as much about hypocrisy as ingratitude. "Last year," he said, "the government of Holland paid exterminators $34 million to take a hundred thousand muskrats out of the big earthen dykes that hold back the sea on Holland's coast. See, the muskrats dig into them and ruin them, allow the sea in on the tulips. The deceit is, they're telling us we can't trap, while they're poisoning muskrats, putting them through an agonizing death that no registered trapper in Canada would even dream of inflicting on an animal."

Murray lit a rollie, inhaled, and exhaled perhaps a cubic metre of smoke. He said, "I'll grant you, making money off of death is not nice. Never was. Then again, the highways are paved with dead animals, roadkill, and you don't hear anybody complaining that we should get rid of cars. I don't have statistics, but I'd be willing to bet there are a lot more animals killed on the roads in this country every day than there are by trappers. I mean, there are often two or three dead animals out on the highway right within sight of the shed here. And there are a lot more killed by industry, in the form of habitat removal and contamination. And there are a thousand times as many killed by the slaughterhouses. And we're not even counting the fisheries and the poultry farms. So going after trappers is just a lot of selective hypocrisy. You might as well get a garment for the death of an animal, as opposed to just a smear of guts or a PCB-riddled skeleton in the wilderness somewhere."

———

At a point during the afternoon, Murray's friend Neil Cedarwall came in with a dozen or so rough-skinned hides for Murray to clean up. With Murray, Neil conducts government-mandated courses in the art and science of trapping. "We teach humane trapping, quick killing, and dignity to the animal," he said. "We're even teaching on the reserves now."

I remarked on the irony of whites teaching Natives about trapping, and Murray said, "They were the originals, but they, too, need reminding these days. People say to me, 'Oh, the early Natives had to trap for survival. You don't have to.' And I tell them I have to survive just as much as anybody else ever did, and if my critics think I'd be doing the world a favour by surviving in the mine or the pulp mill or on the farm, rather than on the trapline, all I can say is they've been drinking too much polluted water. If more people lived as close to the land as I do, and were as protective as I am of six hundred square kilometres of it [the size of Murray's trapline], the planet would be in a hell of a lot better shape than it is. And the animals would be a lot happier, too. Whadda people think, that if I don't trap them they lounge around out there thinking about their retirement? The carnage of nature makes what I do look like a picnic."

Murray has a widespread reputation as a "humane" trapper and in the interest of the quick kill, spends days every summer boiling and cleaning his traps "to get the grease and the rust off." Then he dyes and waxes them, so that they will "throw" quietly, "more like wood than like metal. I dye them different colours, depending on whether they're going onto rock, or soil, or snow. Cleaning them keeps them fast—trapping's dangerous enough without sluggish, unpredictable traps."

Trapping can, in fact, sometimes be as dangerous for the trapper as for the trapped—with the result that, at every trappers' meeting, there is a minute's silence in which those in attendance are invited to remember colleagues who have died in the wilds. "I need every second of that minute just to go through the names of the guys I know who've given their lives to it," says Murray. "They drown, they freeze, they have accidents, they have heart attacks and die lying in a snowdrift looking up at the stars."

Murray can name three occasions on which trapping nearly cost him his own life—two of them in what he refers to as the Cosgrove Triangle, an exceptional segment of the immense wilds of his trapline north of Nipigon. "The triangle is very much a mystic place," he told me. "A sanctuary for breeding—it's wooded, untouched, full of wildlife, lots of moose, always very tranquil. I walk in there just to watch the animals and birds, not to hunt or trap. There's an old trapper's lean-to in there—in fact, it's right at that lean-to that I've twice gotten deathly sick with some kind of unexplainable illness."

On one occasion, several years ago, Murray was so heavily hit by the mystery sickness—"got so weak so fast," as he puts it—that he could hardly walk back to his snow machine a few hundred metres away. "When I got to it," he says, "I lay down—which you never do. Freezing is a nice death, very alluring, and at thirty below it

CHARLES WILKINS

won't take long. So you have to resist. I came round just in time to
turn on the machine and get out to my truck. At the truck, once
again, all I wanted to do was sleep, let them find me—of course,
they won't find you till July."

Half a dozen times on the highway, Murray had to convince
himself not to pull over and sleep. "Nobody's going to stop for
you these days," he said. "I fought unconsciousness all the way
home, walked through the front door and collapsed. Woke up in
the hospital the next day. But they could never diagnose anything.
The thing is, I've got topographical maps, satellite maps, logging
maps—none of them shows anything unusual in the area where I
got sick. But on my geologist's map—my 'green map,' as they call
it—there's a spot that shows a unique rock formation, right where
that lean-to is. Is it magnetite? Is it uranium? Maybe there's some
sort of gas coming out of the ground. I've found gold in there, lots
of things, but I'm not up on my minerals, and I hate to draw official attention to it by inquiring. Before you know it the Ministry
of Natural Resources has a plaque on it, and somebody's taking
eco-tourists out there to buy knick-knacks at the boutique."

———

At a point during the afternoon, Murray and I took a tour of his
property, a kind of backwoods fantasia that may some day fascinate
or stump the archaeologists. A toilet bowl and tank sit on the rise
by the main dwelling, behind which stand a chicken coop and a
drying shack for, among other things, tobacco, garlic and herbs.
And a disconnected satellite dish; and a mountain of buck-length
birch logs; and oodles of rusted-out machinery; and a couple of
old truck campers that Murray identified as belonging to
"Grumpy" or "Lumpy," or somebody. I said to him, "You seem to
know a lot of people by one name only," and he said, "In the bush
you only need one name."

Outside the door to the skinning shed sat a twenty-litre pail
filled to the brim with stringy-looking beaver meat about the
colour of strawberry twizzlers. When I arrived in the morning, a

pair of kick-ass ravens was standing by the pail taking turns jumping onto it and tearing out gobs of protein.

Two or three times a day a pair of weasels enter the shed from somewhere beneath the floorboards, devour whatever scraps of meat they can find, and glance invincibly at their skinned cousins at the far end. "I used to trap them if they got in here," Murray told me. "I didn't like 'em; they ate my chickens. But then I got mice, which chew up the fur, and I needed a weasel or two to pick them off. So, they have free rein in here, and they know it. They're so tame that, when I'm on the phone, they come right up onto my knee and just sit there."

I watched off and on all day, waiting for them to appear, and finally caught a glimpse of a tiny beige dart—actually an elongated "droplet"—that didn't so much walk or run from behind the stove as flow, stopping occasionally, raising its savage little snout, and glaring around with eyes that have become for me the new definition of "beady."

The details of Murray's life are picturesque, anachronistic and, at times, inherently fascinating. On the surface, they are about trapping, politics and cartoon eccentricity. But they are also a consideration of the wider world of nature: of animals, of ecology, of how human beings relate to animals, and how animals relate to one another—in effect, a consideration of the same issues that are faced daily by Steve and Suzanne Lawson from their vastly different perspective.

In the ironic way that fire consumes trees but ultimately preserves forests, trapping is for Murray a means both of claiming and of preserving the wilderness and animals he loves. "That's what I believe," he says. But knowing that some might find the view arguable, or even offensive, he is eminently prepared to defend and rationalize it. "Does trapping deplete animal populations?" he asks with Socratic vigour, and proceeds to explain that, on the contrary, it *builds* populations. "Disease, overpopulation and shortage of food will devastate a species in an area," he says. "We as human beings should understand this. Look at certain Third World countries—starvation, disease, overpopulation. Animals suffer from those things, too." A trapper, Murray says, would be unable to trap the last animal in an area even if he wanted to. "The only thing that'll get the last one is disease. And overpopulation is one of the most prevalent causes of disease. If you get a diseased beaver at the headwaters of, say, the Jackpine River, it'll kill every beaver in that river chain."

Murray's trapline is a compelling lesson in his brand of conservation. It is immediately south of a line that has not been trapped for some time. "Mine is trapped heavily," he says. "I take up to two hundred marten a year. Some trappers only take fifteen or twenty. The old guy who trapped my line before I did didn't take many, so I started by taking seventeen or eighteen. Then thirty-one. Then forty-four. Right up to two hundred. The more you take, the more there are to take. Look at beaver. If any animal was ever going to be trapped into extinction, it would be that one. We've been harvesting them heavily for three hundred years, and there are more of them today than there were at the height of the fur trade." A recent visitor to Murray's trapline pointed out that there was "almost a line in the snow" between Murray's trapping territory and the trapline adjacent to it. "When you drive off my line, the animal tracks just disappear, or go way down in number," Murray said. "On my side there are tracks all over the place: fox, weasel, rabbit, wolf, lynx. When you hit that line, leaving my place, it's like a dead zone. If some government biologist could see my trapline, they'd have to throw the quotas they impose on me right out the window."

Asked for a layman's explanation, Murray responded that removing predators from the food chain allows not just prey to thrive, but other predators—of all species. "An adult lynx will eat 250 rabbits a year," he said. "If I trap one lynx, it not only frees up all those rabbits for, say, foxes and marten, but it allows more food for other lynx. So lynx thrive. And so do foxes and marten. In years when there's too little food, adult marten eat their young. Lynx don't even bear their young if they can't feed them—they abort naturally, sometimes seven or eight years in a row. There are years when I've seen wolves and deer dead of starvation, and bears so hungry they're breaking down cabin doors. But not where I trap. There, everybody's got food. If I see lots of lynx tracks, I'll take more lynx. Same with, say, foxes."

Nature, Murray says, works in seven-year cycles. "Populations of wolves, for example, will peak every seven years, and then decline, sometimes almost to nothing. What I'm doing, in effect, is taking off the highs and lows of the cycle—managing so that all the populations stay strong. Mind you, if I stop trapping, there are going to be problems. That's why I'm no fan of the fairweather trapper. The committed trapper is a caretaker of nature. I'm out there trapping even when the prices go into the tank. Lots of years I lose money. But if we don't keep doing it, we're not going to have the populations."

———

Late in the afternoon, I asked Murray if he could predict what lay in store for the beaver pelts he had worked on that day. "These are good ones," he said without hesitation. "After they're tanned, they'll go to Europe, probably Germany or Austria, where they'll be put on a vacuum plater and sheared right down, so that they look and feel like velvet. Then they'll be dyed—purple, black, white, you name it."

The wearing of fur has, to a degree, always been about appearances. But these days it is more often than not about false appearances— "deceptions," says Murray. "They make the fake stuff look real, the real stuff look fake. By the time these become a garment, Bob Barker and Brigitte Bardot and the other hypocrites in the anti-fur movement won't know whether to spray them or not, because they won't know if they're an animal or if they're plastic!"

One of the trade's more successful deceptions of recent years was developed by Canadian fur designer Paula Lishman, who buys some ninety thousand high-grade beaver pelts a year at auction. "She's married to Bill Lishman, the guy who guides the geese in his ultralight," reported Murray. "They made a movie about him, *Fly Away Home*. She sells furs, and he's an animal lover. It's a good example of what can happen when two people respect one another's points of view."

Paula's gig is to cut her beaver pelts into what Murray calls "mile-long shoelaces," which she dyes a variety of colours before knitting the strands into garments. "The fur comes out on both sides of the knitting," Murray explained. "It's as light as a feather, but has the warmth and the beauty of fur." An additional advantage to the wearer, of course, is that nobody can tell she (or he) is wearing an animal skin—except for Paula Lishman and the likes of Murray Monk, who says that what makes him "so damn crotchety about the need for subversion is that while the antis are raging against us, damning us as killers and heathens, the fake-fur industry that they support is busy filling the world up with its plastics and acrylics, and so on, which are non-biodegradable and non-renewable. If you leave fur outside for even a few days, the bugs and micro-organisms are into it—it's programmed to return completely and harmlessly to nature. Meanwhile, the manufacturing of synthetics kills kids in Third World countries, destroys landscapes and villages, blows horrible chemicals into the air, destroys the ozone layer. Do you think any of these companies that make this stuff care half as much as I do about what's really going on with the environment—here, or in Mexico, or China?"

As Murray revved up on the subject, he ceased work and simply stood by his table, gesturing with preacherly gusto as his congregation of one sat by the stove, nodding. "You tell me what's ethical here!" he said. "This is no simple issue, and the antis have been able to convince a lot of simple-minded people that it is."

————————

Several times during the weeks after my visit with Murray Monk, I heard him and his fellow trappers referred to as "a dying breed." ("I know a lotta people who hope we are," Murray responded when I told him.) But the breed is far from dead yet. At the moment there are some eighty-five thousand registered trappers in Canada, harvesting some $100 million worth of furs annually. "And by the time those furs hit the salons," Murray said, "they're easily worth a billion." So trappers are not exactly an economic nonentity.

Still, the value of the trade is not what it was. Today, there are fewer than six thousand registered trappers in Ontario (about half of them Native), while at one time there were seventeen thousand. "That was in the days of the thousand-dollar lynx," said Murray, in reference to an animal whose skin is now valued at about sixty-five dollars.

Certainly, no one in the business will deny the efficacy of the anti-fur lobby. Yet the industry as a whole still affects a million jobs, including trap makers, fur graders, tannery workers, coat designers, stitchers, retailers, advertisers and, less obviously, the snow-machine makers and dealers, the wilderness outfitters, the government administrators and others, at least part of whose livelihood depends on those who go into the wilds to bring back skins.

Murray recently resigned the presidencies of both the Ontario Fur Managers Federation and the Canadian Trappers Alliance, so that he can concentrate on trapping. But he is not going without fanfare. Last winter, his regional trapping association named him their Trapper of the Year, and the OFMF presented him with its highest annual award—to the Ontario resident who, in a given year, has "done the most for trapping and for the fur industry." Murray's second stated reason for quitting the busy political life is that he would like to find love—"and to give love," he says. "Sometimes I think the ideal woman would be one you could have beside you on the trapline. And yet you need that time alone

————————

with Mother Nature, too, when you're not dealing with business or marital concerns or phones. Men and women both need it, of course. And I intend to get it."

Murray's six-hundred-square-kilometre trapline spreads east off the ancient basalt palisades that rise on the southeast bay of Lake Nipigon, about 150 kilometres north of Lake Superior. "We're not just talking forest," he said to me. "We're talking wilderness. Big trees, undisturbed lakes—holy ground. I'm the only person out there these days, but it wouldn't surprise me if there'd been human habitation there off and on for five or six thousand years before I came along. I've found arrowheads, pottery, old copper, gem-stones, even the remains of old graves."

Murray intends to spend not just time but eternity on the site and, when the time (or absence of time) comes, has arranged to have his ashes sprinkled from the basalt cliffs along the west side of his line. He has a gravestone picked out and will transport it to the site this summer, for future reference. "There are people I can get to sprinkle my ashes," he said. "My problem is that if I die out there, as I probably will someday, there may not be anybody to come and get me. And the food chain makes pretty quick work of a carcass that lies around for too long."

To encourage quick interest in his remains—interest at least from human beings—Murray carries a one-hundred-dollar bill on his person at all times, and lets the fact be known to all and sundry, with the hope that, if he "turns up missing one day," some cash-hungry soul will head out to get him, for the money if for no other reason.

At the risk of being a party-pooper, I asked if he didn't think that, these days, even the most venal mercenary would have to be awfully "cash-hungry" to go out on such a dreary mission for a hundred dollars.

"With inflation," he submitted, "I'm probably going to have to raise the stakes. I guess my hope is I'll be found by a friend who isn't in it for the money, and the money'll just cover some expenses."

As I was preparing to leave, Murray said, "Really, I'd like to stay out there year-round. I could do it with great pleasure."

Apparently savouring the thought, he turned to the fridge, lifted a Budweiser from the door, and extracted another beaver pelt. He advised me that there weren't many guys who had both "the skill and the will" for a long-term venture in the wilderness. But he felt he was one of them.

Then he unrolled the pelt. "Look at this guy," he said quietly. "No scars on the backside. That's my kinda beaver." And, having sipped at his beer and retied his apron, he threw the pelt on the skinning beam, picked up his knife and went to work.

Chapter Thirteen

bout ten years after Murray Monk came into the north—"into the country," as they say in Alaska—I myself took the plunge, moving north from southern Ontario. For nearly a decade now, the city of Thunder Bay and its vast uncivilized surroundings have been a kind of stage set for my life and imagination, not to mention the stimulus and setting for much of my writing, including twenty or more magazine articles, hundreds of CBC Radio commentaries and several books. The writing is a testament to what I know and like best about this part of Canada: Lake Superior, the forests, the inland lakes, the old mountains, the wildlife—and of course the people, most of whom have, in one way or another, been dreamed and dealt, and sometimes damned, by the landscape they inhabit.

Not everyone shares my enthusiasm for the territory. At a recent Christmas gathering, a 250-pound drunk in a hand-finished black suit said to me, "Are you the jerk who used to talk on the radio?"

When I acknowledged that I had at one time talked on the

radio, he said, "Well, I dunno how *anybody* can say the things you say about this godforsaken part of the country." He went on to tell me, in more or less these words, that the rock up here is too hard, the lakes too cold, the summers too short, the mosquitoes too numerous, the distances too far, the winters too long . . .

Realizing at a point that he was at least not going to knock my teeth out, I said, "If you hate it so much, why do you live here?"

"I live here," he said, glaring at me as if at some small, alien insect, "because it's my home!"

———

While hindsight provides an unquestionable tracery of one's fate, I could have reported at any time over the years that, since the period during my late teens when I spent two or three weeks at a stretch hitchhiking the Trans-Canada, I had felt a deep attraction for the land and water along Lake Superior's north shore. At a point in perhaps September 1971, in the shadow of the roadside palisades that look out over the lake just east of Thunder Bay, I recall telling my then-girlfriend and hitchhiking partner that if life worked out for me (I was still green enough to imagine life did such things for people), I felt I would somehow, someday, live beside Lake Superior.

At another time, alone, unable to get a ride at perhaps midnight, near Nipigon, I remember thinking it the most natural development in the world simply to walk down the right-of-way within sight of the lake, unroll my sleeping bag and crawl in for the night.

In light of those early stirrings, the phone call I got in April 1991, asking if I'd be interested in becoming writer-in-residence at the Thunder Bay Public Library, seemed less an invitation than a long-delayed confirmation of this sense of where my life would eventually lead.

In late September of that year, we packed our old blue station wagon until the tailgate bulged, stacked the roof with anything that would take the weather and, as we rolled west along the Trans-Canada, must have presented a passable approximation of

———

the Joads, or even the Beverly Hillbillies, on their westward push to the New Jerusalem. The library had rented us what they described to me as a "furnished house"—described quite generously, as it turned out, in that the total furnishings, stretched across seven rooms, consisted of a vintage Arborite table and a single wingback chair. But the absence of distractions inside invited emphasis on the more permanent furnishings outside—particularly on the view, which took in immense tracts of wilderness, three-hundred-metre cliffs, ships at harbour, and perhaps 150 square kilometres of Lake Superior.

We took not just to the view but to the viewed: to long drives and hikes along the lakeshore, to Ouimet Canyon, to the Sibley Peninsula and the three-hundred-year-old pine forest at Greenwood Lake. We visited our friends' rural saunas, and cross-country skied.

For me, at least, one of the unfashionable pleasures of the move was that, after seventeen years of relative exile—in the Bahamas for a year, on the prairies for a dozen, in southern Ontario for four—I was back on a part of the planet where I could pick decent quantities of wild blueberries. The foraging of my childhood was a timid match for the primitive satisfaction of getting out on a logging cutover north of Thunder Bay on a morning in late August or early September, wandering the edge lands and logging roads, hearing the ravens, and speculating on the presence of bears, moose, foxes, wolves and lynx. And of course picking blueberries—not by the quart as we did in Muskoka during the late 1950s, but by the five-gallon pail. On the Labour Day weekend of our second summer here, my wife and Matt and I picked ten six-quart baskets in the timber clearings out along the Armstrong Highway. An acquaintance and his family picked a *hundred* baskets in two days near Ignace, Ontario. The operative word for good berries in these parts is "lovely." Exceptional berries are "the size of grapes." It is pleasingly symmetrical that the grapes grown north of Superior—the lovingly tended few that make it through to maturity—are the size of blueberries.

In December 1993, we added a daughter, Georgia. And a year later another, Eden. I remember thinking it well-omened that the room at the Port Arthur General Hospital in which Georgia was born had a striking view of the icy harbour and lake.

In the meantime, my sixteen-month appointment at the library had ended, and we had decided to stay put—had, in fact, bought a house, one with a view every bit the equal of what we had had.

Still, though, I resisted the idea of the north as a permanent home. We continued to spend summers in Muskoka. Then one steamy August day in, I think, 1995, after too much driving, too many parking lots and too much hassling in downtown Toronto, I found myself thinking not only that I'd rather be somewhere else, but that I'd rather be home on the north shore of Lake Superior.

On the Labour Day weekend that year, as we returned to the Lakehead, we stopped—five of us—on an isolated stretch of shoreline west of Sault Ste. Marie, spread a blanket or two on the beach and, with the greatest show on earth rolling across a moonless, cloudless sky, spent the last night of summer huddled together between the flying sparks of a bonfire and the waves crashing twenty metres below us on the beach.

In the autumn of that year, I started a series of weekly "excursions" on local CBC Radio, each consisting of a fifteen-minute rap, loosely scripted, on a walk I had taken or a building or place I had visited in or around Thunder Bay. Over a period of a couple of years, I visited every street and alley, and every inch of waterfront, in town. But for the first of those broadcasts, I travelled no further than the Main Street and Central Avenue bridges, both of which lead from the residential and business parts of the city into the industrial and waterfront areas of the port.

It would not have occurred to me to mention these bridges either on the radio or here, except that they are a kind of pedestal from which the essence of this wilderness city can be seen and heard and sniffed. From their summits you can see mountains, ski hills, grain elevators, pulp mills, islands, churches, every major landform and structure, in every direction, within twenty kilometres of the city. You can see twenty kilometres out onto the lake, and can peer straight down into the rail yards, where, on the various sidings and lines, you can sometimes count as many as eight hundred cars, most brimming with wheat, lumber or logs. From the Main Street bridge at dusk, you can watch the deer come out of the poplar woods to the east to feed on the grain along the tracks. I have seen as many as thirty of them, and have seen a dozen or more ravens feeding, in turn, on an unlucky doe. You can hear crows, ravens, gulls, geese, the occasional ship's whistle, and always in the distance the persistent rumble, sometimes just a hum, of wheel and rail. You can smell the sweet fermenting sludge of wet grain, and the rotting fecundity of the lakeshore and the surrounding marsh.

On a perishingly cold day in mid-December that year, in preparation for my Christmas broadcast, I crossed the Pacific Avenue bridge to the so-called East End, the oldest part of the city, site of the original fur-trading post, Fort William, built in 1804. Through the early 1900s, this workaday parish was a kind of mustering grounds for Italian, Polish, Ukrainian and Slovak immigration. It was called the "the Coal Docks," because coal headed for Western Canada was transferred from boats to trains along the north side of the Kaministiquia River, which is the southern boundary of the neighbourhood.

As I walked along Connolly Street past the Slovak Catholic Church, an elderly man in a stylish fur hat came gingerly up the street toward me. "Hello, sir," I said. "Could I ask you a few questions about the neighbourhood?"

"Go ahead," he said amicably. "I've lived here seventy-two years."

We chatted briefly, and when I was about to say goodbye he said, "Why don't you let me show you around? I'm blind, but if you'll let me take your arm I'll be fine."

And thus I toured the cradle of the city—in many ways the cradle of the industrial north—arm in arm with Johnny Zack, who until recently had owned Zack's meat and grocery store on Pacific Avenue, founded in 1919 by his father. We went first to the rail yards and the site of the old fort by the river, where, at John's request, I read aloud the inscription on the granite monument commemorating the activities of the fur traders. Then, hunched against the wind, we tramped the streets, most of them named for the Scottish officers of the North West Company of fur traders: past the site of the old Belluz Winery, Covello's pool hall, Rocky Presidente's barbershop, the abattoir, the stockyards, the (Italian) Workers' Co-op, Purity Bakery and the Fort William Broom Company, which at one time had a contract to supply brooms to the CPR. "I can see them all now in my mind's eye," John told me, "and I can hear them and smell them"—the grapes, the fermentation, the cigar smoke, the clacking of the balls, the talc, the hair oil, the squeals of the animals, the acrid rendering of the carcasses, the yeast and rye flour, and the kielbasa and headcheese at his own family's store. John explained that, during the early days, when a ship came up the river, the captain and officers would beat it over to Rocky Presidente's for a haircut, but that they were often so short of time, they had to buy their way into line by paying for the haircuts of everyone ahead of them.

The notion of a blind man who knew his neighbourhood, past and present, in this detailed, sensory way, and could convey those details so provocatively to a man with full sight, suggested a kind of conjuring to me—both a potency and a poignancy. What's more, it reminded me of the many times I had told writing classes that, in the interest of their work, they should apply their senses and imaginations to their surroundings with the same practised acuity that a blind person might apply his sensitivities to, say, sound or smell or touch.

At one time, John recalled, there were five bakeries and six skating rinks in the East End, an area not much bigger than the average nine-hole golf course. The immigrants arrived from Italy or Eastern Europe and found living space in musty, overcrowded boarding houses or, if they were married, in drafty, ill-heated houses, some of which were little more than shacks. They filched stray chunks of coal from the docks, kept immense vegetable gardens, and raised children by the job lot. At night, the men listened for the whistles of the incoming ships, which brought many of them hustling to the river's edge for work. People in more affluent parts of the city viewed the area with contempt, dismissing its inhabitants as a lesion on the character of the city, necessary only in the enactment of the Empire's dirty work. "It was a lot of malicious nonsense," protested John. "The East End was a peaceable, thriving, bustling, vigorous community."

At a certain point I ran back and got the car, and we finished the tour in the warmth of the front seat. Then I drove John home. "In the old days we sang songs," he told me as we sat in his driveway, emphasizing that they were not "the generic kind" that are played today on the radio, "but songs about ourselves." One he remembered about the East End told of poverty and love, and of how the men, no matter how deep their passions for their women as they lay in bed with them at night—or how deep their sleep— left "one ear on the windowsill," listening for the ships' whistles, which would jolt them upright into their pants and then off into the darkness for the coins they could earn unloading coal or grain.

"Would you like me to sing it to you?" he said.

"Sure," I told him, and in a plaintive tenor voice, papery with age, he began to sing—not in English, as I might have anticipated, but in Ukrainian. I won't attempt to describe what it was to sit there on a day of −30°C while an aging blind man in a black fur hat sang passionately for me of a time I hadn't known, in a language I didn't understand. I will say that, as unlikely as it all might sound, it was intimate to a point where, in the end, I had to force back the lump in my throat. When he got out, John paused at the open car door to wish me the best of the season. "I've enjoyed showing you my home," he said. "Nobody cares about the East End any more." His words formed puffs of frozen vapour on the thin air, then the door slammed shut, and he was gone.

———

Of the questions I get asked, one of the more frequent is, Why do you live in Thunder Bay—or, sometimes, Why on *earth* do you live in Thunder Bay? I am asked the question here in town, and in other cities. Wouldn't I do better in Toronto? Isn't it awfully isolated up there? What do you see in the place? A writer friend from Winnipeg told me recently that if I lived in Toronto, I'd have more work than I could handle and twice as much money. I told him I already had more work than I could handle, and that if I lived in Toronto I'd need twice as much money. Anyway, I did once live in Toronto, and had twice as much work and half as much money.

More to the point, I started to tell him, and within seconds found myself in the middle of what has become for me a familiar little rodomontade (nonetheless heartfelt) about a body of fresh water bigger and wilder and more mysterious—and, in my view, more elegant—than any on earth. And primeval forest, and deep skies, and northern lights—and immense silences, and herons and eagles in flight. I explained as best I could the primordial satisfaction of canoeing along a shoreline, or driving down the highway, and seeing, fifty metres ahead, in its natural habitat, a wolf, or lynx, or black bear, or a pair of moose, the continent's largest and most impressive mammal. Or of living among billion-year-old mountains, the oldest on earth. Or of looking out the window from my desk and seeing in the distance the Sleeping Giant, and ships at anchor, and ravens as big as roasting fowl. I told him that if I were to explain Thunder Bay to someone from the far side of the planet, it would seem as exotic as Rio or Shanghai—or even the lost city of Atlantis (which, in its "lostness," is our natural twin to a degree that few places come close to matching).

"Nowheresville," I heard the city called recently by a resident of another part of the province—voicing a view every bit as fossilized and unimaginative as the hellacious view many of our own residents hold of the big cities to the south (of street gangs, road rage and twenty-dollar parking). And yet it is the view many Canadians

———

have of the country's formidable central forests. Northwestern Ontario is bigger than British Columbia or Texas—is integral to both the history and wealth of the country—and yet most Canadians know no more about it than they know of the fabled Siberia, which at least holds political connotations for most of them. Unlike Siberia, of course, we are lost not on the fringe but in the middle of a continent, about equidistant between the Atlantic and Pacific (and yet are a seaport of all things!). So neglected has the territory become by the provincial government, there is periodic talk up here of secession to the West. The problem is, we are as detached from the West as from the East, and would be no better recognized there. The country's transportation machinery is so acute in its disregard of this vastness and its chief city that to reach it by air from Toronto can cost twice as much as to reach Winnipeg or Regina or Vancouver, when flights to those places pass right over our serviceable and modern international airport.

In the ten years my family and I have lived here, we have had (apart from family) a total of two visitors who came *for the visit*, as opposed to dropping in on the way somewhere else, or as a side issue to business or recreation. In the meantime, we have made perhaps a hundred visits outgoing. At a fifty-to-one differential, we might have begun to get something of a complex were we any less stoic in our geographical confidence. When TSN came here in 1995 to televise the World Nordic Ski Championships to 40 million people around the world, their on-air announcers referred to the city repeatedly as "North Bay." So little is known of the distances up here that an otherwise savvy magazine editor asked me recently if I could go and do a quick interview in Sudbury, a city three times as far from Thunder Bay as it is from downtown Toronto. "That's what you get for being so far north," an old friend in publishing said recently, obliging me to point out that we are well south of Saskatoon and Edmonton, and on roughly the same latitude as Vancouver. "Well, so far *away*, then," she said, obliging me to point out that we are smack in the middle of the country.

However, unlike Winnipeg or Regina or Edmonton—where the apathy of Toronto and Ottawa is worn like a fish hook in the lip—Thunder Bay has pretty much shrugged off that apathy as a philiosophical encumbrance. Many of our residents would, in fact, tell you that their line of connection goes not east or west but south through Duluth to Minneapolis, just six hundred kilometres away, where they feel amicably if platonically linked.

A few years ago when I was preparing to write an article on the city for a national magazine, my friend Greg Adams said to me quite seriously, "I wish you wouldn't do things like that," his view seeming to be that we are better served by the false map, or no map, than by the implied advertisement or endorsement. And indeed, there is an attractiveness to the notion of a virtually secret city—by the lake, amid the mountains, in the wilderness. In the same sense that a city such as ours is rendered distant and irrelevant by the bustle and desperation of the metropolis—by skyscrapers and freeways and noise, and by the fixations of the marketplace—so, too, is all of *that* rendered shaky and irrelevant in the presence of silence and forest, and communities of birds and animals whose ties to the waters and pines were established hundreds of thousands of years before any human being thought to sharpen a stick, let alone build a fashion house on Bloor Street or a bank at King Street and Bay.

To say that one city or town is inherently more "geographical" than another would seem at first to be an absurdity. "The Universe is everywhere," as William Steig wrote. But if geography is no more present in this area than another, it is at least more memorable and knowable for its extremity and drama and accessibility. "If Ireland is history," wrote the Irish-Canadian poet Mary Frost, "Northwestern Ontario is geography."

Even in Thunder Bay proper—a city of some 120,000 people—there is barely a smidgen of history or community that cannot be read as a lesson in the complexities of the planet. All over the north side, for example, there are reminders of the rock-hard Finnish lumberjacks of the early 1900s—men who, when life became impossible in Finland, came to Canada, and then homed in on the Lakehead, because the forests north of Superior were pretty much identical to those outside Helsinki and Oulu.

Today, trees are chomped off at ground level by hydraulic steel jaws and hauled from the forest by motorized skidders instead of horses. And the legendary Finnish lumberjack is as rare in the boreal outback as the crested towhee. But his legacy survives in Thunder Bay, in the form of a Finnish-speaking community of some fifteen thousand souls, the largest population of Finns outside Scandinavia. While most of these Finlanders live in the city, literally thousands keep wilderness cabins—"camps," as they are called up here—each with a sauna just a metre or two from the shoreline of whatever lake the camp happens to be on. It is not uncommon to see as many as half a dozen such saunas—miniature houses with erect chimneys and impeccable woodpiles—in a row on neighbouring camp lots. "If you didn't know better," the Lakehead poet Elizabeth Kouhi once said to me, "you'd think you'd come across a community of gnomes."

In the city proper, the legacy of the lumberjack exists in the colourfully scrappy aggregation of stores, restaurants and antique social institutions that endure along Bay Street in Thunder Bay's north ward. The venerable Hoito restaurant offers just slightly edited versions of the meals it served bushworkers for a dime during the years after the restaurant was founded in 1919. The routine breakfast of such men consisted of a bowl of oatmeal porridge, half a dozen Finnish pancakes, an equal number of sausages, a plate-sized omelette and six-inch stack of thickly buttered rye bread (all still available at the Hoito), all washed down with prescription-strength coffee, the Finnish national elixir, of which the Hoito serves some 1500 cups a day. Not a block away, Bay Meats sells Finnish delicacies such as *suolakala* (salt-cured raw salmon), *lenkke makkara* (sauna sausage) and, at Christmas, *liteäkala* (a kind of jellied cod so horrible that even most Finns can't stand it). The Harri and Kivela bakeries offer Finnish rye bread (referred to simply as "Kivela" in the Hoito) and calorie-rich *pulla*, a Finnish coffee bread laced with cardamom and thereby smelling faintly of spruce boughs. The Kangas sauna is just a short walk south and, until a few years ago, when it closed its doors, Saasto's men's wear at Bay and Algoma stayed solvent on the demand for, among other items of loggerwear, heavy plaid bush shirts, Arctic underwear, and those greyish wool bush pants that, in texture, are about halfway between beaver felt and 50-grade sandpaper.

As much as any business on Bay Street, Lauri's Hardware, directly across from the Hoito, is a throwback to the bushworkers and bush camps of old. The store carries lumberjack tools and accoutrements the origins of which significantly predate the chainsaw and motorized skidder. These include tree-climbing spikes, cant hooks, peaveys, broad axes, two-man cross-cut saws, coal-oil lamps, cookhouse kettles and teapots, frying pans big enough to hold several hundred scrambled eggs, lumberjack suspenders as wide as duct tape, spittoons of the sort that were once used in bunkhouses and cook shacks, plus hundreds of more prosaic items, such as blueberry pickers, fish smokers, machetes, ice axes and a gazillion kinds of bush and hunting knives.

Lauri's merchandising policies, almost as much as the stock, tie the store to the plain-dealing lumberjacks of old. "I'm strictly no bullshit," owner Lauri Hietala said to me one day—meaning, most evidently, that he prefers cash to credit cards or cheques, that he doesn't much bother with anything as niggling as receipts, and he rounds every price off to the nearest dollar, tax included. "Gimme ten bucks," he says when asked about the price of a jackknife. "How much to cut a key?" "Gimme two bucks."

Lauri is attended constantly by a little coterie of old-timers— most of them ex-lumbermen or loggers—who, in varying numbers, inhabit the area around the cash register, chattering away in Finnish at any time of morning or afternoon. I once asked Lauri how many of them came in, and he looked at me, astonished, and said, "All of them!"

When I was in recently to buy an axe handle, Lauri dispatched one such friend to the Hoito to fetch me a cup of coffee, and we got talking about his growing urge to retire. A minute into the conversation, he said suddenly, "*You* should buy this place!"

"You need a Finlander here," I told him.

"You are a Finlander," he snapped. "The only thing missing is the vowels."

I suggested he sell to an unemployed bushworker, and he shot back, "Don't laugh! Lumberjacks are gonna make a comeback. All these big fancy bush machines are eventually gonna break down." He showed me a shipment of 42-inch bucksaw blades that had arrived that day. Each was folded into a long strip of waxy brown paper and was coated in a fine film of oil. "You buy this store," he promised, "a few years from now, you won't be able to keep these things in stock."

I asked how much he wanted for the place, and he squinted and said, "For you personally?"

"No, for anybody."

"For anybody, I dunno. For you, you're a writer, you're a Finlander, you know the bush—look at you, you own an axe." He dropped his voice and said, "Gimme a hundred and fifty thousand, no bullshit."

"How much for this?" I said of the contoured stick of white ash in my hand. "For me," I said, "a Finlander."

"Gimme ten bucks," he said solemnly. "And remember what I told you about the lumberjacks."

———

If the Finns came to the Lakehead for what the landscape *was*—a convincing approximation of home—the Italians, who also number about fifteen thousand here, came for what it *wasn't*.

It wasn't Calabria, Italy's southernmost province, where, before coming to the New World, the majority of this area's early Italian immigrants had been impoverished peasants, under the rule of powerful landowning *padrones*. Their arrival, unlike that of the Finns, wasn't so much a geographical reaffirmation as one of shock and foreboding in a landscape where the *padrone* now spoke English and could do you in—in some cases, simply for being Italian—and the climate, at its worst, could be a test of your resolve even to get out of bed and stay upright.

But it was their chance to own land, as they never could back home, and while few of the early arrivals actually acquired any, the formation of the Italian Society of Port Arthur—which thrives today in enormous new digs on Algoma Street—guaranteed that each Italian who made the crossing would at least have a tiny plot of ground in which he could eventually lie down for good.

By far the clearest example of Italian adaptability and proliferation along the north shore of Superior is the railway town of Schreiber, two hundred kilometres east of Thunder Bay. Of the town's two thousand residents, more than half are of Italian descent. Moreover, some 95 percent of those trace their roots to the small Calabrian city of Siderno on the Ionian Sea. "It's as if a few hardy seeds from Siderno were brought here, planted and flourished in this tough little northern garden," I was told a while back by Cosmo Filane, one of the town's prominent citizens. "You'd think no one from a sweltering climate could even survive here, let alone prosper."

There are nights in autumn, in Schreiber, after the grapes are stomped and the wine made, when the smell of fresh fermentation pours from open basement windows, scenting the air from one end of town to the other. Local weddings are celebrated in grand neo-Calabrian style, and are often attended by guests from Siderno. And most of Schreiber's Italian families still get together every Thursday and Sunday for a traditional spaghetti dinner. Twice weekly, my closest friend in Schreiber, Pina Commisso, cooks up three-hundred-litre lots of tomato sauce and prepares hundred-kilo batches of fresh pasta for her restaurant, Rosie & Josie's, which has earned accolades in several Canadian restaurant guides, and has had excellent reviews as far away as Chicago.

––––––

My friends in these parts include tree-planters, paper makers, geologists, ecologists, foresters, wilderness outfitters, loggers, ski-trail operators, ornithologists, canoe makers, freshwater scientists, as well as playwrights and artists and poets whose imagery is the lake or highway or the sounds or silences of the forest. When I tell my friend Elizabeth Kouhi that her poetry sets a world record for use of the word "boreal," she smiles forgivingly and writes another poem about the north. I have a friend who has committed his entire career to the study of pickerel, another to pine trees, another to ancient Aboriginal culture. Others have committed to ravens, ice climbing and reforestation. They are people who know the taste of moose meat, fiddleheads and wild cranberries. Many of them have picked ten times their weight in blueberries and exotic mushrooms. My neighbour Carmen, a champion gardener, reads the northern soil and growing season as a virtuoso stage director might interpret a limited script to maximum expressive effect. And more of them than you might imagine have, at one time or another, committed the modern malfeasance of raising a scoped rifle and putting a .30-06 bullet into the brain or rib cage of a deer or moose—or have emptied a 12-gauge into a mallard or goose on the wing.

Even in the absence of bloodletting, life up here can be as dramatic and unpredictable as a Jack London novel. My friend Claude Liman hit a moose on the highway last summer (a form of bloodletting), wiping out not only the animal but his car and (he told me) the vestiges of his youthfully dismissive illusions about mortality. Another friend got trapped on an ice floe on Lake Superior. My neighbours across the street, Gerry and Lila Siddall, who are both in their sixties, teach courses in wilderness survival and are key members of the district Search and Rescue team.

As Lila returned from an air search near Lake Nipigon on a winter night of −30°C about a decade ago, the engine of the search crew's Cessna 206 four-seater cut out above dense bush some thirteen kilometres outside Thunder Bay. "I knew immediately we were going down," Lila told me. "What was strange was that I felt no panic at all, just a clear-headed calm, a sense that I was in destiny's hands, even though I felt we were probably going to die. I ripped off my headset [the link between searcher and pilot], braced myself, and in seconds we were clipping the treetops. It was deafening—like being in a steel drum that was being beaten by baseball bats. Then suddenly we hit the crown of a tree we couldn't get past, and we just stopped and dropped—about thirty feet down into deep snow. As it happened, a medevac helicopter had heard our mayday, and had followed us and landed, so that within seconds of kicking our way out the emergency door, we were on the way to the hospital."

It was not until Lila and Gerry visited the crash site the following day that they realized the extent of the miracle that had saved Lila's life. "If we'd travelled another two hundred feet," she told me, "we'd have smashed head-on into a stone cliff. If we'd been fifty feet further east, we'd have hit high-tension power lines and been flipped off our axis and crashed—or perhaps hit one of the big steel power-line stanchions. Remember, our pilot was flying blind, couldn't see any of this in the darkness." The concluding note of grace was that the temperature was just cold enough at −30°C that, instead of bending and springing when the airplane hit the poplar trees, the trees snapped like candy canes, allowing the plane to keep moving forward, gradually slowing, until it stopped and simply sank. "If it had been a few degrees warmer," Lila said, "we'd have been caught and flipped by the first tree, and that would have been that, because we were travelling at tremendous speed."

Lila grew up in the rural bushlands outside Thunder Bay, and has always cherished trees. She said, "As a token of gratitude for my life being spared, I went out to the crash site in the spring, where all these trees had been chopped off, and I planted new ones, mostly pine and spruce. I still go out every year just to sit for a while and see how they're doing."

Thunder Bay's street-side architecture is one of the weaker links in the city's ubiquitous rapport with the earth. On the other hand, our really big buildings—our pulp mills and grain elevators and shipbuilding sheds—are a function of the forests and waters to a degree unseen in cities where banks, stadiums and corporate towers are the most obvious agglomerations of concrete and steel. Rudyard Kipling came to the Lakehead during the 1920s and pronounced the grain elevators "castles of industry." But he left no quotable metaphor for the pulp mills that I myself have sometimes thought of as a version of Baal among the Canaanites—snorting and unsightly and pervasive in agenda. Whatever else they are, the mills represent a fierce utilitarian relationship between humanity and the planet—a representation balanced in this town by the turn-of-the-century brick buildings of the Port Arthur Shipyards. That institution's capacious old machine shop connects land and water and sky in a way that even the finest waterside architecture can for the most part only hint at. The shop is one of two big buildings left at the yards; and while its new metal cladding has obscured its windows, when I last visited the place, the daylight entered it through thousands of overhead panes, creating an illumination similar to what you see in the paintings of Rembrandt or El Greco.

It was in this shop (and others now gone) that the shipyard produced the makings of its historic corpus of freighters, corvettes, minesweepers, tugs and ferries—129 of them in all, some still afloat, some rusting silently on the floor of the Atlantic, or perhaps out beyond the peninsula in our own freshwater sea.

One of the more intriguing footnotes to the shipyard's history is that, during the early 1930s, the company's electrical superintendent, Fenton Ross, cobbled together the prototype for a Gothic-looking four-sided arena clock, a "SporTimer," that was the natural offspring of the fabricating capability of the plant and the region's almost pathological obsession with hockey. The shipyards built several such clocks, one of which hung for more than thirty years in Maple Leaf Gardens, another in the Montreal Forum, from where their televised images were sent weekly into the living rooms of millions of Canadians.

———————

Last year, on the thirtieth anniversary of the amalgamation of the old cities of Port Arthur and Fort William to create Thunder Bay, I was asked for my opinion of the city's greatest asset and greatest cause to celebrate. It was an easy choice, because I know, as on some level we all know, that the lake that laps up to our doorstep is the marrow and mystery (and, in many cases, the money) of our days. There are so many things you could say about Lake Superior and the local waterfront—about the comings and goings of the ships; about the harbour, the tug docks, the shoreline parks; the storms, the ice, the wildness of the shore features and islands—and, of course, about the immense aesthetic and spiritual power of the water. During storms, I can look out my window and, from nearly two kilometres away, watch fifteen-metre lashings of spray shooting up off the breakwater. In clear weather, the view extends forty kilometres out onto the lake—takes in sailboats, ships, the old harbour lighthouse and breakwater; and further out, the Sibley Peninsula and Isle Royale. At night, the lights of the ships at anchor look like villages on a distant plain. I have seen the bay in almost every colour of the spectrum, including blue, mauve, white, grey, silver; red and orange at dawn; and a bright greenish turquoise as the ice was going out last spring.

There is a sense in Thunder Bay, as in, say, Vancouver, that no matter where you are in the city—in back lanes, in junkyards, in shopping malls—you are never far from some elegant expression of the unreconstructed planet. In particular, the water. You come down Dawson Road, or over the hill west of County Fair Mall— or out of the bank, or the library, or around a building in some dire industrial park—and there it is, a shot to the heart: Lake Superior, the harbour, the Sibley Peninsula, Pie Island, the shoreline spruce and pines, a constant for the eye between the impenetrable water and the ultimately unknowable sky. Pie Island is surely the most distinctive and appropriately named island on earth. If you took a pork-pie hat, flipped its brim down, floated it on the water, crown up, and then expanded it a million times, you would have Pie Island—or at least the island's defining south end.

The Sibley Peninsula is a forty-kilometre-long hook of mountainous rock and forest, a kind of hockey-stick shape, the blade tip of which is attached to the mainland at the village of Pass Lake, while the handle drops southwest out into Superior, forming the famous Sleeping Giant. The structure as a whole provides both physical protection for the city's outer harbour and a kind of psychological temple wall for a city that, like most, I suspect, would rather see shelter in its geography than the helplessness suggested by a five-hundred-kilometre fetch of Lake Superior.

One of my constant waterfront interests over the years has been the nameless little settlement of Metis squatters who live in cabins made of bark and board scraps from the planing mill, just south of the Richardson grain elevator. While these days the expansion of the seaplane port to the north has reduced the settlement, it is still there, and you can occasionally spot an inhabitant or two—cutting wood, working on their homes or, in summer, fishing, or just sitting in lawn chairs by the water. On a spring day a while back, I ventured in, ignoring a hand-lettered sign: METIS LAND— WHITE MAN KEEP OUT. Sweet-smelling woodsmoke rose from at least two of the cabins' chimneys as I padded along the sawdust entry lane, and I had a strong sense of being observed. But I could see no one, and was unable to raise an answer at any of the three doors on which I knocked. I stood for a minute looking around, then feeling increasingly intrusive and uneasy, retreated down the path, my admiration for these latter-day survivalists undiminished.

I am a more frequent visitor at Dock 5, just south of Marina Park, where I go for no other reason than to see what's up with the harbour's other resident survivalists, the tugboats. Tugs are not sleek craft, but they are shapely—Botticellian—and no matter how ravaged they get, they never seem to lose the good-natured inno-cence and likeability that comes with their bright paint and jaunty little bridges and stacks—and, of course, their unimpeachable work habits.

On a balmy October night a couple of years ago, my son, Matt, and I went out on an overnight harbour mission on the *Point Valour*, the city's largest tug, co-owned by its chief engineer, Rollie Frayne, a Great Lakes fixture of some fifty years' experience. Like so many veteran sailors, Rollie is as tough as chainlink—has battled cyclones, deck bullies and balky freighters—but he is so knowl-edgeable and well-spoken, you might take him for a professor of history. During our own trip with him, he shortened what would otherwise have been a long night (shifting a Monrovian freighter from elevator to elevator along the waterfront) by telling us sea stories, among them an account of three days of peril on the Gulf of St. Lawrence, during the annual Equinox Gales in the autumn of 1951, when he was an upstart coal stoker on an old Paterson steam vessel called the *New Brundoc*.

"We got caught in hundred-and-twenty-knot winds, forty-foot waves," he said, and he described how for three hopeless days the ship had been tossed around, and how on the third day, with everybody numb, the captain of a nearby Greek freighter had radioed, asking the *New Brundoc* to come to his boat's rescue because it was almost certainly going down. "Looking back," Rol-lie said, "it's hard to express how desperate I felt as a young sailor when our captain radioed them that he couldn't do anything to help, because he was pretty sure we were going down, too. I'll tell ya, that water suddenly looked a whole lot blacker and colder."

By the kindest of meteorological shifts, and some nifty seaman-ship, both vessels survived. But Rollie has known ships that did not. On a November night in 1975, he was upbound on Lake Superior, chief engineer on a ship called the *Lake Winnipeg*, when the captain of a downbound ship began sending radio messages that his vessel was taking on water through the hatches, but that he figured they could cope. "Loss of contact was as sudden as that,"

Rollie said, slapping the instrument panel in front of him. He was talking, of course, about the *Edmund Fitzgerald*. "She went down so fast, the men never even got their life jackets on—never even got out on deck."

Rollie's job requires judgement and experience and an extensive knowledge of water, shorelines and weather. One does not normally think of prostitution in those terms, in that it would not seem to require any particular knowledge of geography or of the planet at all, except perhaps the landscape of the human anatomy. And yet a story Rollie told me late that night led me to believe that a harbour escort these days must, in some cases, be as knowledgeable about shorelines and entry ports as is an officer on the bridge.

With no attempt to embellish, Rollie described to me how itinerant hookers will "pick up" a foreign boat at its port of entry or at an early stop—say, in Montreal or Cleveland—and will follow it right up the Seaway by car, then back down, meeting it en route at perhaps Toledo or Milwaukee or Duluth—anywhere they can find a way aboard. A vision emerged of a couple of weary-eyed women, perhaps mid-thirtyish—tight pants, big hair, road map open on the dash, Quarter Pounder wrappers and disposable coffee cups on the floor of the back seat, ashtray overflowing, zipping along Michigan 28 or Wisconsin 43 or the Trans-Canada, in their LeSabre or Ram or Explorer, perhaps in touch with the ship by cellphone, listening to Garth Brooks or Faith Hill, or perhaps Dr. Laura Schlesinger, as the fields and forests roll by and they debate whether it might be possible to catch four or five hours of sleep at the next town's Super 8 and still beat the ship to Superior, Wisconsin, or Twin Harbors, Minnesota, or to the mouth of the Kaministiquia River, where they hope there will be little sleep for a night or two.

Like many tugs, the *Point Valour* is occasionally hired as a water taxi, and will for a fee deliver supplies, or a mechanic, or crew members who've been ashore—or, yes, a pair of hookers—to a vessel at anchor in the outer harbour. The fee for actually guiding a vessel into port is $1,500, and another $1,500 when it leaves—plus $1,500 if it needs its prow shunted, or its back scratched, between times.

Water is far and away the most obvious of our planetary strengths—a source of cleansing, of sustenance, of transport, of great physical power and influence. It is the medium in which life began. But it is also our greatest vulnerability, in that it gathers up contaminants, carries them over rock and ice, through soil and air, into rivers and lakes of its own making, into the food chain and, finally, to every place and organism that it reaches.

Not surprisingly, the city's waterfront has been the site of some of our grandest environmental debacles over the years, not to mention of our grandest reclamations. For decades, the city's great unseen disgrace—indeed, one of the country's unseen disgraces—was a vast harbour-dwelling monstrosity, the "blob" as everyone called it, glommed up of hundreds of tonnes of creosote, which, since the early decades of the century, had been percolating slowly downward into the water through the shoreline soil around the site of the Northern Wood Preservers mill. It is not difficult to imagine what the public might have thought of such a menace had it existed on land, flowing across the city in the form of an arena-sized globule of carcinogenic black goo. But it was conveniently out of sight beneath the surface of the body of water from which we drink—that is, until two years ago when, after a decade of wrangling over whose responsibility it was, various agencies combined to build a "berm" around it, an underwater earth dyke, and then attempted to decontaminate it by applying neutralizing bacteria that have so far been unequal to the task. So the blob lives, at least for now, in its earthen cage, less threatening than it was, but still not the ecological cherry that we are promised it will become.

Its visible soulmate on the harbour has, in recent years, been a revolting old grain elevator, Saskatchewan Pool #6, which through the mid- and late nineties stood partly demolished, adjacent to Marina Park, like a huge rotting tooth. One day as I stood with Jim Foulds, the former deputy leader of the Ontario NDP, at his home on Dufferin Street overlooking the harbour and the ruined elevator, we began speculating on why the original owner, Saskatchewan Pool, a big, profitable company that had extracted many millions of dollars from the community over the years, had been allowed to abdicate its property and the responsibility for it. It had done so by selling it for a dollar—in other words, giving it away—to a company that originally intended to scrap the elevator for its immense tonnage of iron reinforcement and machinery. However, after making a monumental botch of it, the company, unable to finish the job, gave the structure up to another company, etc., etc. Where was Saskatchewan Pool through all this? we wondered. Why were *they* not accountable for the blight their once-profitable building had become?

Jim looked at me squarely and said, "That's why I'm a socialist," his gist seeming to be that a strictly-for-profit culture could not be counted on to look after either the planet or the public's interest. Jim would be the first to acknowledge that the world's experiments in socialism have not thus far been renowned for their environmental sensitivities (Chernobyl is a mere kitten among the environmental offences of the old Soviet Union). But he would also say that socialism, at least in any pure form, should not be blamed, in that, like Christianity, it has never really been tried.

The good news locally is that the elevator is gone, imploded with due ceremony last December at an hour past dawn on an obscenely cold Sunday morning as several thousand people— including me and my daughters, Georgia and Eden—stood bundled at the lookout in Hillcrest Park. At zero hour, we watched as tiny puffs of smoke emerged from the foundations of the structure, listened to the remote-sounding detonations as they came delayed up the hill, and then gawked as the ugly old monster made its grand exit with a rolling, muted rumble.

Even under such earth-shaking circumstances, a hill is an irresistible invitation to play and, during the long countdown to the blast, any number of children in snowsuits, impatient with the wait, began sliding on the downslope in front of us, or rolling down it, in some cases as parents called frantically that if they didn't smarten up, they couldn't hope to be witnesses to history.

The link between landscape and recreation is so obvious only a fool would bother jacking it into prose. Where there is water, we swim. Where there is big water, we sail. Or we scuba dive. Or surf. Or canoe. Where there is ice, we skate, and where there are forests, we hike, snowshoe or cross-country ski.

Where the hills are snow-covered, as they are around here for five months of the year, we slide on skis, or snowboards, or sleds— or (in time-honoured freedom from encumbrance) on our rear ends, assuming our rear ends have not themselves become encumbrances to play.

Unfortunately, the most elegant and dramatic expression of the link between planet and play disappeared from these parts during the mid-1990s, leaving me, at least, with a fan's craving (whetted intensely during my first three or four years here) that I have never been able to replace. I am talking about ski jumping and, in its memory, will say that it is difficult to think of anything in the realm of sport or entertainment more riveting or poetic than the sight of a first-rate jumper as he or she comes off the trestle and describes that incredible trajectoral arc down the mountain. It occurred to me one day as I stood at the top of the 120-metre jump at Big Thunder, wondering at the courage of anyone who'd actually descend the thing, that the sport must surely be the high point in humanity's centuries-old struggle to counteract gravity and to fly unassisted. Leonardo himself worked on the problem, but it never occurred to him to do what the cagey Scandinavians did and put the wings on the feet.

Even the mention of ski jumping reminds me of the excitement thousands of us shared when the World Nordic Ski Championships were held during the mid-nineties just south of the city at Big Thunder mountain, which at the time was a national training site for ski jumpers. Half a dozen years after the fact, I retain almost photographic recall of the 120-metre jumping on the last afternoon of the games, the event undecided, three jumpers left, each with a chance at the gold medal. First came a young man named Weissflog, from Germany, a former world champion, who under pressure launched an inspired jump that propelled him into what everyone believed was an unsurpassable lead. Then came Goldberger of Austria, with a jump that beat even Weissflog's, and put *him* into the lead.

The last jumper was a seventeen-year-old kid named Tommi Ingebrigtsen who had the fading hopes of Norway, not to mention of the local crowd, riding on his skinny shoulders. Down the trestle he came, ninety kilometres an hour, off the lip, into the flight position. From the crowd of perhaps twenty thousand there came first a kind of murmur, then a gasp, and finally a sustained roar, as the young Norwegian soared past Weissflog's mark, past Goldberger's, and so far on down the hill that I remember a sudden fear that he wouldn't be able to pull out of it, that he had become a kind of runaway airplane wing and was going to crash onto the flats at the bottom. He did pull out—but not until he had gone farther officially than anyone had gone before on that hill.

I say "officially" because it is legend in these parts that the same spectator fear had occasionally existed around the jumps of the great Steve Collins, an Ojibwa kid who grew up on the Fort William Reserve south of the city. Collins's ascent to international heroics during the early 1980s began in endless rehearsal on the Big Thunder runs that were now the site of the championship. The accounts are unverifiable, but I have heard that, at times, in practice, when the wind was right—or wrong, depending on how you see it—Collins would hit jumps that exceeded existing world records, and that his resounding claps onto the flats at the bottom of the hill would cause even inured veterans of the sport to bury their faces, unwilling to watch the risk-taking that, for the teenager, was as natural a part of his relationship with the local mountains and landscape as was fishing or hunting.

Within weeks of the ski championships, both the federal and provincial governments announced the withdrawal of their support for the Big Thunder facility, which now sits rotting, rusting, and under waist-high grass or acres of unbroken snow. For a while it was for sale—on whose authority it is hard to say, inasmuch as it was recently padlocked and impounded by the Natives of the Fort William Band, who, reasonably enough, have reclaimed what was theirs for ten thousand years before it was made famous by one of their own.

————————

Big Thunder, it should be said, is part of the Nor'Wester range of mountains, clearly visible from downtown Thunder Bay. Our lakes are spring chickens, but our mountains are Methuselahs, the oldest on earth. However, when I mention this to people from other parts of the country, they inevitably give me the skeptical eye, as if to say, *Prove it!* or *Is that your own assessment? I mean, they're hardly very big at all!* (after which I hear myself explaining that mountains actually get smaller as they get older). What's more, the Nor'Westers are so distinctive, with their cake-shaped crowns and basalt cliffs and skrees that, if I were shown a photo of them among a hundred photos of world mountain ranges, I would know them immediately, whereas I would probably be at a loss to distinguish among more famous, newer mountains, such as the Alps, Andes or Himalayas. The Nor'Westers hug the uppermost curve of Lake Superior, extending southwest along the Slate River Valley, toward the U.S. border. I have driven along logging roads into the Falling Snow area in Pearson Township, southwest of Thunder Bay, up onto Twin Mountains, where the view is like something out of the peyote dreams of Carlos Castaneda. The famous Highway 61—Thunder Bay to New Orleans—takes you more or less through the heart of the range, then across the border and along the Minnesota shore of Lake Superior.

Which brings me to a point where I would do well to contemplate not just Highway 61, or other highways of the region, but highways, period, as a kind of idiom for the limited first-hand experience any of us really have of the expanses of a country as vast and wild as our own. I hasten to mention that my home city is located at the crux of a T formed by two mythic roads, the aforementioned Highway 61, which John Steinbeck referred to as "the backbone of America," and our own legendary Trans-Canada, which, as much as the lakes, woods and rocks, is a fundamental of life in Canada's vast central wilderness—as, in a sense, are all our paved roads. While the towns and cities of the region are connected by rail and airplane and radio, by telephone and e-mail, when an inhabitant of the area thinks of the distance between his town and the next, he thinks not of airports or railways, much less of the "information highway," but of a real highway, a serpentine strip of blacktop, which, when he climbs into his pickup or four-by-four—or even his rusted Toyota—becomes both a means to an end (the next town) and an end in itself, with its implied freedoms and its rich evocations of woods and waters and wildlife.

The Trans-Canada is not so much a "backbone" for these parts, or for the rest of the country either, as a kind of piscine lateral line, a rolling sensory perspective point, pertinent especially in a country where the distribution of people is about as long as the highway and, in some places, not much wider. We travel our highways day and night, from infancy to the grave, to the point where one of our predominant images of the planet after dark—in fact, of our *existence* in a country where some communities spend months on end with barely any sunlight—is not, as one might imagine, the constellations or planets or moon (lights more meaningful in some cultures than in our own), but that of the dual cone of illumination and of the dotted line, lit doubly by the overlapping fields of the headlights, stretching way off into the darkness, or merely to the next bend, or over the hill, into the unseen wilds beyond the windshield. Every Canadian recognizes it, knows what it is to peer out across the black right-of-way, or past the rock cut, or into the tiny lit eyes in the ditch, watching out for skunks or deer or axe murderers, or merely for the cutoff or roadway into another rural town or northern lake.

The highway system is so singular by the time it reaches its most northerly arc over Superior—one road in, one out—that it has become a functional pinch point for anyone wanting to locate a vehicle moving either east or west. They all come through on the Trans-Canada. One of the more heralded results of the bottleneck is that the escape plans of many criminals heading west from southern Ontario (where the assumption is that there will always be an alternative route) have ended at a roadblock somewhere on the north shore of Superior, with nowhere to turn or run, and not even a hostage to take except for a roadside raven or woodpecker, who will of course not be taken. While most of us will never know the desperation (or relief) of having our tires exploded by the police spike belt, many travellers in these parts have had journeys end in shock or despair in the ditch, or the lake, or the deep snow of the right-of-way—or have ended up unconscious or dead, as a 600-kilogram moose, sometimes half-gutted by metal or glass, and invariably with snapped legs, scrambles bawling to free itself from the imploded windshield.

Which is of course all part of the crapshoot up here. A more merciful and exhilarating part is the raving spectacle of the scenery. For my money, no highway in the country—not the Cabot Trail on Cape Breton Island or 93 Highway through the icefields between Jasper and Banff—is more dramatic than the stretch of the Trans-Canada that connects Sault Ste. Marie to Thunder Bay. I have driven the highway so many times in so many kinds of weather, in every month of the year, and have experienced so many of the highs and lows it can dish out, that it has become for me a sort of paradox, an image on one hand of release, independence and space, but on the other of something decidedly more sinister, in that three times over the past seven or eight years, I have come within a hair's breadth of losing my life on its pavement or shoulders. I survived a near miss with a moose in 1993, a high-speed brush with a rock cut in 1995 and, on a night a couple of years ago, an all-but-impassable blizzard as I drove home from Nipigon where, earlier in the evening, a cadre of the (very, very) faithful had gathered at the public library to hear me read from my work.

Because it is the right of every citizen of this remote part of the country to relate an occasional Trans-Canada nightmare—and because it verges on national fable—I shall describe in the briefest terms how, on the night of the above-noted blizzard, as I drove home from Nipigon, a transport whisked by me near the village of Dorion, forcing me ever so slightly onto the shoulder to the right. Under the fatally icy conditions, even my most delicate manoeuvre to pull all tires back onto the road turned out to be an over-compensation, so that suddenly, there I was doing 360s down the middle of the highway, headlights groping the storm, as Bob Marley howled from the tape deck and another eighteen-wheeler came over the hill toward me some two hundred metres away. I remember thinking as I spun that if I had enough momentum to continue across onto the far shoulder, I might not die. Otherwise, there was an almost peaceful sense that I had already departed.

I remember more clearly the elation as my back wheels touched gravel through the deepening snow, and I knew at least that I was not going to come to rest in the oncoming lane.

When, finally, I stopped, it was with my rear wheels hanging a good half-metre over the steep unprotected embankment just metres from the edge of the pavement. And there I sat, for perhaps five hours in the blizzard—like a character in some latter-day Sinclair Ross tale—unwilling to walk for fear of freezing (I was wearing street shoes), unable to stop a transport, yet jumping from my vehicle as each one passed, so as not to get walloped if it lost its traction (as it certainly would have if it had tried to brake).

It was not until dawn, when the snow stopped and the wind died, that I was able to hitch a ride into Thunder Bay.

My adventures on the Trans-Canada have shown me almost every kind of mammal in the boreal forest: bears, moose, deer, lynx, porcupines, foxes, wolves, skunks, beaver, muskrats and a host of smaller creatures. It is my privilege to believe that, on a crisp December morning, in 1995, also near Dorion, I saw a cougar cross the road perhaps two hundred metres in front of me. I have been told by all and sundry that my imagination was undoubtedly working overtime and that what I probably saw was a dog, or pony, or snowmobile, or perhaps just a road devil, or that I had a cougar-shaped speck of dirt in my eye. But the fact remains that I know of no other animal, and certainly no machine, with a metre-long tail and a head the size of a basketball.

I have seen herons, owls and perhaps more vultures than I care to acknowledge, including some twenty of them sitting in trees near Ignace one day as a blood-drenched cow moose heaved her last in the mosses by the roadside.

Before the building of the city bypass during the late 1960s, the Trans-Canada came right through the centres of Port Arthur and Fort William. On North Cumberland Street, in the old Port Arthur end of town, the route is unchanged to a degree that, if you squint slightly as you follow it south across the Current River, you can easily imagine yourself rolling into town in, say, a 1953 four-holer, after a dusty day on the highway, looking for digs for the night. Places are, of course, history and culture and commerce, as well as geography, and the North Cumberland strip is a kind of museum to a life that most parts of the country said goodbye to three or four decades ago. There are still, for instance, thirteen motels on North Cumberland, not one of them corporate-owned: the Relax, the Lakeview, the Lakehead, the Superior, the Modern, the Sea-Vue, the Lakeshore Terrace, the Voyageur, the Old Country, the Imperial, the Swannee Cabins, the King's and the Munro—all mod cons, each given life by, and within view of, what the American poet Walt Whitman, who visited here during the 1850s, called "the great inland sea."

The area is served by businesses with names such as Gary's Auto Sales, Quick Car Repairs, Blackfoot Minnows & Live Bait, and the National Pride Car Wash. No strip malls, no McMuffins, no Whoppers.

Much has changed in this wilderness city since the heady days when the Seaway was in its prime, the grain elevators were brimming, and the Keefer Terminal on the harbour was unloading up to 2500 tons of foodstuffs and packaged goods a day.

The elevators, if it needs saying, are no longer brimming, and the Keefer can go for days without seeing a ship. Our shipyard has shrivelled, our ore dock has closed and our suburbs have doubled in size. Our retail capacity has tripled, and our airport quadrupled. The building that was once Eaton's department store is now a "call centre" employing some six hundred people who sit at computer terminals answering phone calls from hell, and checking credit card numbers, and so on. The area we call Intercity, which, as it sounds, is the space between the old cities of Port Arthur and Fort William, has evolved from a verdant lowland, replete with herons, spruce forest and mushroom bogs, into a ragtag consumer theme park, from which some of the finest trees in the city were eliminated long ago as an inconvenience. Historical photos show that Intercity's Memorial Boulevard, the main road between the old towns, once resembled the tree-lined thoroughfares of the imperial cities of Morocco or, at very least, the fine elm-arched streets of central and south Winnipeg. The trees, I am told, were planted during the early 1920s, when the road was named a memorial to those who died during the Great War. But the eventual building of gas bars and hamburger joints trumped the honour of dead soldiers, and the widening of the umbilical cord between cities mandated the chopping of the trees (the snowploughs, I was once told, would never have been able to "work around" the trees, the precept seeming to be that not even the last-standing angel for the environment would ever be able to "work around" the snowploughs.)

By the early 1980s, the power pavers had reached Intercity and (as in a reprise of the plagues of Egypt) had begun to cover the land with asphalt. By Aldo Leopold's famous definition, the ground beneath the asphalt is no longer even "land" in any ecological sense, but just space, zoning, real estate. In no time, midtown was a patchwork of six-hundred-car parking lots that, in some cases, connected—Wal-Mart with Future Shop with Winners—to form expansive black fields of subcommerce on which not even a blade of grass or a weed was allowed to sprout. In prep for a CBC Radio broadcast, I once paced off the parking lot of the Real Canadian Superstore and found that on more than fifty thousand square metres of pavement, only one living thing, a tiny chlorosis-ridden aster, a Real Canadian Superaster, had managed to find sunlight by channelling up through the hard cap alongside a light standard. I asked a contractor who had worked on the paving why a few plots of garden or spruce couldn't have been spotted here and there across the wasteland, and heard again that the snowploughs, those sacred chimera of our wintry culture, wouldn't have been able to "get around" such inclusions, although they appear to have no trouble getting around the light standards or cart drops.

I note all this because, of course, it is not just the fate of a smallish mid-continental city, but of a hundred cities—of a continent of them and, inevitably, of a planet.

But not to rave.

Good things happen, too. Here, in town, the city is in the process of reclaiming for humanity long stretches of what was once industrial waterfront and turning it into park and recreational land. Not long ago, Waverley Park, one of the oldest and most gracious public lands in Thunder Bay—in fact, the oldest municipal park in Ontario—was saved by public outcry when it was on the verge of being portioned off to developers. Similar things are happening in cities all over North America.

It seems to me that life's most important philosophic question—whether from a moral, a psychological or a sensory point of view—is: What constitutes a life justifiably lived? For me, the answer is partly about place, and attitude to place.

I was introduced recently as a guy who lives in Thunder Bay "by choice," which is true. In a large sense, and as the ecologists are keen to remind us, we all live in the same place. The insecticides sprayed on the cotton crop in Alabama are eventually eaten by children in the Arctic. In a small sense, where else am I going to live? Where is any of us going to live? My neighbour Joel lived with his first wife and family in complete isolation, trapping in the wilderness north of Armstrong, Ontario. My predecessor as writer-in-residence at the Thunder Bay Public Library, Veronica Ross, told me, years after the fact, that she and her husband had made a mistake in returning to southern Ontario when their term here was up. My friend Jack Haggarty, a psychiatrist, and his wife, Holly, a writer, who come from the London area, left these parts after a couple of years here to return home. And then a year later came back, realizing they were already home. The writer Wayland Drew, who died in 1999, told me his lifelong ambition was to move to Lake Superior when he retired from high school teaching in Bracebridge—but he didn't live long enough. Wayland's best friends here, Diana and Grant Stephenson, couldn't wait to get home to southern Ontario when Grant retired.

Thunder Bay is not the first place I have lived in which I felt close to the planet. In fact, I cannot think of a place where, in my way, I did not feel close: Nassau, Muskoka, Deep River, Cornwall, Winnipeg, Dundas, Toronto. I love big cities but, like my mother and dad, have perhaps been more myself in smaller places. When I asked my dad recently what he remembered or liked best about living in Deep River, way up north of Ottawa, during the 1950s, he said without hesitation that he had enjoyed getting out into the forest and hauling home deadfall spruce and birch to cut up and split for the wood furnace in our house on Parkdale Avenue. "There was a little added thrill about it," he said. "I always expected somebody to step out of the woods, and tell me what I was doing was illegal on Crown land, but they never did."

Cornwall had tremendous natural surroundings—the St. Lawrence River, the Adirondacks, idyllic old fields and woodlots. But I was never fully at home there—maybe because for the first time in my life I was cut off from the evergreen forests and wilds.

As I got into my teenage years, I wanted not the wilds of the forest but of the city—of Toronto—where I eventually went to finish high school and attend university.

When I began writing all of this down, it was not to convince anybody to take up the backcountry, either as a pastime or a dwelling place—or that such territory is by any means the "right" place to be or to live. It is merely my place.

If I lived in the city, I'd be as interested in the planet as I am here—but would not have the access to its wilds and to the range of its stimulations and exotica. Nor would I have what has become for me a cherished model for my imagination.

———

In writing this book, I have thought a lot about home—about "ideas of shelter," as my friend George Amabile, a Winnipeg poet, put it. One of the more impassioned commentaries I heard on the subject during my travels came from Wayne Maxted in Comox. As we said goodbye, he told me that one of the tactical errors made by those who wanted to raze Macdonald Wood and replace it with condos was to suggest, as Wayne put it, "that we were doing what we were doing for our 'homes'—for real estate values or some foolish thing—when we were doing it for our home in a bigger sense, the place we lived, the place we cared about and wanted to preserve and give meaning to. For gawdsakes, many of us risked *losing* our literal homes. We were prepared to remortgage, even sell if we had to, to carry this thing off. I remember thinking at the time: Isn't the notion of preserving the integrity of one's home, one's surroundings, the very *best*, instead of the worst, rationale for doing something like this? Imagine if everybody was absolutely determined to preserve their home, their town, their forest, their park. The possibilities blow your mind."

———————

I recall on the night of my homecoming from the lakes and Seaway, standing out on deck as the *M. V. Paterson* came slowly around Thunder Cape, into sight of the lights of Thunder Bay—recall seeing it all with a kind of nervousness, perhaps a function of some inner turmoil of the moment. But it is true, too, that in the time we are away, home changes. We change. The act of leaving in itself changes us. We arrive back in darkness, perhaps in trepidation, unsure of the bridge between the place we left and the one to which we return.

Home was again on my mind on the afternoon of September 28 as I sat on the beach at Gargantua Harbour, having hiked over from Rhyolite Cove, where I had spent the past nine days, a sojourn documented earlier in this book. During the late afternoon, the sky had clouded over, and for a few minutes it rained. Then it cleared again, although there was an uncertainty, a wintriness, to the sky. The sun set with a bruisy fierceness, and I sat by my fire, reluctant to give it up. I made coffee; I ate apricots. The wind came up, and I tried to read by the firelight. For the second time in several days, I was sure I saw a flicker of light down the beach. If it was a ghost, I told myself, at least I had the coffee on. I took my notebook out of my pack, and wrote: "Have decided not to stay another night." Then, on a whim, crossed out the word "not."

When we had lived in Thunder Bay for perhaps a month, Matt, then three years old, awoke one night beside where I was reading in the bedroom, sat up like a rifle, and said, "Let's go home!"

I said, "We are home."

"I mean to our real house," he said.

"This is our real house," I told him.

———————

After a silence he said, "Is this where we live?"

I told him it was, and he said, "Why don't we live in our other house any more?"

"Because we live here," I said. "Someone else lives in our other house now."

I told him someone else used to live in this house, too, and he said, "The same people who live in our house now?"

"I don't think so," I told him.

He lay back down, and after a longish silence, said, "Can you live anywhere?"

"You can if you want to," I told him.

"Do we want to?" he said.

"Sometimes," I said.

———————

Back at Gargantua, I put on gloves and an extra sweater, and as the twilight deepened walked over to the van to stash some of my gear.

As I came back onto the beach I could see my fire, as remote and sad as a star, seeming almost to belong to somebody else. In fact, as I walked back toward it, I half expected to see somebody sitting beside it. But of course there was no one. It was my fire— my light and heat.

In the morning, I would take the long trail out, and head down the highway toward Thunder Bay. But for now, I did what I had done my first night out—I dug a long, shallow depression in the ground, then spread my groundsheet and sleeping bag. I heaped wood on my fire until it blazed nearly waist-high, and built a foot-high dyke of sand on its northwest side to protect it from the wind. Then I crawled into my sleeping bag and laid my head on the doll's pillow that had served me well.

Because I had slept during the afternoon, I did not drift off immediately, but lay there watching small patches of stars appear and disappear among the clouds. I listened to the fire and the waves. On the day I'd left home, Matt had told me I would get lonely on my own in the wilds. "Hey," I'd told him, "I'm already lonely," and we had laughed, and I had given him a hug. For the most part, as it happened, my days alone had been a tonic against loneliness. I had seldom felt more connected or alive.

When drowsiness came, perhaps an hour after dark, I burrowed deeper into my sleeping bag, edged toward the fire and closed my eyes. Through the blood that coursed in my eyelids, I could see a splash of varied colour, and then the dim pink outline of the flame.